PLAINS HISTORIES

John R. Wunder, *Series Editor*

EDITORIAL BOARD

also in plains histories

America's 100th Meridian: A Plains Journey
by Monte Hartman

American Outback: The Oklahoma Panhandle in the Twentieth Century
by Richard Lowitt

Children of the Dust
by Betty Grant Henshaw; edited by Sandra Scofield

From Syria to Seminole: Memoir of a High Plains Merchant
by Ed Aryain; edited by J'Nell Pate

Railwayman's Son: A Plains Family Memoir
by Hugh Hawkins

Ruling Pine Ridge: Oglala Lakota Politics from the IRA to Wounded Knee
by Akim D. Reinhardt

RIGHTS IN THE BALANCE

79798

RIGHTS IN THE BALANCE

Free Press, Fair Trial, and
Nebraska Press Association v. Stuart

mark r. scherer
Foreword by James W. Hewitt

TEXAS TECH
UNIVERSITY PRESS

This book is typeset in Filosofia. The paper used in this book meets the minimum requirements of ANSI/NISO Z39.48-1992 (R1997). ∞

Designed by Lindsay Starr

LIBRARY OF CONGRESS CATALOGING-IN-PUBLICATION DATA
Scherer, Mark R.
  Rights in the balance : free press, fair trial, and Nebraska Press Association v. Stuart / Mark R. Scherer ; foreword by James W. Hewitt.
    p. cm.
  Summary: "A multiple murder case in Nebraska in October 1975 attracted massive media attention, spawning a collision between the rights of free press and fair trial. Scherer details the criminal prosecution and the ensuing legal battles that led to a landmark constitutional ruling regarding these rights by the U.S. Supreme Court"—Provided by publisher.
  Includes bibliographical references and index.
  ISBN-13: 978-0-89672-626-0 (hardcover : alk. paper)
  ISBN-10: 0-89672-626-6 (hardcover : alk. paper) 1. Free press and fair trial—United States. 2. Free press and fair trial—United States—Cases. 3. Freedom of the press—United States. 4. Fair trial—United States. 5. Nebraska Press Association. 6. Simants, Erwin Charles—Trials, litigation, etc. 7. Trials (Murder)—Nebraska—Lincoln County. I. Title.
  KF9223.5.S34 2008
  342.7308'53—dc22

                                                          2007042111

PRINTED IN THE UNITED STATES OF AMERICA
08 09 10 11 12 13 14 15 16 / 9 8 7 6 5 4 3 2 1

TEXAS TECH UNIVERSITY PRESS
Box 41037, Lubbock, Texas 79409-1037 USA
800.832.4042 | ttup@ttu.edu | www.ttup.ttu.edu

For Ben, who would have been a great historian

Free speech and fair trial are two of the most cherished policies of our civilization, and it would be a trying task to choose between them.

JUSTICE HUGO BLACK
Bridges v. California, 314 U.S. 252 (1941)

contents

ILLUSTRATIONS

foreword

I s there a "legal" culture on the Great Plains? Is there a "journal-istic" culture? Do lawyers and judges and media representatives in the nation's heartland differ in meaningful ways from their colleagues on the east and west coasts of the nation?

Mark Scherer—lawyer, historian, constitutional scholar—uses the vehicle of one of the Great Plains' most heinous murders to scru-tinize how Nebraska's legal community clashed with print media and broadcasting interests as both sides worked to produce a fair and open trial for a despicable man who had committed an awful crime. Lawyers and judges labored valiantly to keep confessional material from being revealed to the public, so that the pool of potential jurors would not be tainted by prior knowledge. The media worked just as diligently to make sure that the trial was open in every aspect, so that no vestige of the Star Chamber would pollute the proceedings.

The collision of important constitutional rights led ultimately to one of the more important pronouncements ever issued by the Supreme Court of the United States on freedom of the press. The col-lision of the First Amendment's guarantee of the press's right to pub-lish without prior restraint and the Sixth Amendment's guarantee of a speedy and public trial by an impartial jury reverberated across Nebraska, the Great Plains, and finally the nation. On the Plains, the contending interests demonstrated clearly that they knew the Con-stitution and were willing to fight for the principles they felt to be involved. In doing so, they conducted themselves with a degree of zeal and sophistication worthy of anyone anywhere in the country.

The important rights set forth in the Bill of Rights, as the first ten amendments to the Constitution are popularly known, are not prioritized. Is the First Amendment more meaningful than the Second? Or the Fifth? Or the Sixth? Scherer discusses at some length the conditions surrounding the original ratification of the Constitution that led to the subsequent adoption of the Bill of Rights. He spells out James Madison's drafting of seventeen amendments, ultimately reduced to twelve. What is now the First Amendment was originally the third, but it moved up two places when the first two amendments failed to be ratified. Thus placement in the amendment pantheon is not as critical as one might have supposed.

Over the years, conflicts between the First and Sixth amendments have occurred with some degree of frequency. Sometimes the press has prevailed, and sometimes it has not. A classic case of media extravagance is detailed by Scherer in the Cleveland murder trial of Dr. Sam Sheppard, who contended his wife was murdered by a "bushy-haired intruder." Such a conflict arose almost immediately in the case of Ervin Charles Simants, brought to trial over the October 1975 slaying of an entire family in Sutherland, a small town in Nebraska's spacious Lincoln County.

With Simants's immediate confession to his own family members and the Lincoln County Sheriff's swift public warning to citizens of a killer on the loose, the press descended upon Sutherland. A Denver television station chartered a helicopter that arrived shortly after midnight. Reporters from media outlets questioned rescue-squad and law-enforcement personnel through the night and, after Sheriff Gordon Gilster's press conference early the next morning, reported faithfully to their readers and listeners—setting off the chain of events that occasions this book.

Unlike Truman Capote, who wrote of the similar extermination of a Kansas family in his classic *In Cold Blood,* Scherer spends little time in psychoanalyzing Simants and his background. Instead, his focus is almost exclusively on the lawyers, both on the prosecution and defense, on the judge who struggled to make sure that Simants could be tried as fairly as possible in a community where his defects were well known, and on the members of Nebraska's media and their attorneys, who viewed the overturning of gag orders on the media as virtually a holy crusade.

Because Simants had confessed, by now in writing and to authorities, prosecutors—needing a showing sufficient to bind Simants over for trial—and the public defenders appointed to represent Simants both felt that restrictions should be placed upon the reportage of the preliminary hearing. When laboratory evidence arrived, establishing sexual assaults on the three deceased females, the lawyers viewed it as even more imperative that word of the awful nature of the crimes not be released into the surrounding community.

But it is at this juncture that the legal conundrum surfaces. Some thought had been given to closing the preliminary hearing to the public, but such closure was rejected. The complaint against Simants, originally outlining six counts of murder, had been amended to include the sexual assaults. The complaint was a public document, available to anyone who chose to peruse it. Any citizen of Sutherland who decided to attend the preliminary hearing could listen to all of the salacious details of the crime, and go home to tell his or her friends and neighbors what had transpired. What, then, was the justification for telling the media that it could not report the information adduced at the preliminary hearing? Yet that was what happened.

Scherer recounts at some length the angst suffered by the county judge, the jurist of first impression in the case. Urged on by both the prosecution and defense, he concluded that the press should be constrained from publishing details of the crime, so that ultimately Simants could be tried by an untainted jury. He therefore entered an order barring the press from reporting upon the preliminary hearing, and the conflict was off and running.

After the county judge's order, the district judge who would be the trial judge entered a restrictive order of his own, and the media appealed both to Justice Harry Blackmun of the U.S. Supreme Court, and to the Nebraska Supreme Court. Scherer does an incisive job of pointing up the conflict between Blackmun, who grew increasingly exasperated with the Nebraska court, and the Nebraska jurists who followed a long-extant pattern of resenting intrusion by the U.S. Supreme Court into matters properly within the ambit of the state court.

Blackmun entered a gag order of his own, the Nebraska Supreme Court punted, and the case was finally accepted for hearing by the U.S. Supreme Court after Simants had been tried and convicted. Although the specter of mootness was raised, the Supreme Court believed the issue of prior restraint on press publications was important enough to be decided, and decide it did.

What then is the meaning of *Nebraska Press Association v. Stuart?* How does it fit within the template of First Amendment jurisprudence? These questions for historians, lawyers, judges, and passionate defenders of a free press are well considered in what follows. In the final analysis, however, the tension between the two competing ideas has not been resolved. The issue will arise again. Pious protestations about the public's right to know may be tainted by the desire to sell newspapers or attract viewers. Arguments that a defendant's rights must be preserved inviolate against wide disclosure might simply mask a desire to be rid of pestering media representatives. But certain milestones have been erected, certain parameters have been established, and Mark Scherer has painstakingly presented us with a panoramic view of events as they unfolded on the Plains in 1975 and where they stand today.

James W. Hewitt
Lincoln, Nebraska, 2008

preface

While any errors of fact or interpretation in this book are mine alone, many other people deserve credit for whatever merit it may possess. My most profound appreciation goes to Dr. John Wunder at the University of Nebraska-Lincoln for his many years of assistance to me as a teacher, mentor, and colleague. This effort would not have been possible without his guidance and support. I owe special thanks also to Drs. David Wishart, Ken Winkle, and Alan Steinweis at UNL, each of whom offered valuable feedback on early versions of the manuscript. So, too, Judith Keeling, Karen Medlin, and the rest of the editorial and administrative staff at the Texas Tech University Press have been unfailingly kind, patient, and generous with me as we worked together to bring this book to fruition. They have my sincere gratitude for all of their efforts.

All of my colleagues at the University of Nebraska-Omaha have been most supportive of this project as well, offering their constant encouragement and assistance and frequently serving as valuable sounding boards for my ideas and interpretations. I owe special thanks to Drs. Jerold Simmons, Michael Tate, and Harl Dahlstrom in that regard. Funding for travel and research expenses in the early stages of this project came through a grant from the Charles and Mary Caldwell Martin Fund at the UNO Department of History, for which I am also grateful. Mr. Floyd Abrams, one of the true giants in First Amendment jurisprudence and a man whose career I have long admired, was kind enough to read and assess the book prior to its publication and offered me his valuable feedback. It has been a great honor for me to gain his participation and support in this effort.

The staffs of various libraries, archives, and judicial offices have been most helpful during my work in their facilities. Particularly important was the assistance of Anita Childerston, clerk of the Lincoln County District Court in North Platte, Nebraska, and her staff, who went out of their way to help me dig out the records I sought and were unfailingly gracious in letting me set up shop in their already-cramped quarters. Likewise, the administrative staffs of the Nebraska Supreme Court's Clerk's Office and the Office of the Clerk of the U.S. Supreme Court were most cooperative during my quests for relevant records under their control. JoAnn Ross and Jason James of the Schmid Law Library at the University of Nebraska-Lincoln were remarkably generous in allowing me access to their archival materials, at a time when their work spaces were in upheaval due to construction and relocation. Archivist John Jacob at the William and Mary Law School Library helped to produce some fascinating insights gleaned from the Lewis Powell Papers archived there.

A brief but important note on sources and citations: during the past thirty years, a number of journalists, attorneys, historians, and other commentators have analyzed and written about the Kellie family murders and the *Nebraska Press Association* litigation. In the course of their fine work, these scholars have interviewed and placed into the published record the memories of many of the key participants in the case. Among the most notable and valuable of those efforts are the works cited herein by journalism professors Nancy Whitmore and Joseph Russomanno, legal historian Bernard Schwartz, and the late renowned journalist Fred W. Friendly. This book is much the richer for its grounding in those previous works.

In the course of my research, I have also spoken with many of the surviving participants in the case, including journalists, attorneys, and judges who made many of the key decisions in the case. Among the many persons who have graciously and generously shared their time and memories with me are Keith Blackledge, Alan Peterson, the late Stephen McGill, James Koley, Woody Howe, the late Hugh Stuart, Ronald Ruff, and the late Joe Seacrest. When—as was often the case—

the stories these witnesses told me coincided with their previously published accounts, I have chosen, more often than not, to cite their quotations as they appeared in the earlier sources. I made this editorial choice for two reasons: first, to gain the advantage of the greater presumed accuracy that may be ascribed to memories of past events that are recorded closer to the time of the events they describe and, second, to draw the reader's attention to—and properly acknowledge—as many of these previously published accounts as I can.

Finally, my most personal and—until now—private appreciation goes to my family. My parents, siblings, and in-laws have given me constant encouragement throughout the time this book has been in the making. My sons Eric, Philip, and—until his death three years ago—Benjamin have been an abiding source of support and inspiration. Ultimately, my deepest gratitude goes to my wife, Lisa. She has been the glue that held our world together during the trauma of our son's death. She has been my muse and my most loyal colleague and friend. Her love and support have quite literally made this effort possible, and it is to her—and to Ben—that I dedicate the final product.

RIGHTS IN THE BALANCE

INTRODUCTION

*The Continuing Search for a
"Legal Culture" of the Great Plains*

S utherland, Nebraska, seems an unlikely point of origin for either a grotesque mass murder or a historic U.S. Supreme Court decision. Once rather disdainfully described as a "bleak prairie village" by an eastern commentator, the town lies in tranquil obscurity along the South Platte River in western Nebraska, about halfway between Omaha and Denver, and fifteen miles west of the larger town of North Platte, the seat of Lincoln County.[1] Despite its modern anonymity, the Lincoln County region is steeped in the history of American westward expansion, with numerous historical sites—including military outposts, Pony Express stations, and remains of the Oregon Trail—scattered throughout the area.[2] It is, in short, the very epitome of the classic "Great Plains" environment.

Today, Sutherland evokes contradictory impressions in a visitor's mind. Credited with just 1,032 residents in the 2000 federal census, the town's wind-worn homes and businesses seem simultaneously to suggest the dubious economic future and the rugged resilience of small rural communities on the Great Plains. Whatever may be said of Sutherland's present condition or its future viability, its past has been imprinted indelibly with the grisly events that occurred there thirty years ago—events that brought unwanted and tragic notoriety to the town and surrounding region and spawned a landmark decision in American legal history.

On the evening of October 19, 1975, six members of a respected Sutherland family, the Kellies, were brutally shot and killed in their home. The murderer, a local misfit named Erwin Charles Simants, sexually assaulted at least two of the three female victims both before and after their deaths. The tragedy that befell the Kellie family that night set in motion not only two highly charged murder trials for Simants but also a collision of constitutional interests that would ultimately reach all the way to the U.S. Supreme Court. At odds in that historic litigation would be two of the most cherished American constitutional protections—the First Amendment's guarantee of a free press and the Sixth Amendment's guarantee of a criminal defendant's right to a fair trial before an impartial jury.

Simants's crimes are strikingly and chillingly comparable to the macabre murders of the Clutter family in rural Holcomb, Kansas, in 1959—the events so vividly recounted in Truman Capote's 1965 classic *In Cold Blood*. Both storylines involved the brutal murder of innocent men, women, and children by sociopathic criminals. Both sets of victims were well known and respected in their respective communities. Both events created an atmosphere of fear, alarm, and paranoia in what had previously been trusting and open rural environments. Both events left significant legacies—the former leading to one of the most acclaimed books of the twentieth century and the latter leading to one of the most significant legal decisions of the past fifty years. Finally, and perhaps most enigmatically, both storylines emerged from remote and obscure parts of the American Great Plains—places that get little if any attention from mainstream American society unless and until notorious events occur there. Legal scholars continue to debate the issue of whether the Great Plains have spawned a unique regional "legal culture."[3] The full dimensions of that debate are beyond the scope of this book. What is abundantly clear, however, is that the terrible events that occurred in Sutherland, Nebraska, on that fateful night in 1975, like the *In Cold Blood* murders, have become an important part of Great Plains legal history. As historian Kermit L. Hall has aptly recognized, before we can identify a distinctive Plains legal culture, "We simply must learn more about law on the Great Plains."[4] This book pursues that goal.

One thread of the narrative herein will be the criminal prosecution of Erwin Simants for the six murders he committed. Simants would initially be convicted and sentenced to death in the Lincoln County District Court. Two years later, the Nebraska Supreme Court overturned that conviction and remanded the case for a new trial. In his second trial, Simants would be acquitted by reason of insanity. He remains today in the custody of the Lincoln Regional Center in Lincoln, Nebraska, where his mental status is reevaluated annually. If, in one of those annual reviews, a judge determines that Simants is no longer a danger to himself or others, state law requires that he be released from confinement.[5] Thus, it is conceivable, though probably unlikely, that Simants may someday walk free. The murders of the Kellie family and Simants's protracted court battles to avoid the electric chair are still quite sensitive subjects among longtime residents of Sutherland, North Platte, and the surrounding area in western Nebraska, many of whom believe that Simants has thus far avoided what they believe to be appropriate punishment for his heinous crimes.

As meaningful as the murder trials have been, however, there is a second legal story emanating from this tragedy that, at the level of constitutional history, leaves an even larger footprint. The murders of the Kellie family spawned an ancillary contest between the trial court judges in Lincoln County, Nebraska, and local, regional, and national news media organizations over the propriety of a judicial "gag order" imposed on the media during the period leading up to Simants's first trial. That conflict would weave its own complex procedural path through the state court system, ultimately arriving at the nation's highest court for resolution. The result would be the 1976 Supreme Court decision in *Nebraska Press Association v. Stuart*, an opinion that remains today one of the most significant Supreme

Court pronouncements on the delicate balance between the rights of free press and fair trial.

The constitutional dimensions of the *Nebraska Press Association* decision are familiar to judges, attorneys, journalists, and scholars in the field, but the human elements of the underlying story are much more obscure. As legal historian John Johnson has noted, "Any legal case study—even one of historic significance—is, at bottom, the story of individual people."[6] To the extent that the law is, to use Justice Oliver Wendell Holmes's classic phrase, a "magic mirror" that reflects the ebb and flow of American social, political, and cultural dynamics, the human stories that lay at the foundation of important legal decisions ought to be of paramount importance in the academic analysis of our legal and constitutional history.[7]

This book is an attempt, then, to tell the story of the Simants murder trials and the *Nebraska Press Association* litigation through a combination of traditional legal analysis and narrative storytelling that explores the human facets of the saga—not only the stories of victims and criminals but also law enforcement personnel, judges, jurors, attorneys, and members of the print and broadcast media, all of whom sought to perform their jobs, and juggle the competing interests at stake, under the most trying and emotional of circumstances. Ideally, the result will be a story that enriches the historical record in all its dimensions, acknowledging the constitutional intricacies and legacy of the Supreme Court decision while at the same time illuminating the broader historical and regional context in which the decision was made and the human tragedies and achievements that lie beneath the technical legal facade. And perhaps, somewhere along the way, we will gain new insights into an emerging and evolving, yet still quite elusive, Great Plains "legal culture."

one
A Trying Task to Choose

In order to enjoy the inestimable benefits that the liberty of the press
ensures, it is necessary to submit to the inevitable evils that it creates.

ALEXIS DE TOCQUEVILLE
Democracy in America, 1835

One of the enduring fascinations of the U.S. Bill of Rights is
the fact that it is not prioritized. The framers, applying what
historian Leonard Levy has aptly called a "genius for studied
imprecision," consciously chose to use broad and unqualified language in the Constitution and its first ten amendments, leaving to
future generations the problem of sorting out the relative "rankings"
of their various provisions when, as inevitably they would, conflicts
arose.[1] Thus, American courts have repeatedly confronted delicate
and often controversial analytical dilemmas—the constitutional
"balancing acts" that are so often required when eighteenth-century
language confronts twenty-first-century facts.

Perhaps no area of constitutional analysis has been more laden
with these types of concerns than the realm of First Amendment
interpretation and litigation. The familiar and unambiguous guarantee of a "free press" has often collided with other equally valued

and significant interests, such as national security, privacy, or personal reputation. From one generation to the next, American courts have announced various standards designed to "draw the lines" in some of these conflicts, such as Justice Oliver Wendell Holmes's famous "clear and present danger" test for speech that might threaten national security in times of war.[2]

Certainly one of the most troubling of such line-drawing dilemmas arises when the First Amendment's protection of a free press intersects with an equally treasured constitutional imperative—the Sixth Amendment's guarantee of a speedy and public trial by an impartial jury for all persons accused of crimes. Indeed, it would be difficult to identify two specifically enunciated constitutional interests that are both so valued and at the same time so frequently entangled with one another. As Justice Hugo Black noted in 1941, "Free speech and fair trial are two of the most cherished policies of our civilization, and it would be a trying task to choose between them."[3]

Trying though it may be, newspaper reporters, editors, prosecutors, defense attorneys, and trial court judges are routinely called upon to find a workable path through this confounding convergence of competing constitutional concerns. For almost 200 years, they had relatively little guidance from the U.S. Supreme Court to assist them in that task. The 1976 decision in *Nebraska Press Association v. Stuart* was one of the rare occasions upon which the Supreme Court did attempt to shed significant light on this problem.[4] The *Nebraska Press Association* decision emerged from the emotional trauma surrounding the horrific murders of six people in the tiny village of Sutherland, Nebraska, in the fall of 1975, but the critical constitutional issue that the high court finally addressed in 1976 was not only a result of the particular facts that brought that case to the Court for resolution. It was also a legacy of the historical development and evolution of free press and fair trial principles, as they emerged out of centuries of English common law and early American constitutional jurisprudence.

By the summer of 1787, when the delegates to the Constitutional Convention began their work in Philadelphia, the notion of a free press was firmly entrenched in the hearts and minds of most of America's citizenry. Just as significantly, it was anchored in the constitutional jurisprudence of most of the sovereign states that composed the new nation. The American conception of a "free press," moreover, seemed to have developed boundaries that extended well beyond those of English common law. For example, the English notion of free speech and press had been constrained for centuries by the principle of "seditious libel," which effectively prohibited criticism of public officials.[5] In one of the most celebrated trials of the colonial period, New York publisher John Peter Zenger was prosecuted in 1735 for seditious libel arising out of his publication of essays critical of the state's colonial governor. At the conclusion of the trial, the judge instructed the jury that Zenger's publication was in fact seditious and that truth was no defense to that crime. The jury, however, disregarded the judge's instructions and acquitted Zenger, concluding that the question of whether the writing was seditious was for the jury to decide and that truth was a valid defense. The Zenger trial has often been interpreted as a reflection of widespread colonial resentment over royal prosecutors' frequent use of seditious libel as a means of controlling the press. That resentment continued to escalate until, some historians suggest, it became one of the driving forces of the Revolution itself.[6]

During and after the Revolution, the American determination to ensure a free press persisted and became increasingly overt. In a widely disseminated and influential resolution issued in the summer of 1776, the Virginia legislature proclaimed that "freedom of the press is one of the greatest bulwarks of liberty, and can never be restrained by any despotick government."[7] Reflecting that sentiment, the constitutions of Virginia, Pennsylvania, and Maryland—each enacted in 1776 as the Revolution got fully under way—contained sections specifically guaranteeing freedom of the press.[8] In 1780 and 1782, respectively, the states of Massachusetts and Delaware placed almost identical clauses in their newly enacted constitutions. Most other states followed suit, reflecting an ever-growing belief that a free press was one of the sacred natural rights of American citizens.[9]

Despite that apparent widespread support for the principles of free speech and press, the U.S. Constitution, as originally drafted, contained no specific language on that point. On September 14, 1787, just four days before the convention completed its work, delegate

Charles Pinckney III of South Carolina proposed the insertion of a clause providing that "the liberty of the press shall be inviolably preserved."[10] The delegates rejected Pinckney's proposal, on the theory that the powers of Congress extended only to matters expressly delegated to it. Roger Sherman, a delegate from Connecticut, put the matter bluntly, saying of Pinckney's proposal, "It is unnecessary—the power of Congress does not extend to the Press."[11]

As the ratification debates proceeded in the states, however, a countervailing position began to emerge—the notion that Congress might seek to assert "implied" powers as well as those expressly granted to it. Therefore, the argument went, it was necessary to include provisions specifically prohibiting Congress from infringing on the freedom of the press, as well as on numerous other civil liberties of the people. As the ratification process dragged on, several key states, most notably Virginia, agreed to accept the new constitution only after receiving assurances that a bill of rights, guaranteeing freedom of speech, press, religion, and other civil liberties, would be added to the existing document.[12]

During the first U.S. Congress that convened in New York in the summer of 1789, James Madison and others sought to make good on the promise to provide a bill of rights. Madison introduced nine proposed amendments to the recently ratified Constitution, two of which contained language expressly addressing the free press issue.[13] One of those provisions, embedded in the second clause of his proposed Fourth Amendment, stated that "the freedom of the press, as one of the great bulwarks of liberty, shall be inviolable."[14] His second proposal, which comprised his entire Fifth Amendment, provided that "no state shall violate the equal rights of conscience, or the freedom of the press, or the trial by jury in criminal cases."[15]

After debate and alteration in committee, Madison's language with respect to free speech and press emerged as a combined proposal that encompassed religion, speech, and press. There was an attempt in the Senate to limit the scope of freedom of the press and speech by adding the words "in as ample a manner as hath at any time been secured by the common law."[16] The proposed addition was rejected by the full Senate.[17] After much additional debate, the proposal dealing with the freedom of religion, speech, and press was sent to the states for ratification, in its present form, as the third of twelve suggested amendments. The first two, dealing with legislative apportionment and congressmen's salaries, were not ratified by the requisite three-fourths of the state legislatures. As a result, the free religion/speech/press proposal moved up in order to become the present First Amendment.[18]

Similarly, the origins of the Sixth Amendment's guarantee of a "fair trial before an impartial jury" may be found in the evolution of English common law as it filtered through the American colonial experience. Twelfth- and thirteenth-century England witnessed a slow decline in the use of primitive criminal processes, such as trial by ordeal—a procedure in which the accused would be exposed to some physical danger, typically involving either fire or water, in the belief that God would rescue the innocent from harm and allow the guilty to suffer the natural consequences resulting from the ordeal— and a corresponding proliferation of new mechanisms for inquiry into criminal offenses, most notably the use of what became known as "grand juries" to determine whether individuals should be tried for certain crimes.[19] In the earliest stages of these developments, indictment by a grand jury created an almost insurmountable pre- sumption of an accused's guilt. As the process evolved over time, a person indicted by a grand jury acquired the right to rebut the pre- sumption of guilt by "putting himself upon the country"—that is, the defendant agreed to accept the decision of his community with respect to his guilt or innocence, as it would be pronounced by his neighbors sitting on what became known as a "petit jury."[20]

In sharp contrast to modern practice, these earliest trial juries were chosen not for their impartiality, but rather for their knowledge of the case. That is, they sat as "witness juries," qualified specifically because of their knowledge of the defendant and the circumstances surrounding the alleged offense. By the sixteenth century, this use of "witness juries" gave way to a procedure in which the litigants pro- duced the evidence upon which the jury relied, with the juries serving as impartial arbiters of the credibility of witnesses and other "issues of fact." That conception of juries, though originally limited to civil cases, had been extended to criminal trials by 1700 in both England and the American colonies. By the time of the Revolution, the right to be judged by a jury drawn from one's own community had become firmly anchored in American criminal procedure. During the American Revolution, the Continental Congress proclaimed the right of every citizen to have public trials by "their peers of the vicinage."[21] Similar assurances made their way into the constitutions of each of eleven states that drafted them during the Revolution.[22]

Given that firm foundation in tradition and practice, it is not surprising that the proposal to include a specific assurance of the right to jury trial among the first amendments to the constitution was not a particularly controversial notion. In the First Congress, James Madison offered language that provided that "criminal trials shall be by an impartial jury of freeholders of the vicinage."[23] Like his free press proposal, Madison's language was reshaped through committee deliberations until it ultimately emerged as part of what is now the Sixth Amendment: "In all criminal prosecutions the accused shall enjoy the right to a speedy and public trial, by an impartial jury of the state and district wherein the crime shall have been committed." Upon its ratification by three-fourths of the existing states, that language, like the provisions of the First Amendment, became a part of American scripture—a fundamental right that, like freedom of the press, is certainly among the most cherished and fiercely protected of all American civil liberties.

What, then, of the potential conflict between the rights of free press and fair trial? In light of the "studied imprecision" of the language used in the First and Sixth Amendments, their potential clash seems to have been inevitable from the start. If, for example, an unqualifiedly free press reports on a particular crime in a manner that is so thorough and pervasive as to suggest the near-certain guilt of a particular defendant, has not that defendant been denied his equally unqualified constitutional right to an impartial jury? Such scenarios have been common in American history, yet they have spawned only a modest line of Supreme Court decisions dating back to 1807 in which the high court has addressed various aspects of the constitutional dilemma without ever fully resolving it. In terms of the historical context from which the *Nebraska Press Association* litigation emerged, four such precedents bear specific attention.

The first, and certainly one of the most celebrated, judicial commentaries on the meaning of the phrase "impartial jury" vis-à-vis the rights of a free press came in 1807, when Supreme Court Chief Justice John Marshall sat as the trial judge in the treason prosecution of former Vice President Aaron Burr.[24] Burr was charged with involvement in a rather murky and far-fetched conspiracy to create a new "empire," carved out of parts of Spanish and American territory west of the Allegheny River. In view of Burr's notoriety and the dramatic overtones of the charges against him, the case drew overwhelming attention in the newspapers of the day, particularly in and around Richmond, Virginia, where his trial was held that August. Under these circumstances, Marshall was compelled to expend considerable time and effort conducting an extensive examination of potential jurors to determine their impartiality, and he issued a significant opinion on the standards to be applied in such cases.

At the most fundamental level, Marshall reiterated the common-law rule that potential jurors who have formed an opinion about a defendant's guilt or innocence before the trial started should be removed from the panel. The more intricate elements of his lengthy decision, however, relate to his exploration of the degree to which pretrial impressions formed by prospective jurors might negate their impartiality. The essence of his conclusion was that pretrial opinions were unconstitutional, while pretrial impressions were not. In drawing a subtle distinction between the two, Marshall described impressions as thoughts formed before trial that "are so lightly held that they are quite capable of being changed by courtroom evidence."[25]

Marshall went on to note that the determination of whether a prospective juror was, in fact, tainted by pretrial opinion could not be accomplished by the cursory sort of pretrial questioning that was typical in that era. Judges could not merely accept a juror's word on the issue at face value. Only by closely and conscientiously questioning each prospective juror, he held, could a trial judge evaluate the sincerity of a juror's vow to consider the evidence impartially.[26]

The concerns raised in Marshall's opinion in *Burr* neither disappeared over the ensuing generations nor produced any immediate Supreme Court guidance on the issue. It was not until 1878 that the high court addressed the free press/fair trial issue in a substantive

way. In *Reynolds v. United States,* George Reynolds, the personal sec-
retary of Brigham Young, challenged his conviction for bigamy on
numerous constitutional grounds.[27] For purposes of the instant discussion, the most significant of his claims were that his jury had been
prejudiced against him and that the trial court had improperly disal-
lowed several of his attorneys' challenges to the jury panel.

In an opinion authored by Chief Justice Morrison R. Waite that
ultimately affirmed Reynolds's conviction, the Court for the first
time attempted to give trial courts some guidance in dealing with the
difficult issue of what constitutes an impartial juror. Waite announced
three primary conclusions that would prove significant. First, he
held that not all opinions formed by prospective jurors—including
those formed from reading newspapers—are necessarily unconstitutionally prejudicial. As Marshall had done seventy years earlier in
distinguishing impermissible opinions from permissible impressions, Waite drew a distinction between light and firm opinions. The
former were permissible, whereas the latter were not. He defined
prejudicial firm opinions as those so strongly held that "they resist
pressure from the evidence to change."[28]

Second, Waite held that it is the job of the trial judge to determine
juror impartiality as a "mixed question of law and fact."[29] That conclusion brought Waite to the portion of his decision that would have
the most direct and significant impact on later appellate rulings. He
held that the trial court's discretionary judgment on the question of
a juror's impartiality was entitled to great deference from appellate
courts and should be reversed only if a clear or manifest error was
committed. Finally, Waite held that all jurors were presumed to be
impartial and that, therefore, the burden of proof in showing a juror's
prejudice was upon the party that challenged it.[30] Collectively, these
elements of *Reynolds v. United States* provided the procedural rules
and standards of review that would control the debate on these issues
for the next century.

In 1961, the Supreme Court revisited the free press/fair trial issue
in *Irvin v. Dowd.*[31] The case involved an Indiana murder trial that had
resulted in massive publicity in a relatively isolated rural area—publicity that included the publication of the murderer's confession to
police. In its decision reversing the defendant's conviction, the Court

essentially concluded that, in some circumstances, pretrial publicity can be so intense and so pervasive that all prospective jurors in a given geographical area cannot be believed when they assert that they are still impartial. Justice Tom Clark, writing for a unanimous Court, held that jurors' declarations that they believe themselves to be impartial do not automatically make them so, no matter how sincere those beliefs may be. If there is evidence of overwhelming pretrial publicity that has the potential of affecting the judgment of the entire jury panel, Clark concluded, an appellate court must take that into consideration, and may reverse a trial court's determination on that point. After an extensive review of the pervasive publicity that surrounded the Indiana trial, Clark concluded that, "in light of the circumstances here, the finding of impartiality [by the trial court and the lower appellate court] does not meet constitutional standards."[32]

In a compelling and oft-cited concurring opinion, Justice Felix Frankfurter vented his frustration with what he perceived to be an increasingly irresponsible press. He noted that what had happened in the Indiana case was "not an isolated case . . . nor an atypical miscarriage of justice due to anticipatory trial by newspapers instead of trial in court before a jury." He caustically criticized the "distortions," "inflammatory newspaper accounts," and "extraneous influences" that were routinely "violating the decencies guaranteed by our Constitution," and he concluded by reminding the media that "this Court has not yet decided that the fair administration of criminal justice must be subordinated to . . . freedom of the press."[33] In view of the strong language of both Clark's majority opinion and Frankfurter's concurrence, *Dowd* may be seen as a significant swing of the pendulum back toward the side of the Sixth Amendment in the never-ending tug and pull between the rights of free press and fair trial.

Five years later, the Supreme Court was presented with a situation that remains to this day the prototypical example of the potential excesses of "trial by newspaper." In *Sheppard v. Maxwell* (1966), the Court reviewed the conviction of Cleveland, Ohio, neurosurgeon Sam Sheppard for the murder of his wife in 1954.[34] Sheppard's arrest and trial had received rabid coverage in the local and regional press—publicity that resulted in what the Court referred to as a carnival atmosphere surrounding the trial and a Roman holiday for the press.[35]

The full details of the press's excesses before, during, and after the Sheppard trial are beyond the scope of this discussion, but the Court, speaking unanimously through an opinion again authored by Justice Tom Clark, ultimately concluded that the trial court judge had completely "lost his ability to control his courtroom" and that bedlam reigned during the trial.[36] The Court noted that the trial judge had "assigned almost all of the available seats" in the courtroom to the media and had given "absolute free reign" to the "throng of newsmen" from all over the country who flocked to the trial.[37] Many of the constitutional infirmities from which the trial suffered, Clark wrote, could have been avoided if the judge had simply understood that "the courtroom and courthouse premises are subject to the control of the court."[38] On the basis of these and many other findings, the Court ultimately held that "since the state trial court judge did not fulfill his duty to protect Sheppard from the inherently prejudicial publicity which saturated the community and to control disruptive influences in the courtroom, we must reverse [Sheppard's conviction]."[39]

Sheppard was a milestone in the Court's handling of the free press/fair trial issue. For the first time, the justices presented a list of specific steps that trial courts could take to protect jurors from the effects of prejudicial pretrial publicity. Clark outlined eleven specific measures available to trial judges, including limitations on the number of journalists allowed in the courtroom; strict controls on the behavior and decorum of members of the media; extensive questioning of jurors to eliminate those with pretrial prejudice; control of the release of information to the press by participants in the trial such as attorneys and witnesses; strong warnings to the jury to disregard all information other than the evidence they hear at trial; change of venue; delay of the trial until the publicity subsides; and, when absolutely necessary, the granting of a new trial.[40]

The ruling and rationale of the *Sheppard* decision combined with the impact of *Dowd* five years earlier to reshape the dynamics of the free press/fair trial debate, making courts substantially more sensitive to the demands of the Sixth Amendment. In the next decade, trial court judges all over the country, acutely aware of the criticism heaped upon the presiding judge in *Sheppard* and mindful of the increasingly pervasive reach of the media, struggled to find a constitutionally acceptable middle ground between First and Sixth Amendment values. In October 1975, in a tiny and obscure village on the plains of western Nebraska, tragic events would bring those issues once again to the nation's highest court. The story of *Nebraska Press Association v. Stuart* was about to begin.

TWO

The Crimes, the Victims, the Media

Everyone in town who had a gun probably had it
loaded and with them, or knew where it was.

LINCOLN COUNTY DEPUTY SHERIFF DAVID SUTER
October 20, 1975

T
he small town of North Platte, Nebraska, where Erwin Charles
Simants was born in 1945, has received well-deserved recognition and praise for its wholesome heartland charm during
World War II. In 2002, best-selling author Bob Greene's *Once Upon a
Town: The Miracle of the North Platte Canteen* described North Platte as
"the best America there ever was" for the remarkable hospitality and
generosity of spirit with which its citizens greeted, fed, and entertained hundreds of thousands of soldiers traveling by train across
the Nebraska plains to departure sites on both coasts.[1]

That justifiably positive imagery notwithstanding, Erwin Simants's childhood in and around the area of North Platte during the
1940s and 1950s was less than idyllic. The eighth of ten children born
to Amos and Grace Simants, he was raised in a family where money
was always scarce—so much so that his youngest sister had to be
"adopted out as a baby because there were too many children to take

care of."[2] As Simants grew up, alcoholism became increasingly pervasive within the family, eventually afflicting all five of his older brothers and at least one of his sisters.[3] Known as "Herb" or "Herbie" to his friends and family, Simants struggled in school and finally dropped out at age sixteen, having reached only the seventh grade. After quitting school, he drifted from one menial job to another, drinking heavily and acquiring a lengthy police record throughout western Nebraska, with numerous convictions for public intoxication and other nonviolent offenses.

When he was twenty-one, Simants impregnated and then married a fourteen-year-old girl. As a result of that relationship, Simants was convicted of contributing to the delinquency of a minor, adding the first sex-related offense to his growing criminal record. Remarkably enough, that early conviction brought Simants before the Nebraska Supreme Court more than seven years before he became infamous for the Kellie murders. The public defenders who represented Simants on the delinquency of a minor charge in 1967 appealed his conviction in the case, claiming that the language of the statute under which he had been charged was unconstitutionally vague and ambiguous. The Nebraska Supreme Court rejected that argument and upheld Simants's conviction.[4]

The young couple's daughter died at age three of a congenital birth defect. Simants and his wife divorced shortly after the death of their child, and he would later report that the child's death and the ensuing divorce sent him into a deep depression, to the extent that he "didn't care what he did or what happened to him."[5] Simants spent the years after his divorce drinking ever more heavily and drifting aimlessly from one job to another in North Platte and the smaller community of Sutherland, fifteen miles to the west. By October of 1975, he appeared to have hit rock bottom. Unemployed, only semiliterate, and enmeshed in alcoholism and sexual frustration, he lived with his sister and brother-in-law, William and Sandra Boggs, in the basement of their home in Sutherland. As empty as his life appeared to have become, however, Herb Simants was about to make a bad situation unimaginably worse.

On the morning of Saturday, October 18, 1975, Simants accompanied his brother-in-law Bill Boggs on a short trip to North Platte.[6]

They returned to Sutherland at about 2:30 that afternoon and went to the Rodeo Bar, one of the two taverns in town. Simants and Boggs began drinking, with Boggs later recalling that Simants may have finished five or six beers within the first hour.[7] They were soon joined at the bar by Simants's sister Sandra and other acquaintances. Around 8:00 p.m., at Simants's request, Sandra drove him back to the Boggs home. After dropping Herb off and checking briefly on her children, Sandra returned to the bar. Simants entered the house, smoked a cigarette, and talked briefly with his thirteen-year-old nephew, James (Butch) Boggs, who was babysitting the younger Boggs children. Looking out a window, Simants observed ten-year-old Florence Kellie, a next-door neighbor, playing in the yard with the younger Boggs children.[8] Acting on impulses that can still only be guessed at to this day, Simants then went into the Boggses' bedroom, retrieved a .22 caliber rifle owned by his brother-in-law, and loaded it with shells. After telling Butch to "keep the kids in here," Simants left the house and headed toward the home of Henry and Marie Kellie, located next to and directly north of the Boggs residence.[9]

The Kellie family had lived in Sutherland for more than twenty years, earning a reputation as quiet, good-hearted, and hardworking members of the community. Sixty-six-year-old Henry Kellie was semiretired from a lifetime of farm labor. He still raised a few head of cattle and took occasional light farm work to supplement his Social Security income. His wife Marie, fifty-seven years old, worked as a cook at the Moore Memorial Nursing Home in Sutherland. Described by coworkers as "truthful, honest, and sincere," Marie was active and well liked throughout the community.[10] Both Kellies attended the Sutherland Wesleyan Methodist Church and regularly assisted in church services conducted at the nursing home where Marie worked.

Henry and Marie had reared two daughters and a son. Their oldest child, Audrey, was married and had moved from North Platte to Colorado with her family earlier in 1975.[11] A younger daughter, Jennie, died in a car accident in 1966, leaving behind a child, Florence. In the aftermath of that tragedy, the Kellies had taken guardianship of Florence and were raising her in their home. The girl was ten years old in the fall of 1975, a fifth grader at Sutherland Elementary School.

Thirty-two-year-old David Kellie, Henry and Marie's middle child and only son, lived near his parents in Sutherland and worked at a grain mill in the nearby town of Hershey. Divorced for several years, David shared custody of his two children, seven-year-old Deanne and five-year-old Daniel. David and the two grandchildren visited Henry and Marie frequently and regularly ate Saturday evening dinners at the home of the elder Kellies.

One of the tragic ironies of October 18, 1975, is that, until that night, the Kellies seemed to have been almost the only people in the community who had developed any sort of a friendly relationship with Herb Simants. In fact, just three weeks before, Henry had paid a $50 fine to free Simants from jail after yet another of his many arrests for public intoxication. The Kellies' minister, Reverend Nils Ibsen, would later observe that Henry's act of kindness toward Simants was typical of his character, saying, "Henry was well liked and it was just his nature to help people."[12] Another friend of the Kellies echoed that sentiment, noting that "Henry had done this sort of thing for years. If anybody needed a helping hand, he'd give it to them."[13] In the three weeks since Henry Kellie had paid his fine, Simants had been doing occasional odd jobs for the Kellies to repay the debt. As far as anyone knew, no tension or rancor had developed. Marie Kellie had mentioned Simants to her coworkers on several occasions but had never even hinted at any kind of impending trouble. The worst that she had ever been heard to have said about him was that "he was quite a drinker, but we all have our faults."[14] On the very day of the killings, Simants himself was reported to have told people that Henry Kellie "was the best friend he ever had."[15]

Even after the passage of more than thirty years, the horror of Simants's actions that night still lingers in the minds of many of the area's residents and shocks the conscience of anyone who revisits the bloody details. The most definitive, albeit chilling, source for the description of the murders is the confession Simants gave to Sheriff Gordon "Hop" Gilster and Nebraska State Patrol Investigator Donald Grieb on the morning of his arrest. That statement was tape recorded, transcribed, and signed by Simants.[16] In it, he told the officers that he had carried the loaded .22 caliber rifle he had taken from the Boggses' bedroom as he headed toward the Kellies' small white frame home next door. He knocked on the Kellies' door and was admitted into the house by Florence, who had come in from playing with the Boggs children. Grabbing the girl, he shoved her into one of the home's two bedrooms and forcibly removed her clothes.[17] He began fondling Florence's genitals and inserted his finger into her vagina. She cried out, saying that he was hurting her. At that point, Simants retrieved the rifle that he had set in a corner of the room and shot Florence in the right temple at point-blank range.[18] After killing the girl, Simants continued to fondle her genital area and may have attempted to complete penetration of her vagina with his penis. He would later claim that he could not recall precisely what he had done in terms of the sexual assault on Florence or any of the other victims.[19]

A few moments after he killed Florence, Simants heard the girl's grandfather Henry enter the house. Simants went to the doorway of the bedroom, watched Henry walk past, and then shot him in the back of the head. He then dragged Henry's body into the bedroom, leaving it in a heap on the floor next to the bed upon which his granddaughter's body lay.[20] A short time later, Marie walked into the house. Seeing Simants and the two bodies in the bedroom, she had just enough time to murmur, "Oh my God," before Simants killed her with a single shot through her right eye. After Marie fell to the floor dead, Simants lifted her skirt, tore out the crotch of her panties, and proceeded to sexually molest her dead body.[21]

Shortly thereafter, David Kellie arrived at the house with his children Deanne and Daniel. As the two children watched, Simants shot David twice as he entered the home. One bullet struck him in the middle of the forehead and a second entered his cheek just below the left eye. As David lay mortally wounded, Simants shot seven-year-old Deanne once in the head, then turned and shot five-year-old Daniel twice in the head, killing both children instantly.[22] The carnage was over within about forty-five minutes.

Simants returned to the Boggs house, bringing the rifle with him. He unloaded the gun, placed it back where he had found it in the Boggses' bedroom, and then sat down at the kitchen table and wrote a note, saying, "I am sorry to all—it is the best way out—do not crie [sic]."[23] After taking the note downstairs and leaving it on a fan near his bed, Simants told Butch, "I've just killed the Kellies." He

Simants's handwritten "confession" note, October 18, 1975.

proceeded to specifically tell the astonished boy that he had shot Henry, Marie, and "a little kid and a girl." He said he didn't want to kill David but that "he came in and so I had to."[24]

Simants then asked Butch to "call Grandma," referring to his mother, Grace Simants. After Butch placed the call, Simants took the phone and talked briefly with his parents, telling them about the murders and saying, "I'm coming home."[25] Simants then walked to his parents' home and repeated his admission. Amos Simants told his son that he didn't believe the story, but he immediately drove to the Kellie home to check. When he arrived there, he pushed the door open and discovered the gruesome scene.[26] Aghast at what he had seen, Amos returned to his home and called the community power plant, where emergency calls for the Sutherland area were received. Without identifying himself, Amos told Floyd Paulman, who was taking calls at the plant that night, "We need an emergency unit," told him where to send the unit, and then hung up.[27] After placing the call, Amos spoke briefly again with Herb, telling him that he had to turn himself in to authorities. Simants instead left the house. Amos then returned to the Kellie house to await the arrival of the ambulance.[28]

June Lindstrom, a nurse who headed the Sutherland rescue squad, was the first emergency worker to enter the home. A close friend of the Kellies—she had assisted with the delivery of Florence when the child was born—Lindstrom was overwhelmed by what she found: "My first thought was 'My God, what happened!'"[29] Lindstrom and the other rescuers found the victims' bodies scattered all around the house—Marie hunched over by the couch, Deanne crouching in a corner as if she were hiding, Florence on the bed in the bedroom with Henry on the floor beside her, and David lying face down in the hallway with his son Daniel on top of him.[30] Looking more closely at David, Lindstrom noticed "bubbles of blood coming from his mouth" and discovered that he was still breathing.[31] An ambulance rushed David to Great Plains Medical Center in North Platte, but he died shortly after arrival, without regaining consciousness.

Lincoln County Deputy Sheriff David Suter was the first law enforcement official to arrive at the crime scene, getting there just a few minutes before the emergency squad. He was soon joined by Deputies Sterling Tatro and Richard Gibbons and Nebraska State Patrol investigators James Burnett and Terry Livengood. Together the officers secured the crime scene and began their investigation. Speaking with Amos Simants and William Boggs, the officials quickly learned of Erwin Simants's role in the grisly events and transmitted descriptions of him to all law enforcement agencies in the region.[32] Standing outside the Kellie home with rescue squad workers, news reporters, and other onlookers, Amos Simants tearfully confirmed to reporters what he had already told the officers, "My son killed five or six people here."[33] Dozens of additional law officers from North Platte and other nearby communities, along with more state patrol officials and investigators, soon descended on the scene, and a manhunt for Erwin Simants commenced.

Acting on the order of Sheriff Gilster, a dispatcher from the sheriff's office telephoned KNOP-TV in North Platte at 9:18 p.m. Don Feldman, the station's only full-time news reporter, answered the call and was surprised when the frantic caller shouted, "Something terrible has happened in Sutherland. Hop wants you to put the following warning on the air immediately: 'Everybody lock your doors and windows. Don't answer your door without a thorough check of the person knocking or ringing your doorbell. There's a sniper loose with a shotgun, and he's killing people.'"[34] Feeling that he had to confirm the call before broadcasting such an alarming message, Feldman said he would return the call to the sheriff's office and then told the panicky deputy to whom he spoke that he would need more detailed

Florence Kellie, ten years old at the time of her death. Courtesy *North Platte Telegraph*.

Marie Kellie, fifty-seven years old at the time of her death. Courtesy *North Platte Telegraph*.

Deanna Kellie, seven years old at the time of her death. Courtesy *North Platte Telegraph*.

Daniel Kellie, five years old at the time of his death. Courtesy *North Platte Telegraph*.

information than the mere "something terrible has happened." After several more phone conversations, including a radio call to Sheriff Gilster who was at the crime scene, Feldman drafted and aired at 9:37 p.m. an "interrupt bulletin" reporting that there had been a killing in Sutherland and warning viewers to "lock their doors and windows and admit no one." Following this initial bulletin, area radio stations began to broadcast similar warnings.[35]

In an eerily coincidental twist to the night's events, at the time of the murders and the ensuing news bulletins, KNOP was broadcasting a movie titled *The Deadly Tower,* depicting a tragic 1966 incident in which deranged sniper Charles Whitman, shooting from a tower on the University of Texas campus, killed and wounded dozens of people.[36] When KNOP ran the bulletin announcing the murders in Sutherland, it was superimposed over a scene in the movie depicting the sniper being killed by Austin police. Many area residents would later indicate that the juxtaposition of the movie with the real-life bulletins created a widespread perception that a copycat sniper was on the loose in Sutherland.[37]

As news of the murders spread, a fearful siege mentality took hold throughout Sutherland, North Platte, and Lincoln County. Phone lines were jammed as residents talked among themselves about the crimes and outsiders called to try to obtain additional information and check on the safety of their friends or relatives. Rumors circulated that the police were engaged in a door-to-door search and had been issued a "shoot to kill" order if the suspect was sighted. A dance at the local American Legion Hall was shut down, with police advising people to go home and lock their doors. At about 10:00 p.m., officers met three buses bringing the Sutherland High School band back from a contest in Chadron, Nebraska, and stood by at the school as worried parents picked up their children. Later in the evening, roadblocks were set up around Sutherland, with officials stopping all cars and carefully searching each one for the suspect. A long, tense, and sleepless night set in for most area residents.[38]

Meanwhile, Sutherland's city hall became the focal point of frenzied media and law enforcement activity. Phone calls from national news organizations and media outlets from as far away as New York began coming in, seeking additional information. Local and regional reporters and wire service representatives pressed officials for more details. A news helicopter chartered by the NBC television affiliate in Denver, Colorado, arrived in the area in the early hours of Sunday morning, hovering over the crime scene even before the victims' bodies had been removed from the house.[39]

As the night wore on, information trickled out to the media in small doses. County attorney Milton Larson and his deputy, Marvin

Holscher, conducted an informal press conference at city hall, giving the reporters gathered there a physical description of the suspect but not naming Simants as the person being sought. Mayor Herbert Meissner of Sutherland conferred with the press as well, giving reporters the first tentative identification of the victims. Meissner, who owned and operated the grain mill where David Kellie worked, told reporters that David had been a friend for more than ten years, saying, "In a town of 800, you get to know everyone, but some better than others."[40]

As the investigation at the crime scene continued, a large group of reporters took up posts near the Kellie home. Holscher established an informal press "restraining line" along a hedge in front of the house, and tension between officials and reporters escalated. At one point, as the newsmen clamored for more information to meet their approaching deadlines, Holscher shouted, "Goddamn it, I'm not going to try this case on the lawn of the house, or in the media." Frank Santiago, a reporter from the *Omaha World-Herald*, responded, "You're not telling us what happened. You're going to make an ass of yourself, Holscher." Holscher recalled Santiago's comment as the more threatening, "I'm going to make an ass out of you." Regardless of which version of the exchange was accurate, the strain of the night's events on both the law enforcement officials and the reporters was becoming increasingly apparent.[41] Later in the evening, Holscher did reveal that a gun had been recovered that appeared to be the murder weapon. He refused, however, to further specify the type of weapon, other than to state that it was not a shotgun.[42]

Incredibly, as the bodies of his victims were being discovered and news of the crimes began to circulate, Herb Simants walked back to the Rodeo Bar, where he calmly sat down and ordered a beer. Neither the bartender, Jack Humphrey, nor any of the other patrons were aware of the murders at the time. Humphrey later recalled that Simants "didn't appear to be drunk."[43] He served Simants one beer, which he drank and then left. Simants walked down the street to the other bar in town, the Longhorn, where he ordered and drank another beer. Just as at the Rodeo, no one in the Longhorn was yet aware of the murders, so they thought nothing of Simants's presence, nor did they note anything unusual in his behavior. After drinking the second

The Kellie home, shown on the evening of the murders. Reprinted with permission from the *Omaha World-Herald*.

beer, Simants left the bar, apparently with no firm plan for what to do next. While dozens of lawmen looked for him, Simants spent the rest of the night wandering in the weeds and brush in backyards and fields on the outskirts of town, mostly in the area immediately around the Boggs and Kellie homes. Near daybreak, Simants took refuge in a chicken coop at the back of the Boggs property.[44]

Around 7:30 Sunday morning, Simants emerged from the chicken coop and knocked on the door of the Boggs house. Bill and Sandy refused to let him in and called the authorities. Within minutes, Sheriff Gilster and State Patrol Investigator Donald Grieb arrived and found Simants in the backyard. Gilster ordered Simants to put his hands on the side of the house. He complied, and the sheriff proceeded to handcuff and search him. Gilster informed Simants that he was under arrest for the Kellie murders and read him his Miranda rights. By 8:30 that morning, Simants had been transported to the Lincoln County jail in North Platte, booked, and clothed in blue-striped denim jail fatigues. He had also been "Mirandized" at least two more times by various officials. Not yet represented by counsel,

Simants waived his right to remain silent and gave an oral statement to the authorities in which he admitted the murders. The statement was subsequently tape recorded, transcribed, and signed by Simants.[45]

While law enforcement officials were processing Simants and taking his confession, Lincoln County Attorney Milton Larson prepared a criminal complaint formally charging him with six counts of premeditated murder.[46] At 10:44 Sunday morning, authorities brought Simants before Lincoln County Court Judge Ronald Ruff for arraignment. In criminal procedure, an arraignment is a hearing designed to advise an arrested suspect of the nature of the charges against him and address other preliminary matters, such as the defendant's right to counsel and the question of bail. Arraignment proceedings serve to meet the constitutional mandate that a person accused of a crime receive timely notice of the reason he or she is being held.[47] Security in the courthouse was tight for this first judicial proceeding in Simants's prosecution, with officials searching newsmen for cameras and recording devices before they were allowed to enter the courtroom.[48] Judge Ruff began the session by directing the prosecutor to read the charges against Simants into the record. As Larson formally read the complaint, Simants sat quietly with his head down, handcuffed to Sheriff Gilster. Ruff then advised Simants once again of his right to remain silent and asked him if he had money to retain counsel. When Simants indicated that he did not, Ruff appointed Lincoln County Public Defenders Leonard Vyhnalek and Keith Bystrom, both of whom were already present in the courtroom, to represent him.[49]

When Vyhnalek and Bystrom raised the issue of bail for their new client, prosecutor Larson asked Judge Ruff to clear the courtroom of all spectators, inasmuch as the prosecution's resistance to the defense request for bail would require the introduction of evidence "which may be prejudicial to the defendant in securing a fair trial."[50] Judge Ruff agreed and ordered the sheriff to clear the courtroom, after which the judge heard Larson present a statement of the evidence against Simants that had been gathered by authorities to that time. After Larson's statement, Ruff allowed the spectators to reenter the courtroom. In open court, Judge Ruff told Simants that "from the evidence that has been submitted to this court, it appears that the presumption is great and that you have committed the crimes of murder in the first degree in six counts. It is therefore ordered that you be held in the Lincoln County Jail without bond pending further action in this court."[51] Ruff then ended the arraignment by setting a preliminary hearing in the case for 9:00 a.m. on the following Wednesday, October 22. In Nebraska, the preliminary hearing in a criminal case serves the same purpose as a grand jury's indictment—that is, it is a proceeding to determine whether there is sufficient evidence to conclude that a crime has been committed and that there is probable cause to believe that the accused defendant committed that crime.[52] Sheriff Gilster returned Simants to the county jail, with news photographers snapping dozens of pictures as he was being led across the street from the courthouse to the jail.[53]

As the legal proceedings against Simants got under way on Sunday, the media attention to the story continued to intensify. Dozens of local, regional, and national news reporters, wire service representatives, and broadcasters had converged on Sutherland and North Platte by the early morning hours of Sunday. In the ensuing days and weeks, hundreds of newspaper stories and broadcast reports about the case flooded the region.[54] Naturally, the media attention focused primarily on Erwin Simants and his apparent involvement in the crimes. Dan Meyers, a reporter for KAHL radio station in North Platte, conducted an on-air interview with Mrs. Laura Woodard of Sutherland, during which he asked Woodard to describe "the Kellie family which was murdered last evening by Simants."[55] Woodard described the Kellies as a "good, church-going family." When asked if she knew Simants, Woodard replied that she didn't know him that well but that he was "more or less a troublemaker probably, or, I don't know really, if he's a troublemaker, but liquor was his downfall."[56]

Later that Sunday morning, NBC released to hundreds of its affiliates around the country a report on the murders compiled by Jim Lee, a reporter from KOA-TV in Denver. Lee, who had flown to Sutherland by helicopter from Denver the previous night, included in his feverish account the statement that "Simants reportedly confessed to his father after the killings, then fled."[57] That same report would be broadcast nationwide on the *NBC Nightly News* Sunday evening and on NBC's *Today* show Monday morning. KNOP-TV, the only television station in North Platte, aired numerous reports on the murders throughout Sunday, including on-air interviews with Sheriff Gilster, who was quickly becoming a fertile source for the media. Virtually all of Sunday's broadcast reports contained information directly linking Simants to the crimes, often citing Sheriff Gilster as a source. Shortly after Simants's arrest and booking, Gilster held a press conference attended by dozens of print and broadcast reporters in which he repeatedly acknowledged Simants's role in the previous night's grisly events. One KNOP report quoted Gilster to the effect that "Simants had told his father, who lives only a few doors from the scene, that he was responsible for the shootings. Simants's father reportedly told his son to give up, but instead he ran."[58] When a reporter asked Gilster whether he had been surprised when Sandra Boggs called his office that morning to report that Simants was there, he replied, "It didn't surprise me . . . a lot of times they say they return to the scene."[59]

Later in that same broadcast interview, the following exchange between Gilster and the reporter aired:

> Reporter: *You mean after he [Simants] had shot these people, he went in and got a drink in a bar?*
> Gilster: *Yes.*
> Reporter: *Why did he kill these people?*
> Gilster: *I can't say at this time.*[60]

Area radio stations, along with both the AP and UPI wire services, repeatedly broadcast these and similar offerings by the sheriff throughout Sunday afternoon and evening.

Given the timing of Saturday night's events, newspaper coverage of the murders necessarily lagged behind the radio and television reports. The *North Platte Telegraph* did not publish a Sunday edition and, given their deadlines, most of the large regional and national papers could only get the barest early details into their Sunday morning editions. Sunday's *Lincoln Journal and Star*, for example, led with a page-one story headlined "Shotgun Sniper at Sutherland Kills

6 People, Flees on Foot." The article contained a physical description of the man being sought by police, but did not name Simants. Similarly, Sunday's *New York Times* reported the killings in a short article headlined "Six Reported Slain in Nebraska Town by Shotgun Wielder" but included no specifics regarding the victims or the suspect. The story did, however, contain an alarming quote from an unidentified deputy, saying, "I can't tell you much now, but there is a man, and he is shooting people."[61]

Some Sunday newspaper stories, however, had already begun to link Simants with the murders. Sunday morning's *Omaha World-Herald*, for example, contained a front-page account of the killings headlined "Six in Family Gunned Down at Sutherland; Police Look for Neighbor of Victims." The story identified the Kellies as the victims, described Sutherland as an "armed camp" through the night, and named Simants as a next-door neighbor of the victims who police were seeking "for questioning" about the slayings.[62]

Monday, October 20, brought a deluge of newspaper reports directly linking Simants to the murders. Every local and regional newspaper carried extensive coverage of the story, including vivid descriptions of the night-long hunt for the suspect, and Simants's arrest and arraignment on Sunday. Large photographs of Simants, handcuffed to Sheriff Gilster and clad in prison garb, appeared on the front pages of the North Platte, Lincoln, Omaha, and Denver papers. The newspaper coverage repeated much of the information that had already been broadcast on radio and television relating to Simants's background, his criminal record, the statements he made to the authorities, his "confession" to his parents, and his activities before and after the murders.

Understandably, the general tenor of virtually all of the broadcast and print reports on Sunday and Monday was to accept Simants's guilt as a given, with speculation focusing on the possible motives for his horrible crimes. Monday's *Omaha World-Herald,* for example, contained stories headlined "Slaying Motive Remains Puzzle" and "Suspect Stopped for Beers after Slayings."[63] The *Lincoln Star* similarly headlined one of its stories with "Sutherland Residents Wonder—Why?"[64] The *North Platte Telegraph* naturally devoted almost the entire front page of its Monday issue to the murders, with photos

Simants, hand-
cuffed to Sheriff
Gordon Gilster,
walking to the
Lincoln County
Courthouse for
his arraignment,
October 20, 1975.
Courtesy *New York
Times*/Redux.

of Simants and all six victims and headlines such as "Anguish, Disbelief Replace Terror" and "Kellie Paid Simants' Fine."[65] Many of the
stories included interviews with friends and neighbors of the Kellies, who uniformly praised the family as wonderful people who
could not possibly have done anything to provoke such an attack.
Simants, in contrast, was described in various print reports as "a
loner," "a drinker," "a hothead," and "a troublemaker."[66] Monday's
newspaper reports also contained details from those portions of
Simants's arraignment on Sunday afternoon that had been conducted
in open court. Various accounts of the proceedings ominously characterized Simants's appearance and demeanor as "dark-haired,"
"dark-eyed," and "showing little or no emotion."[67]

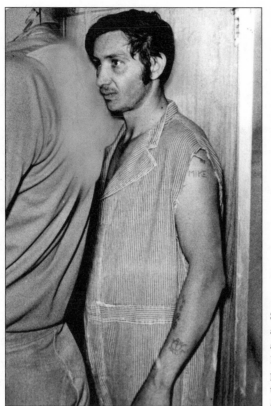

Simants, as he
appeared at his
arraignment.
Reprinted with
permission from
the *Omaha World-
Herald.*

On Wednesday, October 22, the emotional poignancy of the Kellie family murders culminated in a somber funeral ceremony held in the high school gymnasium in Sutherland. More than a thousand mourners filled the gym to capacity and heard the family eulogized as good friends, helpful neighbors, and pillars of the community. The hour-long service concluded at a hillside cemetery outside of town, where the six victims were laid to rest.[68]

As the community-wide trauma and media furor intensified, the key participants in the unfolding legal drama—prosecutors Milton Larson and Marvin Holscher, defense attorneys Leonard Vynahlek and Keith Bystrom, and county judge Ronald Ruff—were quickly growing sensitive to the constitutional dilemma they faced. Each

The Kellie family funeral ceremony, October 22, 1975. Courtesy *North Platte Telegraph*.

came to the belief that the media attention that was saturating North Platte, Sutherland, and the surrounding area posed a distinct threat of tainting the jury pool for Simants's impending trial. Each understood as well the competing legal and strategic interests at stake, and each would soon be forced to make difficult decisions in a dramatic and emotionally charged atmosphere. None of them envisioned that the choices they made and the actions they took in the next few days would leave a lasting imprint on American constitutional jurisprudence.

Lincoln County Attorney Milton Larson was one of the youngest and most inexperienced of the key legal players. Raised on a ranch near Potter, Nebraska, Larson had graduated from Hastings College

in 1969 and from the University of Nebraska College of Law in 1972.[69] He entered private practice with a firm in North Platte in 1972 and two years later was appointed associate county judge. In November 1974, after just six months on the county court bench, Larson ran for and won election as Lincoln County attorney. He was only twenty-seven years old at the time of the Kellie murders, had been in office only ten months, and had never before been involved in a murder investigation or trial.[70] In light of Larson's inexperience, most of the courtroom handling of the Simants prosecution fell to fifty-year-old Marvin Holscher, who had served as a city and county prosecutor in Scottsbluff, Nebraska, for seventeen years before joining the Lincoln County attorney's staff earlier in 1975.[71]

Defense counsel Leonard Vyhnalek found himself appointed to represent Simants at a time when he was trying to leave the public defender's office. In fact, he had already resigned from that post six months before but had agreed to stay on the job during a transition period to enable his successor, Keith Bystrom, time to get acclimated. Vyhnalek, a 1961 graduate of the University of Nebraska Law School, had acquired a good deal of trial experience during his fourteen years of practice and six years as the public defender, but he had never before defended a murder suspect. Bystrom, just twenty-five years old and only six months out of Georgetown University Law School, had almost no experience whatsoever in criminal trial practice. Accordingly, Vyhnalek carried the ball for the defense during most of the litigation.

Judge Ronald Ruff was only thirty-four years old when the Simants prosecution landed in his lap. Born in Grand Island, Nebraska, and reared in North Platte, Ruff had received both his undergraduate and law degrees from the University of Nebraska. After being admitted to the Nebraska Bar in 1967, he moved to Muncie, Indiana, where he taught business administration and business law at Ball State University for five years. For the last four of those years, he also served as a deputy prosecutor for Delaware County, Indiana. In July 1972, he returned to North Platte to run for county judge and won election to the post four months later.[72] In Nebraska, the county court is the lowest court of general jurisdiction, where misdemeanor crimes and small civil actions are processed and arraignments and preliminary hearings are conducted in felony cases. If the county court finds probable cause to believe that a felony suspect committed the crime charged, the accused is "bound over" for trial in the district court of that county.

Shortly after taking the bench, Ruff attended a two-week-long training program for judges conducted by the National College of the State Judiciary. As part of that training, he received instruction in the latest judicial rulings on the question of free press/fair trial tensions and was given a copy of a "model" restrictive order limiting press coverage of pending legal proceedings.[73] In his two and a half years on the bench since that training session, Ruff had never encountered a situation that required him even to consider the use of such an order.

The Simants arraignment and preliminary hearing would be the first, and by far the most notorious, homicide proceeding he would ever handle.

As the preliminary hearing scheduled for Wednesday morning grew nearer, Vyhnalek and Bystrom became convinced that the media coverage of the crimes had already become a serious impediment to their ability to find and seat an impartial jury for their client. Moreover, as if the published reports of Simants's "admission" of the killings to his parents and some of Sheriff Gilster's comments in the press were not bad enough, a new and potentially even more explosive problem had arisen. Initial findings from the autopsies conducted on the victims' bodies indicated that Simants had not only sexually assaulted ten-year-old Florence both before and after he killed her but had also molested the dead body of fifty-five-year-old Marie and perhaps that of seven-year-old Deanne as well. The specter of child rape and necrophilia now loomed over the impending proceedings, raising the possibility of even more lurid and feverish media coverage.

With the autopsy results in hand, prosecutors Larson and Holscher prepared an amended criminal complaint against Simants, alleging that he had committed the six murders "in the perpetration of or attempt to perpetrate a sexual assault in the first degree."[74] In other words, the mystery of Simant's motive for the slayings had now been resolved. The prosecution would seek to show that he had committed the murders while in the act of, and in an attempt to cover up, his sexual attacks on the female victims.

The autopsy findings and the preparation of the amended complaint resulted in numerous telephone conversations between prosecutors and defense counsel on Monday and Tuesday, in anticipation of Wednesday's preliminary hearing. Both sides were becoming increasingly alarmed at the potentially prejudicial impact of the extensive media coverage of the crimes. From the prosecutors' perspective, the primary objective was to ensure that they would be able to impanel a constitutionally acceptable jury—one whose impartiality would survive the inevitable appeal that would follow Simants's anticipated conviction. The defense attorneys' concern was even more immediate—to stop the widespread dissemination of news that strongly suggested their client's guilt so that they might preserve at least a fighting chance to seat an impartial jury. For obvious reasons, Vyhnalek and Bystrom were particularly worried about the possibility of the publication of the autopsy results and any additional published references to the confessional aspects of Simants's various statements.

The attorneys also commiserated over the limited legal options available to them in attempting to deal with the media problem. None of the traditional methods for insulating a jury from potentially prejudicial publicity—such as sequestration, admonitions to jurors from the bench, or a change of venue—seemed adequate to deal with the situation they faced. Sequestration and judicial warnings could only take place once a jury was seated and the trial had commenced, and by then it would be far too late to undo the effects of weeks of intensive media coverage in a lightly populated, rural, and relatively isolated area like Lincoln County. Moreover, under Nebraska law at the time, a change of venue could be granted only to an adjacent county. Given the breadth and depth of the media saturation, the attorneys reasonably concluded that movement of the trial to a nearby county would not solve the problem. Ultimately, both sides agreed that the prosecutors would file a motion seeking a court order restricting press coverage of the impending preliminary hearing. The defense team agreed to join in the motion orally when it came on for hearing.

So it was that on the afternoon of Tuesday, October 21, 1975, a beleaguered young county attorney in North Platte, Nebraska, hurriedly drafted and filed a one-page motion with the local judge—a short and simply worded request that would become the seed from which a historic U.S. Supreme Court decision would ultimately emerge. Styled as a "Motion for Restrictive Order," Larson's request to the court asserted that the intense media coverage of the case had created "a reasonable likelihood of prejudicial news which would make difficult, if not impossible, the impaneling of an impartial jury . . . if testimony of witnesses at the preliminary hearing is reported to the public."[75] They asked the court to enter an order "setting forth the matters that may or may not be publicly reported or disclosed to the public with reference to said case or with reference to the preliminary hearing thereon, and to whom said order shall apply."[76]

With the preliminary hearing scheduled for the following morning, the prosecutors personally delivered the motion to Judge Ruff and asked for an immediate hearing to address the issue. Ruff, too, had become concerned with the intense media coverage and was already pondering his options. In an interview conducted by Nancy Whitmore almost twenty years later, Ruff recalled, "Obviously, one of the main things I was concerned about was whether or not Simants would be able to get a fair trial in Lincoln County, Nebraska. That was the primary concern. There was enough publicity, at that point in time, that I think that most people probably had opinions, and a lot of information was already out that looked like he committed the crime. But the one thing that was absolutely bothering me, that I didn't want the public to know and that I thought would just absolutely be the death of a fair trial in Lincoln County, was the fact that after these people died, he had sex with them. And that was the one thing that I didn't think the public should have."[77]

Like the prosecutors and defense counsel, Ruff felt that his options in dealing with the issue were limited: "And now here's the dilemma—you pick up Nebraska statutes at that time, and in Nebraska all preliminary hearings are [required to be] open to the public. Now how can I as a judge—this is my thought process—how can I as a judge close a preliminary hearing when a state statute says they're open to the public? So I had that problem."[78]

Ruff told Larson that he would take his motion for a restrictive order under advisement and make a ruling before the preliminary hearing scheduled for the next morning. During the next few hours, he consulted with several of his judicial colleagues, including his own associate county judge, Gary Burns, and Judge Richard Myers of neighboring Keith County. The other judges sympathized with Ruff's dilemma but offered conflicting advice. Myers thought Ruff ought to close the preliminary hearing to the press and public, while Burns believed that the proceedings had to remain completely open and unrestricted.[79]

Ruff also consulted with Lincoln County District Judge Hugh Stuart, who would eventually become the presiding judge in Simants's murder trial. Stuart, who at fifty-four was twenty years older than Ruff and a much more experienced jurist, had sat on the district court bench for more than ten years. A native of North Platte, he had developed a reputation as a firm but fair jurist who maintained tight control over his courtroom.

The relationship between Ruff and Stuart was, at best, chilly. Ruff would later tell a reporter that "Stuart once accused me of being the most immature and incompetent judge he had ever met."[80] Ruff dreaded the thought of Stuart second-guessing and possibly reversing whatever decision he made regarding the media coverage, and so he went to the older, more experienced judge for advice. In view of all that ensued, it is not surprising that the two men's recollections of their conversation varied in later accounts. Stuart recalled telling Ruff, "You can't restrain the media" and that to try to do so would be "opening a can of worms."[81] Ruff would later remember Stuart as being much more noncommittal, saying that the older judge ultimately only reminded him of the obvious: "You are the judge."[82]

By late Tuesday afternoon, Ruff had concluded that he should hold some sort of hearing before deciding the issue. He contacted the prosecutors and defense counsel and told them to come to the courthouse at 7:30 that evening to address the matter. Ruff also decided that the media should be apprised of the pending motion and hearing as well. Accordingly, he asked Associate County Judge Dorothy Kriz to assist him in contacting representatives of the local media. Kriz began calling members of the broadcast media, while Ruff called various newspaper representatives, rather cryptically inviting the media to come to the courthouse that night for a meeting to hear "some news that may be of importance."[83] Those telephone calls set off warning bells and a chain-reaction response throughout the Nebraska newspaper and broadcasting community. The plot was about to thicken.

THree
The Initial Legal Skirmishes

When the two rights come into conflict, the right of free press
must be subservient to the right of due process.

LINCOLN COUNTY COURT JUDGE RONALD RUFF
October 22, 1975

L ate in the afternoon of Tuesday, October 21, 1975, the telephone rang in the office of Keith Blackledge, editor of the
North Platte Telegraph. The caller was Lincoln County Court
Judge Ronald Ruff. Ruff told Blackledge that he wanted to notify the
newspaper of what he called a "meeting" he would convene that night
at the courthouse. The judge spoke ambiguously about wanting to
discuss the procedures and limitations he intended to implement
with respect to news media coverage at the next morning's preliminary hearing in the Simants prosecution. He further indicated to
Blackledge that he wanted the press involved in the session to ensure
that they had "first-hand knowledge" of the court's position on the
issue of press coverage.[1]

Blackledge was obviously well aware of the Kellie murders and
Simants's arrest—certainly no newsman anywhere in Nebraska or the
entire Midwest, much less in North Platte itself, could have possibly

avoided hearing about those events—but he had not yet become actively involved in his paper's coverage of the story. Instead, he was immersed in coverage of a high school bond issue that was, on that very day, winning passage by local voters. As Blackledge would later recall, "I was a reluctant participant. On the evening of Judge Ruff's decision, I was celebrating passage of the bond issue."[2]

Despite his preoccupation with the bond issue story, Blackledge was alarmed at Judge Ruff's vague hints about some sort of restriction on media coverage of the impending Simants hearing. He immediately conferred with *Telegraph* reporter Bill Eddy, who had been leading the paper's coverage of the Kellie murders and Simants's arrest. Eddy called AP reporter Kiley Armstrong in Omaha who, in turn, conferred with her boss, Omaha AP Bureau Chief Ed Nicholls. The chain of phone calls and rushed consultations continued with Nicholls phoning G. Woodson (Woody) Howe, executive assistant to the president of the *Omaha World-Herald*. Howe then called Joe R. Seacrest, editor of the *Lincoln Journal*. Both Howe and Seacrest were members of the Nebraska Joint Press/Bar Committee on Free Press/ Fair Trial, an entity that had been created several years earlier by the Nebraska State Bar Association and the Nebraska Press Association as a cooperative mechanism to deal voluntarily with tensions that might arise between the two organizations' respective First and Sixth Amendment concerns. Both men were also active in Media of Nebraska, a recently created lobbying organization that represented a consortium of print and broadcast media outlets throughout the state. Media of Nebraska would become the primary conduit for the collection and distribution of funding for the media's litigation activities, with Howe serving as its chairman.[3] Blackledge, Howe, and Seacrest also hurriedly consulted with other state media leaders about that evening's judicial "meeting" in North Platte, including Frank Fogarty of the Nebraska Broadcasters Association, the Nebraska Press Association's Phil Berkebile, Fremont newspaper publisher Russell Weber, and Larry Walklin, president of Sigma Delta Chi of Nebraska, a fraternal organization for professional journalists.[4]

All the participants in the telephone conferences agreed that the media ought to have legal representation at that night's court session, but the logistical obstacles were daunting. Ruff's meeting was scheduled to begin in just a few hours, and the Lincoln County Courthouse in North Platte was more than 200 miles from both Omaha and Lincoln. Moreover, both the *World-Herald* and the *Journal*'s regular First Amendment counsel were out of town or otherwise unavailable. Alan Peterson, a Lincoln attorney who regularly represented the *Journal,* was sick with the flu when Seacrest contacted him, and could not get to North Platte for Judge Ruff's evening session.[5] Ultimately, Seacrest, Howe, Blackledge, and representatives of North Platte radio station KODY agreed to retain, through the auspices of Media of Nebraska, North Platte attorney Harold Kay to represent the news organizations at that night's session. Kay had represented the *Telegraph* in previous matters and also served as counsel for KODY.[6]

As the 7:30 meeting approached, telephone consultations between Kay and his clients intensified. Given the ambiguities in Judge Ruff's notification to the media, no one knew exactly what to expect. Ultimately, Howe, Seacrest, and the other newsmen instructed Kay that, if it appeared that Ruff intended to impose some sort of gag order on the media, he was to object immediately and vigorously. The media leaders further instructed Kay to argue that any such attempted restriction would be unconstitutional and completely unnecessary and that the affected media were entitled to a more adequate opportunity to be heard and more time to prepare a legal response before such an order should even be considered. Finally, they authorized Kay to assure Judge Ruff that the media groups he represented would voluntarily comply with the existing Nebraska press-bar guidelines regarding the publication of pretrial information in the Simants case.[7] Those guidelines had been drafted in 1970 by a committee including members of the Nebraska bar and representatives of the Nebraska news media. Designed to achieve a reasonable accommodation between the rights of free press and fair trial, the guidelines enunciated specific types of information that were deemed suitable or unsuitable for disclosure and publication. Among the material specifically identified as not appropriate for reporting was "the existence or contents of any confession, admission or statement given by the accused," and "opinions concerning the guilt, the innocence or the character of the accused."[8] As prepared as he could be under the circumstances, Kay arrived at the courthouse at the designated time and waited to see what would happen. About a dozen reporters, broadcasters, and other media representatives appeared as well. Their worst fears were soon realized.

No formal record of the unusual Tuesday night court session was made, so the details of what took place there may be gleaned only from the participants' memories and the next day's news stories and from testimony elicited later in District Court proceedings.[9] From the outset, Kay and the other media representatives were taken aback by the realization that Judge Ruff intended to conduct a relatively formal judicial hearing complete with the presence of the defendant Simants and his attorneys, rather than the rather informal "meeting" that the telephonic notifications had suggested. After a short closed-door conference with the prosecutors and defense counsel in his chambers, Ruff took the bench and announced that he would hear arguments on prosecutor Milton Larson's motion for a restrictive order filed earlier that day.

This was the first time that Kay or any of the news organizations he represented became aware that a formal motion to restrict press coverage had been filed in the case. Larson proceeded to reiterate the essence of his position—that the news media had to be restricted in their coverage of the next morning's preliminary hearing so that the state's ability to seat an impartial jury would not be impaired. As he had promised the prosecutors earlier in the day, defense counsel Leonard Vhynalek endorsed the prosecutor's motion and then went even further, asking Judge Ruff to close the preliminary hearing completely to the press and public. Arguing that the Nebraska open courts law—which mandated that all judicial proceedings in the state be open to the public—did not necessarily apply to preliminary hearings in all circumstances, Vyhnalek contended that barring the press from the hearing was not only permissible under state law, it was absolutely necessary to protect Simants's Sixth Amendment rights.[10] He added that given the extensive media coverage of the case "some damage has been done already."[11] While continuing to press his motion for restricted coverage, prosecutor Larson disagreed with Vhynalek's request for a totally closed hearing, asserting that "permitting the press may forestall any additional rumors that are not true."[12]

Judge Ruff invited Kay to address the issue on behalf of his clients. Kay noted first that, contrary to Vhynalek's argument, state law clearly required that preliminary hearings be open to the public. He went on to assert that "the people are entitled to freedom of the press" and assured the court that "the news media will take no action which would prejudice the defendant."[13] He suggested that a change of venue seemed inevitable in the case, in light of already published "disclosures by law enforcement officials that would violate Nebraska bar-press guidelines."[14] Kay concluded by arguing that a restrictive order against the press would be an unprecedented act in Nebraska. He told Ruff that, as far as he knew, no Nebraska court "has ever applied a gag rule and the press doesn't want a gag rule in this case."[15]

When the attorneys finished their arguments, Ruff announced from the bench that he was denying Vhynalek's motion to close the next morning's hearing. With respect to the prosecution's motion to restrict the media coverage, however, Ruff acknowledged that he had to sort out "some real serious constitutional issues."[16] He announced that he would render his decision the next morning before the preliminary hearing began. Ruff then adjourned the session and retired to his chambers for what he would later describe as a sleepless night of agonizing contemplation.[17]

The preliminary hearing held in the Simants prosecution on Wednesday, October 22, 1975, may well have been the most unusual such proceeding in Nebraska legal history. Preliminary hearings are typically pro forma events, with the prosecution introducing just enough evidence to meet its burden of showing that a crime had been committed and that there is probable cause to believe that the defendant had committed that crime. For its part, the defense usually does little more than sit back and listen, using the hearing to try to assess the strength of the state's case. Such hearings rarely involve more than a few prosecution witnesses—usually only the investigating law enforcement officials and, in homicide cases, coroner's testimony relating to the cause of death as determined from autopsies or other forensic evidence.

The Simants hearing, however, was different from the norm in many respects. It began in unusual and dramatic fashion with a visibly weary Judge Ronald Ruff taking the bench and announcing his decision on the prosecution's pending motion to restrict media coverage. After first acknowledging that the motion presented him with the "toughest decision that I have ever had to make in my relatively young life," Ruff declared that "the power and persuasiveness of the news media are of such significance that courts must at times take strong action to insure that both parties in a criminal lawsuit start equally."[18] He then delivered the kind of strong action he believed the circumstances required, reading from the bench an order that prohibited all persons involved in the case and all persons present at the preliminary hearing from revealing "for public dissemination in any form or manner whatsoever any testimony or evidence adduced during the preliminary hearing."[19] His order further provided that the news media were prohibited from publishing any information concerning the Simants prosecution "other than as set forth in the Nebraska Bar-Press Guidelines for Disclosure and Reporting of Information Relating to Imminent or Pending Criminal Litigation." In yet another indication of the dramatically unusual dynamics of the situation, copies of Ruff's order were distributed to all the spectators and reporters in the courtroom at the preliminary hearing.

Judge Ruff's explicit incorporation of the bar-press guidelines into his restrictive order was a matter of considerable concern for the media. Indeed, for many of the Nebraska news leaders, Ruff's adoption of those guidelines as part of his order would become the *most* egregious aspect of the entire controversy. *World-Herald* executive Woody Howe, for example, would later recall being "infuriated" at the "betrayal" that had been visited upon the media.[20] Most of the media groups had not been enamored with the guidelines to begin with but had gone along with their creation and adoption under the assurance that they were purely "voluntary" in nature. Now, as media attorney Alan Peterson later recalled, they "felt stupid for having been had in regard to having ever agreed to such guidelines."[21] Editorializing on precisely that point just a week after Ruff's order was imposed, Keith Blackledge lamented that the press had been "sandbagged" and vowed that "we will not enter again soon into any socalled 'voluntary' codes."[22]

The Nebraska media objected to the incorporation of the guidelines into the court order for other reasons as well. In the first place, it was obvious to everyone that certain disclosures relating to Simants's involvement in the murders that would be considered inappropriate for publication under the guidelines had long since been broadcast or reported multiple times. For example, Sheriff Gilster's published comments strongly implying Simants's guilt, along with the various references to Simants's purported confessions to his nephew and his parents, had been repeatedly broadcast or printed and now had become common knowledge in and around Lincoln County. In that sense, then, the guidelines were already a dead letter. Their invocation now by Judge Ruff seemed to be merely wishful thinking—a futile attempt to put the proverbial genie back in the bottle.

Beyond that practical reality, the incorporation of the voluntary guidelines into Judge Ruff's order raised troubling issues relating to the local court's jurisdiction and control over out-of-state journalists. News media from all over the country were converging on Sutherland, and most of them had never even heard of the Nebraska bar-press guidelines, much less considered themselves bound by them. It seemed both legally dubious and logistically impossible to suggest that the Lincoln County Court could impose and enforce those types of local standards or, for that matter, *any* limitations on content, on media organizations that operated outside of the court's physical jurisdiction.

At the most fundamental level, however, the Nebraska news organizations were alarmed at Judge Ruff's adoption of the guidelines because that action ran directly contrary to the spirit and intent of the guidelines themselves, which repeatedly emphasized the voluntary nature of their provisions. In their introductory language, the guidelines specifically provided, "As a voluntary code, these guidelines do not necessarily reflect in all respects what the members of the bar or the news media believe would be permitted or required by law."[23] All parties involved in the drafting and adoption of the guidelines had always envisioned them as merely advisory in nature. Now, for the first time, a court had moved to make those voluntary standards mandatory, giving them the force and effect of law. An ominous First Amendment threshold had been passed, and the Nebraska press, already beginning to mobilize, would quickly respond.

In the meantime, however, the preliminary hearing proceeded. Approximately thirty spectators, including about a dozen reporters, watched and listened, all of them bound to silence regarding what they saw and heard by the terms of Judge Ruff's just-announced gag order. Apparently feeling the need to further justify his action, Ruff opened the substantive portion of the hearing with another unusual act—reading into the record a quote from the U.S. Supreme Court's famous *Sheppard v. Maxwell* decision, announced nine years before.[24] In that opinion, Ruff noted, the Court had reversed the murder conviction of Dr. Sam Sheppard because "the state trial judge did not fulfill his duty to protect Sheppard from the inherently prejudicial publicity which saturated the community and to control disruptive influences in the courtroom."[25] Casting himself as the man who had to avoid a *Sheppard*-like result, Ruff declared, "This Judge is not going to abdicate his duty, and in a preliminary hearing in a case of this nature, there should be restrictive protection."[26]

With that statement from the bench completed, the formal presentation of evidence against Erwin Simants commenced. Prosecutor Larson began by formally introducing and reading into the record his amended complaint against Simants, charging him with six counts of first-degree murder while "in the perpetration or attempt to perpetrate a sexual assault."[27] Because Ruff's gag order did not specifically prohibit the publication of the contents of the amended complaint, Larson's filing of the new complaint in the clerk's office, combined with his reading of it in open court, effectively made the sexual aspects of Simants's crimes a matter of public record, although the specific identity of the victims who were subjected to the sexual attacks was not revealed.

In another departure from routine practice, the preliminary hearing stretched on for most of the rest of the day, divided into a morning and afternoon session, with prosecutors offering the testimony of no fewer than nine witnesses. Marvin Holscher, the lead trial counsel for the prosecution, first called Dr. Miles Foster, the pathologist who had performed autopsies on all six victims. Foster testified that all of the Kellies had died as a result of gunshots to the head, with two of them (David and Daniel) shot twice and the others once each. Over the objection of defense counsel, he offered his opinion that all of the fatal wounds had been delivered by a .22 caliber rifle. Foster further stated that powder burns around the entry wounds on the bodies of all of the victims except Marie indicated that they had been shot at almost point-blank range. Finally, he testified that forensic tests revealed that ten-year-old Florence had been sexually assaulted, with her assailant completing the act of "sexual penetration within the meaning of the Nebraska statute."[28] Upon cross-examination by defense counsel Vyhnalek, Foster elaborated on the position and angles of trajectory of the various gunshot wounds but offered no additional details regarding the sexual abuse visited upon the victims.

Holscher next called Herbert Meissner, the mayor of Sutherland, who briefly testified regarding his identification of the bodies as they lay in the Kellie home on the night of the murders.[29] Emergency medical technician June Lindstrom, one of the first rescue workers to reach the Kellie home on the night of the murders, followed Meissner to the stand. She described her friendship with the Kellies and her recollections of the scene of the murders and the location of the bodies in the home. Lindstrom also related her discovery that David Kellie was still alive at the scene, discernible by "the bubbles that were coming through the blood and from the wounds."[30] She sought and received permission to transport David to the hospital in North Platte, where he died about an hour later.

Perhaps the most dramatic and poignant testimony at the preliminary hearing came from Simants's teenage nephew Butch. The boy recalled how his uncle had taken the rifle from his parents' bedroom, loaded it with shells, and then went out the door, telling him, "Don't say anything" and "Don't let the kids go out."[31] When Simants returned to the Boggs home about an hour later, Butch testified, he told the boy that "he shot Henry and Marie and a little kid and a girl . . . he said he didn't want to but he went over there and he said David came up to Henry's house, and he came in. And he said he wasn't going to shoot them but they came in."[32] Butch also testified that he had seen Simants writing a note, which he then took downstairs, and that Herb asked him to "call Grandma," meaning his mother, Grace. After talking with his parents on the Boggses' telephone, Simants left, telling the shocked boy, "Don't say anything to anybody."[33]

Larson next offered the testimony of Amos Simants, who told the story of his son's phone call and visit to his house on the night of the murders, during which he admitted the killings. Inexplicably, Herb told his parents that he "had just beat the Kellies to death."[34] Amos also told of his trip to the Kellie house, his discovery of the gruesome scene there, and his subsequent phone call for an ambulance. When Amos's testimony was finished, Judge Ruff adjourned the hearing for a lunch break.

The afternoon session began with Nebraska State Patrol investigator James Burnett taking the stand, followed by his fellow investigators, Danny Reese and Terry Livengood. Collectively, the three officials described the location of the bodies in the house, and their recovery of eight empty .22 caliber shell casings and one live cartridge from the murder scene. They further testified that they had attended the autopsies of the victims and had taken possession of the bullet fragments recovered from the bodies. Livengood also testified that he had gone to the Boggs home and taken possession of a .22 caliber rifle and several boxes of ammunition, as well as Simants's handwritten "I am sorry to all" note.[35]

Prosecutor Holscher's final witness at the preliminary hearing was Lincoln County Sheriff Gordon "Hop" Gilster. Gilster described his arrest of Simants outside the Boggs home on Sunday morning. Once Simants had been handcuffed, State Patrol Lieutenant Donald Grieb read him his Miranda rights from a small card. Grieb then told Simants to read the card himself. He complied and then indicated that he understood all of his rights. Gilster and Grieb transported Simants to the jail and sheriff's office in North Platte, a trip of about twenty minutes. During that time, Gilster sat in the back seat of the unmarked cruiser with Simants, while Grieb drove. Gilster testified that he had no conversation with Simants during the ride to the jail other than to ask him if he was all right.[36] At the jail, Simants was booked, photographed, and twice more advised of his Miranda rights. He signed a waiver of those rights and proceeded voluntarily to answer questions posed to him by Gilster and Grieb. That interview with Simants was recorded and then transcribed. When the officials presented the transcription to Simants, he read it and then signed it. At the preliminary hearing, Holscher offered that signed transcription of Simants's statement, sealed in an envelope, to the court as State's Exhibit 3. The contents of the statement were not revealed in open court, but when Holscher offered it into evidence, defense attorney Vyhnalek asked for a recess so that he could have time to examine what he called "this confession or this statement."[37]

As he granted the defense request for a short break, Judge Ruff reminded the courtroom spectators of the terms of his order restricting the dissemination of information presented at the hearing. He told observers that "as you leave the courtroom you should be served with a copy of the order, and you are bound by that order."[38] Following a twenty-minute recess, Sheriff Gilster took the stand again, for cross-examination. Vyhnalek attempted to elicit some indication from the sheriff that Simants may have been drunk at the time of his arrest and confession. Gilster firmly maintained that Simants was not drunk Sunday morning but acknowledged that he did appear to be somewhat "dazed" or "hung-over."[39]

With Gilster's testimony concluded and the sealed confession accepted into evidence, the prosecution rested. Following brief concluding arguments from counsel, Judge Ruff announced his ruling from the bench. Ruff held that the offenses charged in the complaint had been committed and that there was probable cause to believe that Simants had committed those crimes. Accordingly, he told Simants, "It is therefore ordered that you be bound over to District Court to stand trial on six counts of murder in the first degree."[40] On the question of bail, Ruff concluded that "the only thing the Court can say is that six people are dead, three of them children. The tragedy and the magnitude of these events are such, and the nature is such, that this Court cannot grant you bond. It is denied."[41] With the entry of that order, jurisdiction over the Simants prosecution shifted from Judge Ruff to the Lincoln County District Court, in the person of Judge Hugh Stuart.

Ironies abound in the events surrounding the Simants preliminary hearing and the entry of Judge Ruff's gag order. In the first place, for reasons that are still not apparent, prosecutors Larson and Holscher introduced far more testimony and evidence than seemed necessary to meet their burden and bind Simants over for trial in the district court. Certainly the medical and forensic testimony of Dr.

Foster, combined with Sheriff Gilster's testimony and the introduction of Simants's signed confessional statement, would have amply demonstrated the existence of the murders and provided the necessary probable cause to hold Simants for trial. Had the testimony and evidence introduced at the preliminary hearing been more limited, there would have been far less material subject to the judge's gag order for the media to squabble over.

Moreover, a great deal of the testimony and evidence presented at the hearing, which Judge Ruff's order now purported to bar from publication, had already been published and broadcast in local, regional, and national media outlets. For example, June Lindstrom had been interviewed and quoted in several AP stories relating to what she saw and did at the crime scene. Sheriff Gilster himself had already released, through interviews or press conferences, most all of the damning inferential evidence his office had gathered against Simants, except for the details of his signed statement and the particulars of the sexual assaults. Perhaps most significantly, Butch Boggs's story of his contacts with his uncle on the night of the murders, as well as Amos and Grace Simants's encounters with their son, and his confessional statements to them, had been reported across the country.

As for the sexual aspects of Simants's crimes, which the prosecutors, defense counsel, and Judge Ruff himself were particularly concerned about, they became a part of the public record with the filing of the amended complaint—the terms of which were not prohibited from publication under the terms of the gag order. As Joe Seacrest, editor of the *Lincoln Journal* and a key participant in the events, would later recall, "The amended complaint fueled rumors and speculation even beyond the truth. Were all six assaulted? Men? All the women? Which females? . . . All kinds of hearsay was being quoted by some members of the public to others."[42]

Adding to the incongruities surrounding the announcement of that first gag order in the case was the fact that Judge Ruff and media attorney Alan Peterson were close friends from their law school days. Peterson would later suggest that, had he not been ill with the flu and been available to appear at the night session before the preliminary hearing, he could probably have "short-circuited this thing—I think I could have talked Ron out of [issuing the gag order]."[43]

Given all that transpired after the entry of the October 22 gag order, perhaps the most extraordinary irony of all is that Ruff himself fully understood all of the inherent flaws in his order but decided to enter it anyway. Remarkably, Ruff would later acknowledge to interviewers that he never anticipated that the order would be obeyed by the press, nor did he have any realistic hope of enforcing its provisions. Indeed, by the end of the preliminary hearing, he had come to the conclusion that the gag order was not even necessary at all. In an admirably candid interview with Fred Friendly conducted several months after the preliminary hearing, Ruff wryly recalled his own perceptions of the limits of his power to restrain the press, saying "Me, gag the powerful *Omaha World-Herald* and the *Lincoln Journal* and the *Chicago Tribune?*"[44] In that same interview, Ruff emphasized his understandable dread at the thought that his antagonist Judge Stuart might second-guess his handling of the preliminary hearing: "I kept thinking of *Sheppard v. Maxwell.* . . . I didn't care what was in the paper; I just didn't want to be reversed."[45]

As to the necessity of the order, Ruff recalled in a 1994 interview conducted by Nancy Whitmore that none of the scurrilous and potentially prejudicial information he was most concerned about had actually been offered in open court:

> I could stand corrected, but I think the confession and [medical] reports were just handed to me, and I don't think the public even saw the thing. . . . And when the hearing was over, *I was of a firm opinion that there was no need to even have a restrictive order . . .* but I'm sitting there saying 'I've been awake now thirty hours, thirty-five hours, forty hours or whatever it was, and I don't know how clear I'm thinking' . . . and I didn't think I was in the frame of mind that I should rescind an order without knowing if I properly heard what I heard. But that was my recollection, why even have an order at this point in time? . . . which is ironic, but at least I had done what I thought I had to do to protect the ability to try and have a fair trial. (emphasis added)[46]

Thus, Judge Ruff's October 22 gag order—which would ultimately lead the Nebraska litigants all the way to the U.S. Supreme Court—

originated as little more than a token gesture—an arguably well-intentioned, but ultimately futile and unnecessary decree issued by a physically and mentally exhausted local judge. From that humble and completely human origin, a momentous Supreme Court decision would be born.

By the time the preliminary hearing concluded on Wednesday afternoon, the Nebraska media organizations were already well on their way toward mobilizing in opposition to the gag order. Reporters at the hearing had quickly relayed news of the order to their bosses in Lincoln, Omaha, and elsewhere. In various telephone conferences, the media executives and their attorneys began debating their legal and tactical options. The most direct and obvious strategy— simply to ignore the order and then challenge its constitutionality in the contempt of court proceedings that would likely follow—was considered and promptly rejected. Several factors account for that decision. First, the Nebraska media attorneys were well aware of a recent decision from the Fifth Circuit Court of Appeals (*United States v. Dickinson*) holding that reporters must obey judicial restraints on press coverage of trial proceedings until such orders are reversed on appeal, even when the restraint seemed patently unreasonable and unconstitutional.[47] Beyond the impact of the *Dickinson* precedent, which seemed directly controlling in the situation they faced, the media decision makers in Omaha, Lincoln, and North Platte also seemed to exhibit what Fred Friendly referred to as a "fundamental conservatism that rejected the notion of civil disobedience."[48] Accordingly, they chose not to defy the court order directly.

The press executives also considered the relatively conventional option of bringing an independent action as plaintiffs in the district court to challenge the propriety of the gag order. That approach was rejected because it carried with it the risk of delay and uncertainty in the court's handling and hearing of the matter.[49] It was conceivable that the court might not entertain such an action for some time, allowing the gag order to remain in effect during the weeks and months leading up to the Simants murder trial.

For these reasons, the Nebraska media representatives and their counsel opted to attempt a unique and innovative procedural strategy. They decided to ask the district court to allow them to insert them-

selves directly into the Simants criminal prosecution as "interve-
nors." From that position inside the criminal case, they believed,
they could then most expeditiously challenge the constitutionality of
Ruff's gag order. As one commentator later noted, when this approach
ultimately succeeded, it put the Nebraska media in "a powerful position . . . with status equal to the prosecutor and defendant."[50] By
becoming a kind of quasi-party in the criminal case, the press gained
the ability to appeal immediately decisions made during the trial
proceedings (such as the gag order) that neither the prosecution nor
the defense might otherwise have challenged.

Late in the morning of Thursday, October 23, little more than
twenty-four hours after the entry of Judge Ruff's gag order, a consortium of news media organizations filed an application in the Lincoln
County District Court, seeking to appear and be heard in connection
with the order entered by Judge Ruff.[51] The named parties in the
application included the Nebraska Press Association, the *Omaha
World-Herald* Company, the *Journal-Star* Publishing Company, the
Western Publishing Company, the North Platte Broadcasting Company, the Nebraska Broadcasters Association, the Associated Press,
and United Press International. Attorneys Stephen McGill of Omaha
and Harold Kay of North Platte drafted and filed the application on
behalf of the media companies. The language they used in this initial
legal volley would essentially become the cornerstone of all the subsequent constitutional challenges in the case.

McGill and Kay contended that Judge Ruff's order violated the
First, Sixth, and Ninth Amendments to the U.S. Constitution, as well
as various provisions of the Nebraska Constitution and state statutes.
They further alleged that "the County Court's blanket gag rule is virtually unknown to our system of justice . . . [and] is repugnant to a
free society . . . [and] smacks of precensorship with the resulting
evil of muzzling a free press." The application concluded with the
request that the media be allowed to formally enter into the criminal
case in order to oppose the gag order, and asked the district court to
"vacate it and hold it for naught."[52]

After filing their application with the clerk's office, McGill and
Kay took it directly to Judge Hugh Stuart, the district court judge who
had drawn the assignment of presiding over the impending Simants

trial. Stuart, known for maintaining tight control over his court-room, had just two days earlier consulted with Ruff about the possi-bility of entering a gag order on the press. While Ruff remembers Stuart as being noncommittal on the issue, Stuart later recalled that he had cautioned Ruff not to enter such an order, telling him that it would open "a can of worms."[53] Now, just as Stuart claimed to have feared, the can was open and the worms were in his lap. The media attorneys asked Stuart for an immediate hearing on their applica-tion, and Stuart agreed to convene a court session that night to address the matter. Notice of the hearing was passed along to the prosecutors and Simants's defense team.

And so at 6:10 p.m. on October 23, 1975, the second rare night court session within three days was held in the Lincoln County Court-house to address the issue of press coverage of the Simants murder trial. As legal proceedings go, it was a rather dramatic affair, lasting more than three hours and including testimony from two sitting judges, accompanied by emotional and sometimes hyperbolic con-stitutional arguments from the attorneys involved. Simants himself was present in the courtroom, along with his attorneys Vyhnalek and Bystrom. Also appearing was prosecutor Larson, this time accompa-nied by deputy county attorney John Murphy. McGill and Kay repre-sented the news media.[54]

For the first forty-five minutes, the attorneys' arguments focused on the threshold procedural issue of the news organizations' right to appear before the court at all in the case. Vyhnalek and Bystrom asked the court to reject the media's application to appear and be heard regarding the gag order.[55] They argued that no precedent existed for allowing news organizations to become, in effect, a "party" to a state criminal proceeding, and that the instant situation certainly did not warrant such an extraordinary step. In response, McGill and Kay contended that the public's right to monitor the operation of its legal institutions constituted a vital and perpetual "third interest" in every criminal proceeding—an interest that could only be protected by a vigilant press armed with free access to open courtrooms and the right to report the activity that takes place therein. McGill and Kay's oral arguments to the court mirrored the language of their written application filed that morning, wherein they claimed that "properly conducted preliminary hearings and trials, in addition to serving the interests of the accused . . . and the interests of the victims . . . maintain the confidence of the community in the honesty of its institutions, in the competence of its public officers, in the impartiality of its judges, and in the capacity of its criminal laws to do justice."[56] Ultimately, Judge Stuart overruled the defense motion to strike the media's application, holding that "the news media have a right to be in the case to a claimed infringement of their constitutional rights."[57] He then granted the defense counsel about an hour to gather their evidence in opposition to the news organizations' arguments and in support of their motion to close all future hearings in the case.

Despite Stuart's decision to allow the news organizations to proceed with their arguments that evening, the precise legal nature of the media's appearance in the district court remained somewhat murky then, as it does now. At the time of the ruling, and in subsequent discussions of the case, media representatives celebrated their innovative and apparently successful tactic of intervening in the criminal proceeding. In a newspaper story published the day after the Thursday evening hearing, Stephen McGill was quoted as saying that "it may have marked the first time that a third party had been allowed to intervene in a criminal case in the state."[58] In later pretrial proceedings unrelated to the gag order, however, Judge Stuart expressly ruled that the Nebraska Press Association was *not* a "proper party to this proceeding," and required the attorneys for the media organizations to remove themselves from counsel tables in the courtroom.[59] In discussions with the author many years later, Judge Stuart indicated that his decision was intended only to allow the media to be heard for purposes of the issues being addressed at that evening's session. He did not, he recalled, intend to grant them all of the access of an officially recognized "intervenor" in the case.[60] As a practical matter, the technicalities of the issue make little difference, inasmuch as the news organizations did gain access to the district court via their application and that access gave them sufficient "standing" to appeal the gag orders to the Nebraska Supreme Court and, ultimately, to the U.S. Supreme Court.

When the hearing resumed around 8:00 p.m., Harold Kay called Associate County Judge Dorothy Kriz to the witness stand. Kriz had assisted Judge Ruff in his efforts to notify the news media of the Tuesday evening court session, at which the court considered the prosecution's original request for a gag order. Kriz testified that she had called representatives of two local radio stations and the local television station, informing them that Ruff had "some news that may be of importance" to them, and asking them to come to the courthouse that evening to receive that news.[61] In reply to specific questions posed by Kay, she acknowledged that those phone messages were delivered to the media representatives even before prosecutor Larson had actually filed his "Motion for Restrictive Order" and further acknowledged that she had not indicated in her phone calls that there would be any kind of a formal hearing that evening on the question of a gag order on the press. Moreover, she acknowledged that no witnesses had testified at the "hearing" that evening and that no evidence or exhibits had been offered or admitted into evidence before Judge Ruff.[62] As Kay began to refer repeatedly to the Tuesday night session as the "so-called hearing," Vyhnalek objected, saying, "This thing is getting bad enough without stuff like that in here."[63] Judge Stuart agreed and ordered all instances of the "so-called hearing" stricken from the record. Kay's point, however, was well made. He had succeeded in showing that the county court session two nights before had been at best a seat-of-the pants proceeding, with no formal evidence of prejudicial or inappropriate news reporting produced or offered into the record. In the final analysis, Judge Ruff had simply accepted at face value the prosecutor's and defense attorneys' predictions about the anticipated impact of the media attention to the crime and Simants's arrest.

Following Dorothy Kriz's testimony, Vyhnalek and Bystrom presented the evidence they had been forced to hurriedly collect in order to defend the existing gag order and bolster their request to extend the restrictions on the press even further. They began by calling Judge Ruff himself to the witness stand to explain and justify the order he had entered the previous morning. On direct examination by Vyhnalek, Ruff testified that he had become aware of a high level of statewide and national media attention to the Kellie murders and the Simants arrest and that he had personally received many telephone calls from news organizations seeking information on the case.[64] During his questioning of Ruff, Vyhnalek also introduced into evidence a file containing fourteen newspaper articles dealing with the case clipped from various editions of the *North Platte Telegraph, Omaha World-Herald, Lincoln Star, Kansas City Times,* and *Denver Post.*[65] Vyhnalek's goal in offering the exhibits was to illustrate the breadth and depth of coverage the case was receiving at the local, state, and national levels. On cross-examination, however, Kay elicited from Judge Ruff repeated acknowledgments that he had not personally read each of the articles introduced by Vyhnalek and that he had not necessarily taken any of those specific articles into consideration in making his decision to issue the gag order.[66] In the end, Ruff testified that he had been only partially swayed by the amount of publicity the case was receiving in the media and had based his entry of the gag order primarily on the statements of the prosecutors and defense counsel, which he admitted "were not of record."[67]

When Ruff finished testifying, all that remained was for the attorneys to make their final arguments to Judge Stuart. Although those arguments did not make their way into the official transcript of the night's proceedings, they were reported in some detail in the next morning's newspapers.[68] At the most fundamental level, the arguments advanced by the Nebraska attorneys that night in that North Platte courtroom would be the same arguments that six months later much more celebrated attorneys, representing much more powerful clients and using much more elegant language, would make to the U.S. Supreme Court. Kay argued that "absolutely no evidence" of inappropriate or irresponsible reporting by the press had been introduced at the hearing before Judge Ruff two nights before, and that the voluntary bar-press guidelines should be allowed to function as they were intended, without judicial interference. He suggested that the court might even use its contempt power to punish irresponsible journalists in the future but it ought never to engage in the kind of prior restraint manifested in the existing gag order.[69]

In his portion of the argument, media attorney Stephen McGill took an even more stridently absolutist position, contending that the courts "should never deny freedom of speech." At one point in his presentation, McGill overreached, stating, "Goodness gracious, we want this man to have a fair trial . . . but I'd let somebody go free who was guilty before I'd deny freedom of speech."[70] In light of the depravity of the Kellie murders and the emotional trauma they had produced, the patronizing tone of McGill's argument did not sit well with the prosecutors, Judge Stuart, or many of the citizens of Lincoln County. Prosecutor Larson quickly countered McGill's point by arguing that the balance of constitutional interests ought to swing the other way, saying, "I would rather stem adverse publicity than have a guilty man go free."[71]

As news of McGill's statement appeared in the Friday papers and circulated on the local grapevine, a backlash of public opinion against the press's position washed through the community, with many people expressing disgust at what they perceived to be the news media's self-serving arguments. An editorial in the *North Platte Telegraph* on October 29 quoted an unnamed local attorney as saying that he hoped the newspaper would "get your pants beat off on this one" because "all you guys are trying to do is sell more papers."[72] In letters to the editor printed in the paper that same day, various local residents expressed fervent support for Judge Ruff's gag order and dismay at the press's seemingly callous disregard for the victims. Lorna Hansen wondered whether McGill would feel the same way about letting a guilty man go free "if it were members of his family that had been injured or killed."[73] Wilma Wyman, purporting to speak for "many citizens who feel that Judge Ruff was absolutely right," was even harsher in her attacks on the press and its attorneys. Calling McGill's statement contemptible, she wrote that the "balderdash claimed by the 'Attorneys for the media coalition' is simply a quest for notoriety and the almighty dollar."[74]

When the Thursday night session finally drew to a close after more than three hours of testimony and argument, Judge Stuart announced his tentative rulings from the bench. Without comment or delay, he overruled the defense motion to close all future pretrial proceedings in the case. On the larger issue of the propriety of Ruff's existing gag order, Stuart expressed acute awareness of the significance of the constitutional conflict at issue and offered the hope that both of the important interests at stake could be protected if the matter was "handled with great delicacy and restraint by both sides."[75] Stuart went on to say, "I must condemn the past courts that are secret.

I have seen many times that secret courts are bad courts. Courts are better off as the light of day shines on them."[76] At the same time, he expressed equally firm disagreement with the absolutist position embedded in McGill's "let a guilty man go free" comment, saying, "This court [is] not willing to sacrifice a fair trial in order to get a free press, and is not willing to go along with Mr. McGill's propositions that mistrials are all right in order to get a free press."[77] In the end, Stuart concluded that he needed more time to study the constitutional issue before making a final decision. He therefore held that Ruff's existing order would continue in effect "on a temporary basis," and promised that he would issue a modified order by the following Monday afternoon.[78]

As the hearing concluded, Stuart showed admirable restraint by not divulging a notable and rather remarkable personal twist to the unfolding story. The constitutional dilemma he faced would not be his only concern over the coming weekend. His only daughter's wedding was scheduled to take place on Saturday, just two days hence. He later understandably acknowledged that it was "another matter of considerable importance to me."[79] Thus, with all those considerations before him—the emotional turmoil of the horrible Kellie murders, the legal arguments of the attorneys, the weighty constitutional issues at stake, and even his own daughter's impending wedding—Hugh Stuart began to confront head-on the "trying task" Justice Hugo Black had described thirty-four years earlier. Stuart would attempt to reconcile a clash between "two of the most cherished policies of our civilization."[80]

Three days later, Stuart announced his decision. Taking the bench at 2:52 p.m. on Monday, October 27, he began by expressing his appreciation to all the attorneys for "their professional attitude and for the assistance they have given me in trying to avoid gross error."[81] He then proceeded to read his decision into the record, with the promise to reduce it to a formal statement in writing "as soon as practically possible."[82] The gag order Judge Stuart entered that day would become the focal point of all the ensuing constitutional litigation in the appellate courts and would ultimately make Stuart himself the named defendant in one of the leading Supreme Court decisions on press freedom in American legal history.

Given the far-reaching effect of the October 27 gag order, its provisions warrant sustained attention. Stuart began by finding that a clear and present danger existed that pretrial publicity could impinge on Simants's right to a fair trial, and that "an order setting forth the limitations of pre-trial publicity is appropriate."[83] He then terminated the existing order issued by Judge Ruff, declaring that it was "too broad," and substituted in its place his own more precisely enunciated limitations on press coverage of the Simants proceedings. Despite Stuart's explicit rejection of Ruff's original language, and notwithstanding his later claim that he had considerably eased the restrictions placed on the press, the fundamental essence of his order proved to be essentially the same as Ruff's had been.[84] That is, he specifically adopted and incorporated the provisions of the voluntary bar-press guidelines as the formal court order controlling the dissemination of information in the case. In an attempt to add more precision and clarity to the order, however, Stuart did set out six specific addenda designed to mold the provisions of the guidelines to meet the particular circumstances present in the Simants prosecution. Specifically, his order provided that (1) the phrase "pre-trial" publicity, as used in the guidelines, would refer to all reporting prior to the impaneling of a jury in the upcoming trial; (2) the reporting of any references to a statement or confession made by Simants to law enforcement officials was specifically prohibited; (3) the reporting of any references to statements made by Simants to his nephew, Butch Boggs, or his parents, Amos and Grace Simants, or references to the confessional note he had left in the Boggs home, were specifically prohibited; (4) the reporting of the technical aspects of the testimony of Dr. Miles Foster at the preliminary hearing—involving the scientific and forensic evidence of Simants's sexual assault on ten-year-old Florence—was specifically prohibited; (5) the reporting of the identity of any of the victims who had been sexually assaulted or the details of any of the sexual assaults was specifically prohibited; and (6) the reporting of the precise nature of the limitations imposed by the gag order itself could not be reported. In other words, the media could report that they had been gagged, but they could not disclose the nature of the information they were being prohibited from reporting.[85]

Four days after the entry of Judge Stuart's gag order, the Nebraska Press Association and the other media organizations filed a notice of appeal in the district court, announcing their intention to take the question of the constitutionality of the new gag order to the Nebraska Supreme Court.[86] While the Simants murder prosecution continued down the path to trial in the Lincoln County District Court, the constitutional litigation on the First versus Sixth Amendment issues was about to enter a new phase, in much bigger arenas.

Four
Entering the Appellate Labyrinth

There is here much drama—and the stuff of
future history books—to watch.

EDITORIAL, *Lincoln Evening Journal*
November 24, 1975

Judge Hugh Stuart announced the imposition of his gag order on the afternoon of Monday, October 27, 1975. For the next several days, newspapers and broadcast outlets across the state and the region weighed in with commentary in opposition to Stuart's action. On October 30, the *Lincoln Evening Journal* ran a long editorial in which it raised the ominous specter of the Spanish Inquisition and the English Court of Star Chamber as examples of the dangers attendant to secret court proceedings, and the paper warned that the Stuart gag order "imperiled Americans' constitutional protections."[1] Other major newspapers echoed that sentiment, including the *Chicago Tribune*, which decried the perils of a court order that "prevented news reports of a public proceeding in a public court."[2]

The *Omaha World-Herald* was just as strident in its opposition to Stuart's gag, arguing in an October 29 editorial that "the idea that one right is subservient to the other is a latter-day invention of lawyers

Editorial cartoon by Bill Mauldin, *Omaha World-Herald,* October 29, 1975. Copyright 1975 by Bill Mauldin. Courtesy of the Mauldin Estate.

and judges, and stands as one of the most potentially destructive concepts in the judicial system, when it is abused as it has been in the Simants case."[3] Accompanying the editorial was a cartoon depicting a spiked boot labeled "totalitarianism" stomping on a set of eyeglasses representing "press freedom." The caption read "First Step."

Even before the issuance of Judge Stuart's version of the gag order, the *North Platte Telegraph* had made its editorial position quite clear, running a cartoon by Carl Bieber in its October 24/25 edition depicting four journalists bound and gagged, suggesting their ability to hear the court proceedings but not to comment on them. Sarcastically titled "Hearing the hearing," the cartoon also showed two of the gagged journalists thinking, "He's sure a Ruff judge!"

As attention from the regional and national press increased, representatives of the Nebraska news organizations who were directly

Editorial cartoon by Carl Bieber, *North Platte Telegraph,* October 24, 1975. Courtesy
North Platte Telegraph.

involved in the litigation deliberated in Omaha at the offices of *World-Herald* Vice President G. Woodson (Woody) Howe, who had become one of the leading spokesmen for the group.[4] Omaha attorney Stephen McGill, accompanied by his partner James Koley, briefed his clients on the impact of Stuart's ruling and the legal options available to them in the appellate courts. There was no doubt among the participants that Stuart's order had to be challenged. Indeed, Howe had already publicly declared that the media would not accept a continuing gag. On October 28, the *North Platte Telegraph* quoted him as vowing that "the media cannot and will not endorse, in any way, a new order by the District Court which inflicts prior restraint on the constitutionally protected right of free speech. . . . Any order interfering with the exercise of the people's right to a free press must and should be opposed."[5]

Thus, the only question to be resolved was one of tactics. What procedural strategy should be used to mount a legal assault on the gag order in the appellate courts? The answer came on Friday, October 31, when the media's attorneys initiated a two-pronged line of attack. On one front, North Platte attorney Harold Kay, representing the various news organizations involved in the litigation, filed a simple notice of appeal in the Lincoln County District Court. Kay's notice advised the prosecutors and defense counsel in the Simants criminal proceedings that the media outlets affected by Judge Stuart's order were appealing its constitutionality to the Nebraska Supreme Court.[6] The appeal would be taken directly to the state supreme court because, at that time, Nebraska was one of the few states in the country that did not have an intermediate court of appeals. Thus, any and all appeals from the district courts were entertained by the state's highest court.[7]

After filing the notice of appeal, Kay contacted Judge Stuart to make an oral request that Stuart stay (that is, temporarily delay enforcement of) his gag order. On that day, Stuart happened to be presiding over other unrelated proceedings in Ogallala, Nebraska. When Kay reached him by telephone and asked him for the stay, Stuart declined, indicating that he would take no further action on the matter of the gag order until he returned to North Platte the following week. As was normal procedure in such appeals, Kay also filed a formal request with the clerk of the district court and Judge Stuart's court reporter in North Platte, asking them to prepare transcripts of the proceedings held in the district court and to file those transcripts with the Nebraska Supreme Court. That appeal proceeding would be docketed in the state high court as case number 40445.

At the same time that Kay was filing his notice of appeal in North Platte, McGill and Koley were implementing the second prong of the media's appellate strategy. In a rather loosely phrased document titled "Application for Leave to Docket," entered in the Nebraska Supreme Court as case number 40471, they asked the state high court to allow the news organizations and individuals affected by Judge Stuart's gag order to "commence an original action in the nature of a Writ of Mandamus (or any other original action—however designated—authorized by the Constitution and laws of the State of Nebraska and appropriate in these proceedings)."[8] In other words, in addition to the appeal from Judge Stuart's gag order, the news organizations also sought to initiate an original proceeding in the Nebraska Supreme Court aimed at overturning Stuart's gag order.[9]

The writ of mandamus referred to in McGill and Koley's application is an ancient, but still frequently invoked, common-law remedy whereby a superior court is asked to issue an order to a lower court or other governmental entity to take some action in accordance with the inferior tribunal's legal duties. By naming Judge Stuart as the respondent in this proposed mandamus action, the news organizations, as relators, were asking the Supreme Court to issue an order requiring Judge Stuart to vacate his gag order.

Along with that uniquely crafted "application," McGill and Koley filed a twelve-page petition in the Nebraska Supreme Court, setting out the factual, legal, and procedural events that had brought the news media to the high court's door. The petition outlined the basic facts of the Kellie murders and described in some detail the unusual evening court sessions that had led to the two separate restrictive orders entered against the press by Judges Ruff and Stuart. In describing the October 23 hearing before Judge Stuart, the media's attorneys emphasized that "there was no showing of danger to the administration of justice or to the denial of a fair trial to the defendant," nor, they argued, was there any "evidence of misconduct of any kind on the part of the press."[10]

After reciting verbatim in their petition most of the provisions of Stuart's gag order, McGill and Koley proceeded to attack its constitutionality on numerous grounds. They argued first that, by leaving members of the public free to discuss what they heard and saw at the preliminary hearing, the order placed the press "in an inferior position with respect to their exercise of first amendment rights to the general public . . . who attended these hearings in open court."[11] They went on to point out that most of the material barred from publication under the order was "information that was either publicly testified to in open court during the preliminary hearing or is contained in documents filed in that court, which are matters of public record in the State of Nebraska and to which any interested citizen may have access."[12]

In paragraph 11 of the petition, the attorneys vigorously attacked Stuart's adoption of the Nebraska bar-press guidelines, calling that portion of his order "an abuse of discretion that is not in the best interests of the administration of justice in this state."[13] They contended that "the language of the guidelines was not designed for inclusion in court orders; rather, the guidelines set forth statements of broad general principle subject to varying interpretations."[14] By effectively converting the guidelines into law, they continued, Stuart had perverted their spirit and intent since they were "never intended to be law thrust upon the press by the bar."[15]

The legal arguments contained in McGill and Koley's petition to the state high court culminated in a declaration that Stuart's gag order constituted a direct and continuing violation of the news organizations' rights and responsibilities under the First, Sixth, and Fourteenth Amendments to the U.S. Constitution, as well as a blatant violation of Nebraska's "open courts" statutes.[16] They asked the court to issue an "immediate stay" against the operation of the existing gag order and to conduct an "immediate hearing" on the validity and constitutionality of the order.[17] To further emphasize the urgency of the issue, the media attorneys also filed a "motion to advance appeal," relating to the separate appeal proceeding initiated that morning by Harold Kay in North Platte. That motion sought to invoke a provision of the court's operating rules which called for expedited handling of cases that involved "issues of great public interest which, if not advanced, heard and disposed of forthwith, will become moot or fruitless."[18]

In addition to their application, petition, and motion to advance appeal, the media attorneys also filed with the supreme court an eleven-page statement in support of the court's jurisdiction. In that document, they sought to convince the state high court that it had the jurisdictional authority to issue a writ of mandamus against Judge Stuart, because his gag order constituted a direct prior restraint on speech in violation of the news media's and the public's rights under the U.S. Constitution. McGill and Koley argued that Judge Stuart had "no discretion to issue an Order in direct violation of the Constitution" and that, accordingly, "mandamus will lie" to compel Stuart to vacate his existing order.[19]

With the filing of all of those documents in the district court and the state supreme court on October 31, the Nebraska news organizations set in motion a labyrinthine eight-month legal contest in the appellate courts.[20] The case bounced back and forth between the Nebraska Supreme Court and the U.S. Supreme Court on several occasions, placing the two tribunals in a delicate, and often testy, jurisdictional battle of wills. Indeed, for the first month of the appellate litigation, tedious procedural and jurisdictional peculiarities, rather than lofty constitutional principles, would dictate the flow and progress of the case.

Despite the news organizations' repeated requests in their pleadings for immediate, expedited, or advanced relief, the state court's initial response was silence. On Tuesday, November 4, McGill contacted the Office of the Clerk of the Nebraska Supreme Court to ask when the court might take action on the media's pending requests for relief. The clerk of the court, George Turner, told McGill that the next available date for submission of such a matter would not come until December 1, 1975, and that the documents filed on behalf of the news organizations would be scheduled for consideration by the court on that date.

In other words, the Nebraska Supreme Court expressed no intention of taking any action, or even fitting the matter into its schedule, for almost another month. Although judicial sluggishness is not at all uncommon, and one month amounts to only a blink of the eye in routine appellate litigation time, the news organizations believed that they had already been abundantly indulgent by complying for more than two weeks with what they considered to be two blatantly unconstitutional court orders in the Simants prosecution. Feeling that a continuing constitutional violation occurred every day that Judge Stuart's gag order survived, the Nebraska media now moved on to the court of last resort. They took their case to the U.S. Supreme Court.

At 10:45 p.m. on Wednesday, November 5, 1975, the Nebraska news organizations filed an emergency application for stay in the Supreme Court, seeking immediate relief from Judge Stuart's gag order. The operating rules of the Supreme Court provided then, as now, that such an application (most typically used in last-minute death penalty appeals) would be referred for handling to the member of the Supreme Court responsible for the circuit from which the case arose.[21] For a case emanating from Nebraska, that meant the Eighth Circuit, for which Justice Harry A. Blackmun was the presiding circuit justice.

So it was that, little more than a week after Judge Hugh Stuart entered his gag order against the Nebraska media in North Platte, Nebraska, the constitutionality of that order made its way to the Washington, D.C., desk of Supreme Court Justice Harry Blackmun. A native Minnesotan, Blackmun had been appointed to the Court by President Richard Nixon in 1970 as an anticipated "Minnesota Twin" for recently appointed conservative Chief Justice Warren Burger. Though many of his early rulings justified that expectation, Blackmun's judicial legacy is considerably more nuanced than can be captured with traditional labels of liberal or conservative. Indeed, for much of his tenure on the Burger Court of the 1970s and early '80s, Blackmun served as a key swing vote between the Court's generally conservative voting bloc of Burger, Byron White, William Rehnquist, and John Harlan, on the one hand, and the liberal faction of Thurgood Marshall, Lewis Powell, William Brennan, and John Paul Stevens, on the other.[22] Ultimately, Blackmun created for himself a widely respected legacy as a pragmatic justice whose judicial philosophy is generally seen as undergoing an evolutionary shift from the right to the left during his twenty-four years on the high court.[23] Upon his death in 1999, Blackmun would be eulogized by the American Civil Liberties Union as a man of "great courage, passion, and eloquence" who had, by the end of his tenure, "found his voice as a defender of civil liberties."[24]

Antiabortion advocates, of course, will always view Harry Blackmun in far less flattering terms. At the time of the Nebraska Press Association litigation in the fall of 1975 (and to this day) Blackmun was certainly most acclaimed, or vilified, for his authorship of the majority opinion in the Court's controversial 1973 *Roe v. Wade* decision, which held that first-trimester abortions were constitutionally protected by a woman's right to privacy.[25] Fortunately for the justice, his other claim to fame during his early years on the court arose from an opinion that addressed a much less controversial topic. In 1972, he had become the champion of many baseball fans (and certainly all Major League owners) for his lyrical, almost poetic, paean to the game of baseball in *Flood v. Kuhn,* a decision upholding Major League Baseball's exemption from antitrust laws.[26]

Notwithstanding Blackmun's rising profile as a key member of the Court, in 1975 his record on First Amendment issues was unremarkable. The minimal record on free press issues that he had created, however, could not have given much comfort to the Nebraska news organizations that now sought his assistance. In 1971, Blackmun had cast one of three dissenting votes (Burger's and Harlan's were the other two) in the Court's landmark First Amendment decision in *New York Times Co. v. United States.*[27] The majority opinion in that case had denied the federal government's request for an injunction prohibiting the *New York Times* from publishing what had become known as the Pentagon Papers, classified documents detailing American involvement in the Vietnam War.[28]

In his dissent, Blackmun complained that the case had been rushed before the Court with unseemly and inappropriate procedural haste and reminded the press that "the First Amendment, after all, is only one part of an entire Constitution."[29] "I cannot," he declared, "subscribe to a doctrine of unlimited absolutism for the First Amendment at the cost of downgrading other [Constitutional] provisions."[30] He went on to express his judicial sympathy with the government's claimed justifications for restraining the press, suggesting that the publication of the documents "could clearly result in great harm to the nation . . . [in the form of] the deaths of soldiers, the destruction of alliances, the greatly increased difficulty of negotiation with our enemies, the inability of our diplomats to negotiate, the prolongation of the war, and further delay in the freeing of American prisoners."[31]

The media's application to Justice Blackmun for a stay, prepared and filed by McGill and Koley, was docketed in the Supreme Court as number A-426. It recounted in some detail the factual, legal, and procedural events that had given rise to Judge Stuart's existing gag order and alleged that the news organizations' ability and responsibility to perform their function of informing the public of the operation of the criminal justice system had been "almost totally frustrated by the direct prior restraint imposed by the District Court's order."[32] The application further advised Blackmun that the "District Court and the Nebraska Supreme Court have declined to act on the requested relief," and culminated in the request that he "stay the order of the District Court and, after hearing, declare it void, vacated, and of no further effect."[33]

Blackmun responded quickly to the news organizations' request. On the morning after their application reached his office, his clerks dispatched notices to the Nebraska attorney general (as representative of Judge Stuart), Lincoln County Attorney Milton Larson, and Simants's attorneys, Leonard Vyhnalek and Keith Bystrom. Those notices requested that the attorneys file responses to the news organizations' application by the following Tuesday, November 11. All of them complied promptly, sending written briefs to Blackmun's office during the next several days. All of the responses made essentially the same points—that the gag order was necessary to protect Simants's right to an impartial jury, and that the Nebraska Supreme Court should be given more time to rule on the issue before Blackmun intervened. In his response on behalf of Judge Stuart, Nebraska Attorney General Paul Douglas told Blackmun that, during the week the news organizations filed their requests for relief in the Nebraska Supreme Court, the court was already committed to hearing arguments in fifty-seven previously scheduled cases. Thus, he argued, it was self-evident why the state high court had not yet acted on the matter.[34] Prosecutor Larson's response specifically assured Blackmun that the Nebraska court would "act promptly and diligently to bring this matter to conclusion."[35]

In the meantime, however, the Nebraska Supreme Court had taken note of the news organizations' action in Washington and responded with an unusual procedural decree that seemed to suggest at least mild resentment at the high court's threatened intervention in the matter. On November 10, the Nebraska justices issued a *per curiam* statement in which they announced that "we are reliably informed that the relators have filed with the Supreme Court of the United States an application or a request that that court act to accomplish the same purposes to be accomplished by their request to us to exercise our original jurisdiction."[36] In legal usage, *per curiam* means "by the court" and is used to denote an opinion issued on behalf of the entire panel of an appellate court, with no single identified author. Such opinions are typically issued in routine jurisdictional matters to reflect unanimity within the court, but they are also used on occasion to conceal disagreement among the court panel. In its November 10 statement, the state supreme court went on to note that the filing of the application in the U.S. Supreme Court put it in the position of possibly exercising parallel jurisdiction with the high court—a situation that the Nebraska justices deemed to be inadvisable.[37] Accordingly, they announced that they would refrain from taking action in the case "until the Supreme Court of the United States has made known whether or not it will accept jurisdiction in the matter."[38] The procedural dynamics of the situation recalled the old joke about a cowboy whose horse gets its own hoof caught in one of the stirrups. The cowboy tells the horse, "If you're getting on, I'm getting off." Similarly, the Nebraska justices were telling Justice Blackmun, "If you're getting into this case, we're getting out."

When Blackmun learned of the state court's statement two days later, he responded with a similarly unusual and rather confrontational procedural decree of his own. On November 13, again acting in his capacity as the circuit justice for the Eighth Circuit, Blackmun issued an in-chambers opinion in which he scolded the Nebraska Supreme Court for failing to take more expeditious action on the news organizations' requests for relief.[39] He reminded the Nebraska justices that Judge Stuart's gag order "obviously imposes significant prior restraints on media reporting[, and] it therefore comes to me bearing a heavy presumption against its constitutional validity."[40] He went on to point out that, if no action could be anticipated from the state court until December 1 at the earliest, "the day-by-day duration of that delay would constitute and aggravate a deprival of such constitutional rights, if any, that the applicants may possess."[41]

Based upon his interpretation of the state court's *per curiam* statement of three days before, however, Blackmun decided that he would give the state high court a bit more time to take action. He announced that he would temporarily defer ruling on the media's application for a stay so that any action on his part should "not be deemed to stultify [the Nebraska Supreme Court] in the performance of its appropriate constitutional duty."[42] He further announced, in unusually firm language, his expectation "that the Supreme Court of Nebraska, forthwith and without delay, will entertain the applicants' application made to it, and will promptly decide it in the full consciousness that 'time is of the essence.'"[43] Blackmun concluded by reminding all the parties (including the Nebraska justices) that he would step in immediately if "prompt action was not forthcoming" from the state high court.

As the litigants shifted their attention back to Lincoln, Nebraska, and as news of Blackmun's ruling began to circulate in the press, the state high court's indignation at Blackmun's pressure grew more palpable. A front-page article in the November 14 *Omaha World-Herald,* quoting what the paper referred to as high court observers, indicated that "for a U.S. Supreme Court justice to virtually direct a state supreme court to consider an application, and promptly, is highly unusual."[44] In a sidebar piece printed in boldface type next to that same article, the chief justice of the Nebraska Supreme Court, Paul W. White, issued a rare public statement on a pending case. White defended his court's handling of the matter and fired a not-too-subtle shot back toward Blackmun: "This court has always acted promptly on matters and at the same time maintained balance by proper deliberation and consideration."[45]

In light of Justice Blackmun's own dissenting opinion in the Pentagon Papers decision four years earlier, White showed admirable restraint in not parroting Blackmun's own words back to him. In that opinion, Blackmun had strongly criticized the majority of his own court for allowing themselves to be "pressed into [a] hurried decision of profound constitutional issues on inadequately developed and largely assumed facts without the careful deliberation that, one would hope, should characterize the American judicial process."[46] Now Blackmun was himself directing the Nebraska Supreme Court to move more quickly on an almost identical "profound constitutional issue." His prodding of the state court might well have been seen as ironic at best or hypocritical at worst.

For another full week after Justice Blackmun urged the state supreme court to entertain the matter "forthwith and without delay," no further word was heard from Lincoln. On Monday, November 17, media attorney Stephen McGill again called the court to see if any action had been taken on the case. Clerk George Turner replied that he knew of none. Based upon that response, McGill dispatched a telegram to Justice Blackmun that evening, advising him that the state court had still not ruled on the matter, and asking him to take action immediately, as promised in his November 13 opinion.

The following morning, the Nebraska high court issued a docketing order announcing that it would hear arguments on the gag order case one week later, on November 25. The court's order reiterated its justification for its deliberate pace, stating, "The nature of the issues in this case indicate that oral argument is advisable. Procedural due process requires that we not act summarily . . . [and] that all interested parties . . . be given an opportunity to be heard."[47] Dismayed at the thought of another week's delay, and encouraged by the tone and import of Blackmun's earlier opinion, McGill sent another telegram to the justice's office, advising him of the state court's latest announcement and formally renewing the news organizations' application for an immediate stay of the Stuart gag order.

By then, Blackmun too had run out of patience with the state court. On November 20, he issued another in-chambers opinion— this time directly addressing the merits of the Stuart gag order. Blackmun first noted that, by the time the state supreme court heard arguments in the case on November 25, "at least twelve days will have elapsed, without action, since the filing of my in-chambers opinion [of November 13], and more than four weeks since the entry of the District Court's restrictive order."[48] Concluding that the state court's delays had now "exceeded tolerable limits" and that "the likelihood of irreparable injury to First Amendment interests" required him to act, Blackmun proceeded to issue a partial stay of the Stuart gag order. Inasmuch as this second in-chambers opinion by Justice Blackmun would go a long way toward framing the constitutional issues that would later be addressed by the full Supreme Court, it bears close examination here.

Blackmun began his analysis by turning aside a procedural objection raised by Nebraska Attorney General Paul Douglas, Lincoln County Attorney Milton Larson, and Simants's defense attorneys, Leonard Vyhnalek and Keith Bystrom. In their opposition to the news organizations' application for a stay, all of them had argued that a Supreme Court justice's statutory authority to issue such a stay could be exercised only against a state court's "final judgment or decree."[49] Inasmuch as Judge Stuart's gag order had not yet been ruled upon by the Nebraska Supreme Court, they argued, it was not a "final judgment" upon which Justice Blackmun could act.

After first acknowledging the complexity of the issue under the existing circumstances, Blackmun concluded that the state court's delays had, in effect, lent "virtual finality" to the Stuart gag order. He held that, in cases involving a direct prior restraint on freedom of the press, "each passing day may constitute a separate and cognizable infringement of the First Amendment. The suppressed information grows older. Other events crowd upon it."[50] To that extent, Blackmun continued, "any First Amendment infringement that occurs with each passing day is irreparable."[51] Thus, by delaying action on the news organizations' claims until November 25 at the earliest, the state high court had, in effect, decided that prior restraint would persist during the intervening days. In that sense, Blackmun concluded, "delay itself is a final decision."[52]

Blackmun then proceeded to address the substantive constitutional conflict at issue in the case. He first acknowledged the delicacy of the balance between the competing rights at stake, noting that there is "no litmus paper test" for drawing a line between the two and that "some accommodation of the conflicting interests must be reached."[53] Still, he left no doubt concerning where he believed the burden of persuasion lay in such contests, holding that "the governing principle is that the press, in general, is to be free and unrestrained" and that those who would seek to limit the reporting of news "bear the burden of showing that publicizing particular facts will irreparably impair the ability of those exposed to them to reach an independent and impartial judgment as to guilt."[54]

Agreeing with one of the most fundamental arguments that had been persistently advanced by the media attorneys, Blackmun held that the most troublesome aspect of Stuart's gag order was its wholesale incorporation of the Nebraska bar-press guidelines.[55] Those standards, he concluded, were merely suggestive, and their language was necessarily vague.[56] As a particularly egregious example of the guidelines' imprecision, he cited their admonition that publication of an accused's prior criminal record "should be considered very carefully" and "should generally be avoided." Such phrasing, he held, did not rise to the level of specificity necessary for a court order infringing on First Amendment rights. "If a member of the press is to go to jail for reporting news in violation of a court order," Blackmun stated, "it is essential that he disobey a more definite and precise command than one that he consider his act 'very carefully'."[57] Finding the Nebraska bar-press guidelines to be riddled with that type of vague and indefinite language, he concluded that "the best and momentary course is to stay their mandatory and wholesale imposition in the present context."[58]

As he continued his analysis, Blackmun concluded that there was "no persuasive justification" for paragraphs 4 and 5 of the Stuart gag order, which prohibited the publication of Dr. Miles Foster's testimony at the preliminary hearing relating to his autopsy findings and the publication of details of the sexual crimes and identities of the victims who had been subjected to sexual assault. Those kinds of facts, Blackmun noted, "do not implicate a particular defendant" and their publication, therefore, "could not infringe upon the accused's right to a fair trial of the issue as to whether he was the one who committed the crimes."[59] Accordingly, he immediately stayed those portions of the gag order as well.

Despite his purge of large portions of Judge Stuart's existing order, Blackmun explicitly reminded the parties that he was not issuing a blanket prohibition of any and all judicial limitations on pretrial reporting in the Simants's prosecution. Noting that judicial restraints of the press "are not necessarily and in all cases invalid," he proceeded to specifically identify those portions of Stuart's order that survived his scrutiny. To the great dismay of the news organizations, Blackmun declared that certain facts that were "strongly implicative of" or "highly prejudicial to" a criminal defendant could be restrained, and suggested that "a confession or statement against interest [by an accused] is the paradigm" for items that might be permissibly prohibited from publication.[60] Thus, he left intact the portions of the Stuart gag order (paragraphs 2 and 3) that prohibited pretrial publication of Simants's confession to law enforcement officials, his admissions to his parents and nephew, and the contents of the "I am sorry" note he left in the Boggs home. As the media had been arguing for weeks, virtually all of that material had been offered in public court proceedings, or was available in documents that were part of the official court files in Lincoln County District Court. Nevertheless, the "gag" on the media relating to those items remained intact.

Blackmun concluded his November 20 opinion with language that placed the burden of continuing the constitutional analysis back upon the Nebraska Supreme Court. Acknowledging that the state court was closer to the local situation and better able to gauge the "consequences of community opinion that have arisen since the commission of the [Kellie murders]," he suggested that the Nebraska high court could and should continue to "evaluate the [other] details of the restrictive order."[61] He had, he reminded the state court justices, addressed only those aspects of the Stuart gag order that appeared to him to "require resolution immediately and without one moment's further delay."[62]

With the Stuart gag order now partially stayed by Justice Blackmun's November 20 opinion, the focus of the constitutional conflict returned yet again to Lincoln, Nebraska. As the hearing before the Nebraska Supreme Court on November 25 drew nearer, national attention to the case increased, and the drumbeat of commentary in the press continued to grow in volume and intensity. In an editorial published the night before the Supreme Court's hearing, headlined "High Drama Here Tuesday," the Lincoln Evening Journal suggested that the state high court had never before been thrust into the national spotlight as it would be the next day.[63] The column predicted, with notable accuracy, that the case "may result in a landmark interpretation of the First Amendment" and closed with the observation that "there is here much drama—and the stuff of future history books—to watch."[64]

When the Nebraska Supreme Court took the bench to hear arguments in the case on the morning of Tuesday, November 25, the panel of attorneys at the bar before them comprised many of the same men who had carried the litigation to that point. Stephen McGill and James Koley argued for the news organizations, while prosecutor Milton Larson and defense counsel Leonard Vyhnalek appeared in defense of the existing gag order. No transcript of the hearing survives, but some of the exchanges between the attorneys and the justices made their way into newspaper reports published the next day.[65] The media attorneys continued to advance their fundamental points—that the

gag order was a blatant and continuing violation of the First Amendment and the Nebraska "open courts" statutes. Larson and Vyhnalek
continued to argue that Stuart's restrictions on the press were narrowly and appropriately drawn so as to accommodate reasonably the
competing constitutional interests at stake.[66]

Koley again emphasized all of the less restrictive options available to the trial court to protect Simants from prejudicial publicity,
including a delay of the trial or a change of venue. He also contended
that massive publicity about a pending case had never been conclu-
sively shown to affect potential jurors and cited as an example the
recent Watergate prosecutions in Washington, D.C. Despite the
overwhelming media attention to those cases, he claimed, hundreds
of potential jurors had been found who claimed to know absolutely
nothing about the Watergate affair. To that line of argument, Vyhnalek dryly countered, "Our people out here are better informed
than they are in Washington."[67]

At least one of the justices, John Newton, expressed considerable
skepticism at the notion that jurors could truly remain free of bias in
a highly publicized case. He asked McGill, "When a bunch of jurors
say they're not prejudiced by what they hear and read, do you think
that's true? Isn't there a residue of influence?" McGill could only
reply that he hoped that "when jurors are sworn to tell the truth
[about their possible biases], they will." Newton seemed unper-
suaded by that response, telling McGill, "You have some [unique]
understanding of human nature, I take it."[68]

When the hearing concluded after some seventy minutes, Chief
Justice Paul White announced that the court would take the matter
under advisement and issue a decision by the following Monday. Five
days later, on December 1, the state high court kept that promise,
issuing its only substantive decision on the merits of the case. The
court's *per curiam* opinion, in effect, created a third incarnation of the
gag order in the Simants prosecution and, at the same time, provided
the final judgment of the state court that would ultimately be taken up
for consideration by the full U.S. Supreme Court.[69]

The court's opinion began with an analysis of the same procedural
and jurisdictional complexities that had troubled Justice Blackmun—
that is, the overlapping exercise of authority between the state and

federal courts that had existed for more than three weeks. At the least, the court suggested, that situation seemed to threaten "the regrettable possibility of collision [between the two courts]."[70] The court observed that, if it was to be entirely consistent with its previous actions, it ought to again refrain from acting "because we are now in the position of exercising concurrent jurisdiction with the U.S. Supreme Court for which there is no precedent."[71] Nevertheless, five of the seven members of the court concluded that pressing issues of state procedure, combined with the need to provide guidance to the local courts as well as a final order to be considered by the U.S. Supreme Court, compelled them to decide the merits of the case.

Although the state court's decision was issued *per curiam,* which generally indicates unanimity within a court, there was in this instance significant disagreement among the justices about the proper disposition of the jurisdictional issue. Associate Justice Lawrence M. Clinton filed a strong dissent from the majority opinion, which was joined by Chief Justice White. Clinton declared that, by invoking the jurisdiction of the U.S. Supreme Court, the news organizations had become *estopped* from continuing to argue the case in a state court.[72] Clinton observed that "there is no precedent or authority for this court and the Supreme Court of the United States to exercise concurrent jurisdiction in matters relating to the construction of the federal Constitution. Either we have jurisdiction in this case, or the Supreme Court of the United States has jurisdiction."[73] Accordingly, both Clinton and White concluded that the news organizations' request for relief in the state court "ought to be dismissed . . . because of the intervening jurisdiction of the Supreme Court of the United States."[74]

Clinton's dissent also offered clear evidence of the underlying and ongoing tension between the state court and Justice Blackmun. He set out in some detail the procedural constraints that had prevented the Nebraska court from acting more quickly in the case. He noted, for example, that when the news organizations' challenges to the gag order reached the court, "We were engaged in the first of six days of oral arguments in cases pending before us [that were] already irrevocably scheduled."[75] The court could not and should not, he argued, shortcut its procedures "on the basis of telephone calls from counsel, or telegrams."[76] Clinton went on to observe caustically that "apparently, both the relators and Justice Blackmun expected that we would act summarily without notice to all interested parties and without a hearing. We did not do so, I think for reasons that should be obvious."[77]

The complexity of the jurisdictional question and the mixed feelings among the Nebraska justices on the issue were further evidenced by the fact that two other justices, Harry A. Spencer and John E. Newton, filed a separate concurring opinion in which they expressed full agreement with the opinions expressed in Clinton's dissent. Nevertheless, those two joined in the majority opinion so as to "resolve the immediate controversy in this jurisdiction" and put the matter to rest.[78]

Having made the threshold determination to proceed with the disposition of the case, the majority next addressed another procedural issue—the ability of the news organizations to intervene in the criminal case in the first place. Prosecutors and Simants's defense counsel had been arguing for weeks that the news media had no right to intervene in—and in effect become a "party" to—a pending criminal prosecution. Even the media attorneys had been mildly surprised at their success in implementing that strategy.[79] Now the Nebraska Supreme Court concluded that Judge Stuart's decision to allow the media to intervene in his court and challenge the gag order had in fact been an error. The court held that "no third party has any right to intervene in a criminal prosecution. The matter at issue in such cases is the guilt or innocence of the accused. In legal contemplation, no third party has or can claim an interest in the matter."[80] Accordingly the court dismissed case number 40445, involving the news organizations' appeal from Judge Stuart's gag order. That left for consideration only the news organizations' request for a writ of mandamus against Judge Stuart—the proceeding docketed as number 40471.

Before they proceeded to a consideration of the substantive constitutional issues involved in that matter, however, the justices addressed two more lingering jurisdictional questions. From the beginning of the controversy in the Lincoln County Court at the time of Simants's arrest and arraignment, the media attorneys had argued that Judge Ruff could not enforce a gag on the press because he lacked "personal jurisdiction" over the news organizations he sought to restrain. Even as he issued the first gag order in the case, Judge Ruff had expressed his own serious doubts about his power to enforce such an order.[81] Now the Nebraska Supreme Court agreed with those misgivings, rebuking Judge Ruff with the conclusion that "it seems clear enough that the county court had no jurisdiction over the persons of the relators. . . . [Judge Ruff's] order purports to restrain 'the news media.' The courts have no general power to enjoin or restrain 'everybody.' Even when acting with jurisdiction in proper cases, orders must pertain to particular persons or legal entities over whom the court has in some manner acquired jurisdiction."[82] The court even went so far as to suggest that, given the jurisdictional infirmities of Judge Ruff's original order, the news media could have simply ignored it, thereby perhaps avoiding all of the messy litigation that ensued.[83]

On the other hand, the court held that Judge Stuart in the district court clearly had possessed proper jurisdiction over the media. Because the news organizations had themselves invoked that court's authority through their motion to intervene, they had voluntarily submitted to Stuart's jurisdiction. When Stuart granted their motion to intervene (albeit erroneously, in the Supreme Court's view), he had acquired jurisdiction over those parties that could not now be disavowed.

Having thus dispensed with all of the complex procedural and jurisdictional peculiarities of the case, the state high court was left with only the news media's substantive request for a writ of mandamus ordering Judge Stuart to vacate his gag order. Resolution of those claims brought the justices at last to the consideration of the fundamental First versus Sixth Amendment issues at hand. Bravely, they waded into that morass.

The court began its constitutional analysis by reiterating the familiar premises that both the First Amendment guarantee of a free press and the Sixth Amendment guarantee of fair trials are cherished rights of American citizens and that the Constitution establishes no hierarchy among them.[84] Citing with approval such well-known First Amendment decisions by the Supreme Court as *Bridges v. California* (1941) and *New York Times Co. v. United States* (1971), they acknowledged the established principle that prior restraints on the press bear "a heavy presumption of unconstitutionality."[85] The court went on to observe, however, that the U.S. Supreme Court had not yet "spoken definitively" on a scenario such as the one then confronting them—where "a clash between these two preferred rights was sought to be accommodated by a prior restraint on freedom of the press."[86] They noted that several Supreme Court decisions, including *Branzburg v. Hayes* (1972) and *Irvin v. Dowd* (1961), had at least suggested that a prior restraint might be permissible under some circumstances.[87] *Branzburg,* in particular, seemed particularly noteworthy to the state court. In rejecting a news reporter's claim that he could not be compelled to testify before a grand jury, Justice White's majority opinion in that case had included language to the effect that newsmen "may be prohibited from attending or publishing information about trials if such restrictions are necessary to assure a defendant a fair trial before an impartial tribunal."[88] While the Nebraska court acknowledged that *Branzburg* had not involved an attempted prior restraint of the press, and the language quoted above was merely *dicta,* the majority still observed, with appreciable logic, that "the implication is . . . that if there is [only] a presumption of unconstitutionality then there must be some circumstances under which prior restraints may be constitutional for otherwise there would be no need for a mere presumption."[89]

Thus, the ultimate issue before the court was whether the evidence before Judge Stuart of a threat to Simants's right to an impartial jury was sufficient to overcome the heavy presumption of unconstitutionality that attached to his gag order. To answer that question, the court embarked upon an extensive analysis of the evidence and physical factors confronting Judge Stuart at the time he issued the order. The court noted that the widespread notoriety and publicity surrounding the Kellie murders had resulted in newspaper stories and broadcast reports that "contained hearsay information and purported statements of counsel, which, if true, tended clearly to connect the accused with the slayings."[90] The justices further observed that the "tainted" atmosphere against Simants in Lincoln County had even been acknowledged by the media's own attorneys, who had stated in one of the hearings before Judge Stuart that it was "already doubtful that an unbiased jury could be found to hear the Simants case in Lincoln County."[91]

The court also weighed the various other procedural, demographic, and logistical considerations that had confronted both Judge Ruff and Judge Stuart as they dealt with the enormous tide of publicity that accompanied the Kellie murders and Simants's arrest. Taking notice of the exceedingly low populations of the western Nebraska counties adjacent to Lincoln County (which were the only counties to which Simants's trial could have been moved under Nebraska law at the time) and the saturation of news coverage among those populations by the local and national news services, the court ultimately concluded that Ruff and Stuart's concern that pretrial publicity might have prevented the seating of an impartial jury for Erwin Simants was not ill founded.[92] Thus, they held, unless the absolutist argument advanced by the news media—that *no* prior restraint of the press is *ever* permissible in such circumstances—was constitutionally correct, "it would appear that the District Court acted properly in restraining publication of certain information which might or may have been adduced at the preliminary hearing."[93]

What, then, was the state court's reaction to the absolutist position advanced by the news organizations' attorneys? The justices concluded that the media's fervent defense of First Amendment freedoms "assumes too much" and could not be wholly upheld. The court held, "It is difficult to accept the [media's] position that the press must be completely unrestrained even if the cost is that a criminal cannot be tried."[94] Repeatedly characterizing the press' arguments as extremist, the Nebraska justices concluded that "society as a whole loses a great deal when a criminal has to go free because he cannot be tried. . . . The absolutist position of relators assumes that each and every exercise of freedom of the press is equally important and significant and that any impingement whatever may be equally disastrous for our state and nation. Such a position cannot, we believe, be supported."[95]

With all of that constitutional analysis as prologue, the Nebraska Supreme Court arrived at its somewhat surprising final disposition of the case. Despite their rejection of the media's absolutist position and their obvious appreciation of the difficulties confronting Judge

Stuart, the *per curiam* majority ultimately held that his existing gag order had to be set aside because it "impinges too greatly upon the freedom of the press."[96] Consistent with Justice Blackmun's November 20 opinion, the court specifically determined that Stuart's adoption and incorporation of the Nebraska bar-press guidelines was inappropriate, inasmuch as those standards "were not intended to be contractual and cannot be enforced as if they were."[97]

The Supreme Court then proceeded to do just what Stuart himself had done when presented with Judge Ruff's original order. It created and put into place a gag of its own—the third such order to emanate from the Simants litigation. The new order issued by the high court prohibited the publication of only three categories of information: confessions made by Simants to law enforcement officials; confessions or "admissions against interest," given by Simants to any other third parties; and finally (and most problematically) "other information strongly implicative of the accused as the perpetrator of the slayings."[98]

The Nebraska Supreme Court's December 1 opinion constituted the state courts' final judgment on the matter. When combined with Justice Blackmun's November 20 opinion, the net effect of the Supreme Court's decision was to eviscerate the bulk of the Stuart gag order; create a new, more narrowly drawn order; and establish a rather pronounced tilt toward the press' view of the conflict. And yet, from the news media's perspective, both decisions fell far short of a complete victory. Ominous concerns still lingered. Most alarmingly, both Blackmun and the Nebraska Supreme Court had failed to confirm what was, for the media, the most fundamental issue at stake—the principle that the press has an *unrestricted* right to publish information gleaned from a public hearing in open court or material contained in public documents, such as court records, that were within the public domain. Moreover, the disturbingly ambiguous prohibition on the publication of information "strongly implicative" of an accused's guilt remained in place. Spurred on by the loud support of columnists, commentators, and media groups across the country, the Nebraska news organizations headed back to the U.S. Supreme Court to try to gain the complete victory to which they felt entitled.

FIVE

The Paper War in the Supreme Court

There is no grander sight in the land than the American press on a
white horse riding into metaphorical battle for its own freedom.

New York Times COLUMNIST ANTHONY LEWIS
December 13, 1975

The Nebraska news organizations viewed Justice Harry Blackmun's November 20 opinion as only a partial victory at best.
Omaha World-Herald executive G. Woodson (Woody) Howe,
who had become a leading spokesperson for the press litigants,
expressed mild satisfaction with the justice's conclusion that Lincoln County District Judge Hugh Stuart had been wrong to incorpo-
rate the Nebraska bar-press guidelines into his gag order. He also
grudgingly acknowledged that "the public's right to know is a bit
better off in some ways" as a result of Blackmun's ruling.[1] Howe's
boss, *World-Herald* president Harold Anderson, echoed that ambiva-
lence, declaring that he was at least partially "encouraged by the fact
that Justice Blackmun recognized the importance of the issue and the
need for prompt appellate action."[2]

Notwithstanding that tepid appreciation for the partial victory
Blackmun had given them, the Nebraska media expressed much

greater dismay at what he had *not* done. Specifically, news organizations were alarmed that Blackmun had not expressly held that the press could *never* be restrained from publishing information that was presented in public hearings in open court or material that was contained in public court documents. Indeed, his ruling seemed to suggest that just the opposite was true—that is, he explicitly left open the possibility that, in some cases, a trial court judge *could* restrain the press from publishing such material. By condoning the possibility of that kind of prior restraint, most First Amendment advocates believed, Blackmun's ruling represented an extremely dangerous precedent—one that could not remain unchallenged.

Throughout late November and early December, columnists, editors, broadcasters, and journalists' organizations from all over the country offered increasingly strident commentary on the Nebraska case, virtually all of it critical of Justice Blackmun's November 20 ruling.[3] In a widely published AP wire story, Jack Landau of the Newhouse News Service suggested that Blackmun's ruling had left the Nebraska media no better off than they had been prior to the entry of Judge Stuart's gag order. "They haven't achieved any results by spending all this money and all this effort," Landau declared. "They're just going around in circles. I think what [Blackmun's decision] is going to do is to encourage papers to start breaking gag rule orders."[4]

In an op-ed piece published in the *World-Herald* and headlined "Hello Gag Rule, Goodby [sic] Liberty," syndicated columnist Carl T. Rowan fumed over Blackmun's decision, declaring that it threatened "the very heart of our system of justice, of checks and balances in government, of restraints on tyrannical power."[5] He went on to point out that, while Blackmun seemed to accept at face value the notion that a gag on the press ensured Erwin Simants a fair trial, his decision ignored the fact that "thousands of defendants in our history got a fair trial only because there was no gag on the press."[6] Tom Wicker, a columnist with the *New York Times* News Service, echoed Rowan, declaring that Blackmun's ruling "would permit judges to suspend part of the press's function as a check upon government, including the administration of justice, when it is those same judges to whom that administration is largely entrusted."[7]

Other influential voices offered similar opinions. The editor of the *Chicago Tribune,* Clayton Kirkpatrick, called Blackmun's ruling an extraordinary intervention that threatened to subvert the protections guaranteed by the Bill of Rights.[8] "Among men and women whose forbears fought and died for the rights written into the Constitution nearly 200 years ago," he declared, "the willingness of the courts to accept the evils of closed and secret trials should be shocking."[9] Well-known syndicated columnist and CBS's *60 Minutes* television commentator James J. Kilpatrick couched his reaction in even more dramatic tones. Calling Blackmun's order a bombshell that "dwarfed the Pentagon Papers" in its potential impact on press freedom, he argued that it would "invite every defense attorney, in every important case, to move for a gag; and trial judges, thus encouraged, will stop our presses."[10] Kilpatrick proclaimed the press's "unabridgeable right to print the news, and to print it now," and exhorted his Nebraska colleagues to challenge the Blackmun ruling by every means available.[11]

At least one notable commentator, however, suggested that the press may have been overstating its case. In an op-ed piece published in the *World-Herald* under the headline "Another Point of View: Does the Press Protest Too Much?" *New York Times* syndicated columnist Anthony Lewis emphasized the unique factual circumstances that had produced the Nebraska gag order and pointed out that the restrictions on the press imposed by Judge Stuart were only temporary in their duration—they would be in effect only until a jury was seated in Simants's upcoming trial.[12] With dripping sarcasm, Lewis observed,

> There is no grander sight in the land than the American press on a white horse riding into metaphorical battle for its own freedom. . . . When Justice Blackmun refused to set aside all the restrictions [contained in the Stuart gag order] the nation's media trembled with outrage. They told us that two hundred years of law were threatened, that American liberty was at the edge. . . . [T]he order that we are told threatens our liberties [is one that] briefly forbids what might make a fair trial difficult in a single criminal case. Does that really shake the foundations of our constitutional system? Is it indeed unreasonable?[13]

Lewis went on to argue that the proper framing of the issue should involve less self-righteousness and hysteria from the press and more analysis of the competing values at stake in each particular case. "The press rarely seems to concede that there is more than one value at stake in these cases," he declared.[14] "For example, it would be well to stop saying 'prior restraint' as if those words ended all argument. Courts routinely restrain false advertising and all sorts of things without violating the 1st amendment. The real issue is the values involved."[15]

By the time much of this clamor made its way into print, Nebraska's news organizations had long since collectively made up their minds to challenge Justice Blackmun's order. On November 21, Omaha media attorneys Stephen McGill and James Koley filed a motion addressed to the entire Supreme Court panel, asking the full Court to vacate Justice Blackmun's chambers opinion issued the day before.[16] More particularly, the motion asked the Court to set aside the portion of Blackmun's order that left intact the restraint on publication of information brought out in open court or contained in court documents that were matters of public record. The attorneys described the Blackmun order as a restraint that was even broader and more restrictive than the one the Court had rejected in the Pentagon Papers case four years earlier and argued that it "sweeps within its net untold amounts of information directly or indirectly connected to a criminal justice proceeding."[17]

McGill and Koley were not alone in their attempts to gain the attention of the full Court. Of all the groups and individuals who offered encouragement and support to the Nebraska media during the gag order litigation, the most tangible assistance came from an organization called the Reporters Committee for Freedom of the Press (RCFP), a legal defense group for news personnel whose attorneys had played a significant role in the Supreme Court appeal. Created in 1970 as a nonprofit entity dedicated to the protection of journalists' rights under the First Amendment, the RCFP remains today one of the country's leading advocacy groups for freedom of the press.[18] Just five years old at the time of the Nebraska case, but already well-funded and increasingly influential, the RCFP took interest in the litigation almost from the outset. Within several days of the issuance of Judge Ronald Ruff's original gag order in the Lincoln County Court, the RCFP dispatched attorney Larry Simms to Omaha, to consult with the Nebraska press organizations and assist them in their early attempts to have the order set aside. In a November 1 *World-Herald* article, Simms described the committee as "the only national organization concerned exclusively with protecting freedom of the press," and he warned that judges' "increasing use of gag orders . . . carried the dangerous potential to establish a system of secret justice in this country."[19]

As the appeals to Justice Blackmun and the Nebraska Supreme Court took shape in early November, the RCFP's involvement in the case grew into an almost full-fledged participatory partnership. By the middle of the month, the committee had retained Washington, D.C., attorney E. Barrett Prettyman, Jr., to assist the Nebraska media in their efforts before the high court. A partner in the international law firm of Hogan & Hartson, Prettyman was then, and remains today, a prominent and widely respected Washington appellate attorney, with vast experience before the Supreme Court.[20] As a former clerk for Justices Robert Jackson, Felix Frankfurter, and John Harlan, Prettyman's connections to the Court were long and deep, as were his family's roots in the Washington legal community. (The federal courthouse in Washington is named for Prettyman's father, the longtime chief judge of the U.S. Circuit Court of Appeals for the D.C. Circuit.) Prettyman would play an increasingly influential role in the litigation before the high court, ultimately taking the lead in presenting oral argument on behalf of the news media several months later.

Prettyman and the RCFP initially appeared in the case before the Supreme Court as *amicus curiae,* a Latin phrase that translates as "friend of the court." *Amicus* documents are commonly submitted to the Court by professional organizations or interest groups that are not formally involved in a case as actual parties but claim to have some compelling stake in the outcome. Given their interest in the case, and the specialized knowledge they purport to have on the subject matter, *amicus* parties offer written, and sometimes oral, arguments as assistance to the Court in its deliberations.

The Supreme Court's operating rules control the admission and consideration of proffered *amicus* filings.[21] In general, those rules provide that organizations may enter cases as *amici* if they have obtained consent from all the actual parties to the action, or from the Court itself. Most such requests are routinely granted. In the Nebraska gag order litigation, more than sixty newspapers and press organizations, led most prominently and actively by the RCFP, would ultimately appear in the case as "friends of the Court."

In an *amicus* memorandum filed in support of McGill and Koley's motion to the full Court asking for review of Justice Blackmun's ruling, Prettyman argued that Blackmun had "effectively determined that direct prior restraints of the press are constitutional . . . and effectively extinguished the light of the First Amendment for all Nebraska citizens."[22] He went on to urge the full court to act immediately to stay the order, lest it become a "signal to trial courts across the country that such orders are acceptable."[23]

The requests to the full U.S. Supreme Court for review of the Blackmun chambers opinion were filed on November 21— when the parties were still waiting for the Nebraska Supreme Court to take some definitive action in the case. (Recall that the state supreme court had scheduled a hearing on the case for November 25, four days hence.) The fact that the Nebraska high court had not yet ruled on the case made an already cloudy procedural situation all the murkier. The full Supreme Court was being asked to vacate a temporary order that had been issued—reluctantly and with serious jurisdictional reservations—by one of its own brethren while the highest state court with jurisdiction over the matter was still contemplating action of its own on the case. In light of those complexities, it was probably fortunate that the full Court was in recess from November 21 until December 5. By then, of course, the Nebraska Supreme Court had issued its final judgment in the case. Inasmuch as Justice Blackmun's November 20 order expired on its own terms at the time the Nebraska Supreme Court ruled, the messy procedural scenario cleared considerably. Now the *only* operative order at issue in the case was the Nebraska Supreme Court's December 1 opinion, which had modified, but not destroyed, Judge Stuart's gag order. Almost immediately, the media attorneys shifted targets, focusing the full force of their attack on that opinion.

On December 4, McGill and Koley, joined by Prettyman and the RCFP as *amicus,* filed an application addressed to the full Supreme

Court asking for a stay of the Nebraska Supreme Court's order.[24] At the same time, the media attorneys filed a motion and supporting memorandum asking the justices for an emergency hearing on the request for a stay. In that motion, they informed the Court that Simants's trial for the Kellie murders was scheduled to begin in just one month—Judge Stuart had set a trial date for January 6, 1976. Thus, they argued, if the Court did not agree to hear and decide the matter in an expedited fashion, the trial would be over and the gag order would have expired long before the Court ruled. Emphasizing the continuing nature of the First Amendment violation at issue, the attorneys urged the justices to act immediately, telling the Court that "typewritten briefs could be filed within hours or days and arguments could be held forthwith thereafter."[25]

The media attorneys also filed a rather unique *ad hoc* procedural request asking the Court to treat all of their previously filed papers in the case (the pending motions and memoranda seeking to overturn Justice Blackmun's November 20 order) as a "petition for a writ of certiorari."[26] Like the *amicus* procedure discussed above, the matter of *certiorari* merits brief explanation. Literally translated, a *writ of certiorari* is an order from a higher court to a lower court directing the inferior tribunal to transmit and certify to the higher court a record of all the proceedings conducted in the court below. If issued, the writ causes a case to come before the Supreme Court for disposition, with the high court reviewing the actions of the lower court in order to determine whether or not some sort of error has occurred. The party who sought the writ becomes the petitioner in the Court's nomenclature, while the opposing party becomes the respondent. During the last century, the writ of certiorari is the method by which the vast majority of cases have come before the U.S. Supreme Court for consideration.[27] In the 1970s, certiorari accounted for approximately 90 percent of the Court's workload for any given year.[28]

The decision to grant a petition for certiorari is discretionary with the Court. Rule 10 of the Court's operating procedures provides that certiorari will be granted only when there are special and important reasons to do so.[29] The rule also offers a list of noncontrolling criteria that the justices may consider in exercising their extremely important, but often underappreciated, function of "deciding what to decide." Among the factors considered by the Court before granting such a petition are whether there is a conflict among the lower courts on an important point of law; whether the highest court of a particular state has decided a case in such a way as to conflict with decisions of other state high courts or lower federal courts; and whether a state high court or a federal circuit court has "decided an important federal question in a way that conflicts with relevant decisions" of the Supreme Court.[30] Ultimately, as many commentators have pointed out, these considerations offer little specific direction or guidance for predicting the types of cases the Court will choose to hear.[31] In the final analysis, the nine individual justices of the Court decide for themselves which cases are sufficiently special and important to be "cert-worthy," and the odds against such a determination are daunting. In 1975, when the Nebraska gag order litigation came to Washington, the Court received 2,352 petitions for certiorari and granted 244, or only about 10 percent.[32]

The members of the Court meet in conference at regular intervals to discuss pending requests for certiorari. Usually without much debate or discussion, the justices vote, in order of seniority, to grant or deny the petition. By informal custom known as the rule of four, the Supreme Court will grant certiorari when at least four justices vote to do so.[33] If a petition does not pique the interest of four or more members, certiorari is denied, and the decision of the lower court is left in effect, effectively becoming the final decision in the case. By asking the Court to consider all of their previous filings as a petition for a writ of certiorari, the Nebraska news organizations were essentially attempting to clean up the case procedurally. If granted, the motion would place directly at issue the constitutionality of the only gag order that was still in effect in the case—the Nebraska Supreme Court's December 1 ruling.

As a result of all of these filings by the Nebraska media, by the time the full Court took up the case in conference on December 5 the questions before the justices were numerous, but relatively clear: Would they issue a stay of the Nebraska Supreme Court's order? Would they agree to consider all of the media's previously filed paperwork in the case as a request for certiorari? If so, and most important, would they vote to "grant cert"—that is, would they agree to hear the case on the merits? Finally, if the justices did accept the case for review, would they also grant the motion to expedite the hearing of the matter and move it forward immediately on the Court's calendar? The answers to those questions came quickly.

On December 5, eight sitting members of the U.S. Supreme Court met in a regularly scheduled conference session and considered the Nebraska gag order case. These conferences are among the most secret proceedings conducted within the federal government. No one other than the justices attend, and their deliberations are not recorded or published in any official form, nor do they become a part of the "record" of the case that is available to the public.[34] The incoming ninth member of the Court, John Paul Stevens, would not be confirmed and take his seat on the Court until December 17, 1975. Thus, he took no part in the deliberations over whether to accept the Nebraska case for review.

At the December 5 conference, the justices immediately and unanimously agreed to grant the media's request to treat all of the papers filed in the case as a petition for a writ of certiorari. On the disposition of the other motions before them, however, there were significant differences of opinion among the justices. In an indication of initial support that the Nebraska media petitioners had to find encouraging, Justices William Brennan, Potter Stewart, and Thurgood Marshall voted to grant the request for an immediate stay of the Nebraska Supreme Court's December 1 judgment. The other justices, however, believed that a decision on the request for a stay should be deferred until the state of Nebraska and the other parties involved in the litigation had an opportunity to file responses to the news organizations' motions. Accordingly, notices were dispatched immediately to the attorney general of Nebraska, the Nebraska Supreme Court, Judge Stuart, and Simants's attorneys, inviting them to submit responses quickly to the news media's pending motions.

On December 8, the Court issued a short procedural decree in the case, officially announcing the action taken in its conference three days earlier. The Court's order formally granted the media's request to have their papers treated as a petition for a writ of certiorari.[35] The order went on to state, however, that a final decision of whether to accept the case for review, and a ruling on the accompanying motion for a stay of the Nebraska Supreme Court's judgment, would be deferred by the Court "until the requested responses thereto have been received or until the close of business Tuesday, December 9, 1975."[36] In other words, the Court was announcing that it would wait at least one more day before making a final decision of whether to accept the case for review and whether to expedite it for hearing.

On that same day, December 8, responsive pleadings arrived at the Supreme Court from the Nebraska attorney general's office, representing Judge Stuart, and from Lincoln County Prosecutor Milton Larson, representing the state of Nebraska. Larson himself had prepared and signed his memorandum, and the response for Judge Stuart was prepared by Assistant Attorney General Harold Mosher. Both responses were relatively short and straightforward, consisting primarily of restatements of arguments that had already been advanced repeatedly in the state courts and before Justice Blackmun.[37] As before, the attorneys defended the gag order by arguing that the extraordinary facts and circumstances surrounding the Kellie murders and Simants's arrest—the horrific nature of the killings and the accompanying sexual depravities, along with the overwhelming publicity in the small and close-knit rural community—created an "exceptional case" that justified Judge Stuart's "narrowly-drawn" restraint on publication.[38] They also contended that the demographic realities of rural western Nebraska, combined with the vagaries of Nebraska state law limiting a possible change of venue to only a neighboring county, had effectively left Stuart with no viable alternatives to the gag in his effort to preserve Simants's Sixth Amendment rights. Thus, they concluded, the gag order ought to be considered an entirely appropriate accommodation between the First and Sixth Amendment interests at stake.[39]

On December 11, the full Supreme Court met again to consider the case. The following day, the justices issued another order in which they announced their rulings on all of the procedural issues before them.[40] First and most important, they agreed to grant the Nebraska media's petition for a writ of certiorari, thereby accepting the case for review. The vote to "grant cert" was 6-2, with Rehnquist and Burger in the minority. Justice Powell's notes from the Court's conference sessions show that Burger recognized the need to address the weighty constitutional issues presented in the case at some time in the future, but he felt that the Nebraska case was "a poor vehicle."[41] Most of the chief's colleagues apparently disagreed with that assessment. Powell noted, for example, that Blackmun felt "this is one of the most important issues we will have this term."[42]

On the remaining procedural issues, the justices' opinions varied considerably. With respect to the motion to expedite the matter for emergency hearing, Justices Brennan, Stewart, and Marshall felt that the case presented issues that necessitated that type of treatment and voted to grant the motion. For the same reasons, those three justices—as they had done three days before—voted to grant an immediate stay of the Nebraska Supreme Court's December 1 decision. On both those points, however, Brennan, Stewart, and Marshall were outvoted by their brethren. Four other members of the Court (Justices Burger, Blackmun, Powell, and Rehnquist) announced that they were convinced that the constitutional issues involved in the case "should be decided only after adequate briefing and argument and ample time for mature consideration."[43] Therefore, they denied both the media's request for an immediate stay of the gag order and their request for expedited handling of the case.

Justice Byron White expressed yet a third view of the procedural issues before the Court. Adopting an approach that seemed to indicate agreement with the Nebraska media's primary point of contention, he voted to grant the requested stay of the Nebraska Supreme Court's judgment "to the extent that its order forbade the publication of information disclosed in public at the preliminary hearing in the criminal case out of which this case arose."[44] Despite that sentiment, White agreed with the rest of the Court that the issues at stake required "careful and deliberate consideration." He therefore joined in the denial of the motion to expedite the case. In his view, granting the requested stay would have eliminated any ongoing First Amendment deprivation, while denying the motion to expedite would allow the Court to consider the constitutional issues involved in the case with the mature deliberation they deserved.[45]

Notwithstanding those differing viewpoints among the eight sitting justices, the net effect of the Supreme Court's December 12 ruling was to announce that the nation's highest Court intended to decide the constitutional validity of the gag order imposed on the Nebraska media in the Simants litigation. Because the Court refused the media's request to hear the case immediately on an emergency basis, however, no decision on the propriety of the gag order would be forthcoming until well after Erwin Simants's trial, scheduled to begin in early January 1976, had taken place. To the media's great dismay, the existing order of the Nebraska Supreme Court would continue in effect until a jury was seated in the Simants trial. For the attorneys, the Court's December 12 order meant that the pressure of time had been eliminated, as far as the constitutional issues were concerned. The case was placed on the Supreme Court's regular calendar, and both sides began to prepare for what would prove to be a historic contest before the high court.

The procedural progression of a case once it is has been accepted for review by the U.S. Supreme Court is dictated by generations of custom and tradition, which have, through the years, been codified by the Court in the form of a rather elaborate and detailed set of operating rules. The process begins with a notice from the clerk of the Supreme Court to the clerk of the lower court that the justices have granted the requested writ of certiorari. The lower court's clerk is asked to certify and transmit to the high court a record of all the proceedings conducted in the lower court.[46] Working from that record below, as well as other documents and transcripts from previous hearings in the case, the parties before the Supreme Court are then required to create and file a joint appendix.[47] The rules direct the parties to work cooperatively in the preparation of this appendix and to include in it all of the relevant judgments, decisions, and docket entries issued by the lower courts in the case, as well as "any other parts of the record that the parties particularly wish to bring to the Court's attention."[48] In other words, the joint appendix is designed to serve as an abridged and easily managed version of the full record of the case developed in the courts below, so as to ease the Court's consideration and disposition of the specific issues before it.

In the Nebraska case, the parties filed their joint appendix with the Court on January 26, 1976. Totaling more than 150 pages, it contained transcripts of the hearings conducted by Judges Ruff and Stuart on the gag order issue, as well as the text of the restraining orders issued by each of the judges. Also included were various pleadings, exhibits, affidavits, motions, and memoranda filed in the Nebraska Supreme Court action and, of course, the text of that Court's decision issued on December 1, which had created the third and final version of the gag order—the only order that was still technically at issue before the Court.

With the granting of the writ of certiorari and the filing of the joint appendix, the Court's briefing schedule kicked into effect. "Briefs," the appellate attorney's stock in trade, are written legal arguments to a court, typically containing extensive analysis of previous judicial decisions addressing the same or similar issues as those presently before the court. Like all other procedural aspects of the Supreme Court's operations, the preparation and filing of briefs is controlled by the Court's rules, which establish detailed requirements and limitations for the parties' briefs, including page limits, size and style of typesetting, formatting, and even the color of the covers attached to the parties' respective briefs.[49]

By January and February 1976, when the briefs in the Nebraska gag order case were flowing into the Supreme Court, the arguments that both sides would be advancing had already been made, with varying degrees of success, at no fewer than four previous stages of the litigation. County Court Judge Ronald Ruff, District Court Judge Hugh Stuart, the Nebraska Supreme Court, and Justice Harry Blackmun had all heard and considered the same constitutional claims and issues that now came before the full Court. There was little new to say. All that remained was for the attorneys to marshal their arguments once again, restyling them in their loftiest shades of eloquence and sophistication for their final and most important audience.

Writing on behalf of the petitioners, Omaha attorneys Stephen McGill and James Koley filed their brief with the Court in early January 1976. They were joined in their drafting efforts by E. Barrett Prettyman, Jr., the Washington-based attorney who had, in the prior weeks, filed the RCFP's *amicus curiae* brief. Late in December, the Nebraska Press Association and the other news organizations retained Prettyman to serve as co-counsel with the Omaha attorneys. He, McGill, and Koley worked together closely and amicably on the case thereafter.

As had been so often the case in the litigation, before the attorneys could argue the substantive constitutional merits of the case in their brief, they first had to address a significant procedural issue. That issue was the doctrine of mootness. Article III of the U.S. Constitution grants to the Supreme Court and the other federal courts the authority to adjudicate actual cases or controversies. If an issue before the court is resolved or extinguished by the passage of time or the occurrence of some other event, the case is said to have become moot, and the Court traditionally will refuse to entertain it. If, for example, a high school student sued his school district claiming that the district's dress code violated his constitutional rights and, although the case remained pending, the student graduated from the school so that he was no longer subject to the code, his case would become "moot" and would most likely be dismissed by a federal court.[50] The potential applicability of this principle to the Nebraska gag order litigation was obvious. Because Simants's trial in North Platte, Nebraska, was about to begin, and because the gag order expired by its own terms once a jury had been seated in the trial, it was apparent that the judicial restraint on the Nebraska press would be eliminated long before the Court ruled on the case.

Nevertheless, the Supreme Court has carved out an exception to the mootness doctrine for cases involving "short term orders, capable of repetition, yet evading review." That is, if an issue arises frequently but is likely to continually escape judicial resolution because of the mootness principle, the court will proceed to hear the case. First enunciated in *Southern Pacific Terminal Co. v. Interstate Commerce Commission* (1911), the "capable of repetition" exception had been confirmed and reiterated by the Supreme Court many times over the years.[51] Now, the media attorneys argued, the circumstances surrounding the Simants's gag order presented a classic example of a situation to which the exception applied.[52]

They contended that, unless the Court proceeded to hear and resolve the substantive issues at stake, it would be confronted with a plethora of such cases in the future—cases that would invariably arise "in the context of hastily briefed motions for a stay, which, by their terms, expire quickly enough to raise serious questions of mootness."[53] "In addition," they claimed, "lower courts will continue to be confused and at odds with each other over the constitutionality of prior restraint orders."[54] For all of those reasons, they claimed, the *Southern Pacific* exception clearly applied, and the Court should proceed to decide the merits of the case. Besides, the attorneys added, since the justices had accepted the case for review knowing that Simants's trial was imminent and had still denied the petitioners' motion to expedite the case, the Court itself had already implicitly decided that the case was not moot.

Passing beyond the threshold issue of mootness, the primary substantive argument presented in the petitioners' brief was, of course, that the gag order issued against the Nebraska press was a wholly unjustifiable deprivation of the media's First Amendment rights. With respect to the prohibition on publication of information that either was publicly testified to in open court during Simants's preliminary hearing or was contained in documents on public file, the brief contended that prior Court decisions clearly and unequivocally prohibited such an egregious prior restraint. The precedents cited by the attorneys on that issue seemed to be directly on point and were impressively compelling. In *Craig v. Harney* (1947), for example, the Court held:

> A trial is a public event. What transpires in the court room is public property. . . . Those who see and hear what transpired can report it with impunity. There is no special perquisite of the judiciary which enables it . . . to suppress, edit, or censor events which transpire in proceedings before it.[55]

Likewise, in *Estes v. Texas* (1965), the Court observed that "reporters of all media . . . are plainly free to report whatever occurs in open court through their respective media."[56] And again, in *Cox Broadcasting Corp. v. Cohn* (1975), the Court held that "once true information is disclosed in public court documents open to public inspection, the press cannot be sanctioned for publishing it."[57] Based upon those and other similar rulings, the brief argued, the Nebraska Supreme Court's bar on the reporting of what the press had observed in open court or in public files was patently unconstitutional and should be summarily reversed.[58]

Despite the apparent controlling applicability of those precedents, the media counsel worried nevertheless about the effect of language in the Court's decision in *Branzburg v. Hayes,* rendered just four years earlier, that seemed to indicate that reporters could, in some circumstances, be barred "from attending or publishing information about trials." The Nebraska Supreme Court had cited and relied upon that language in fashioning its own version of the gag order, and now McGill, Koley, Prettyman, Abrams, and the other media attorneys knew they would have to deal with those problematic words. Ultimately they decided they would have to confront the possible "Branzburg problem" head on.[59] After first pointing out that *Branzburg* was not a prior restraint case and that the language in question was merely *dicta,* they proceeded to argue that the state supreme court had "misread" *Branzburg.* That decision, they contended, actually only stood for the proposition that the press may be denied access to a certain narrow category of court proceedings (*e.g.,* grand jury hearings) and could therefore not report on those proceedings. To the extent that the *Branzburg* dictum relied upon by the Nebraska court suggested otherwise, they concluded, "It is inconsistent with the body of prior restraint case law previously established [in the Supreme Court] and it should be overruled."[60]

If the only troublesome aspect of the Nebraska gag order had been its attempt to prohibit the press from publishing information gleaned from open court proceedings, the media attorneys' legal analysis could have stopped there. The Nebraska Supreme Court's order, however, also purported to prohibit the publication of "confessions or admissions against interest made by the accused" and, even more ambiguously, "other information strongly implicative of the accused." Because that language seemed to encompass information that the news media might have obtained *outside* of open court records or proceedings in the normal course of its news gathering responsibilities, the media feared that the order could become "the fatal first step in the censorship, subjugation, or destruction of a free press."[61] Thus, the attorneys stated, the constitutional issues required further comment.[62]

In the remaining forty pages of their brief, the media attorneys enunciated three broad lines of argument in opposition to the gag order. First, they attempted to recast the fundamental nature of the debate by arguing that, despite all of the rhetoric about resolving the conflict between the First and Sixth Amendments that had permeated the litigation to that point, the case actually presented no real conflict between those two constitutional interests at all. At least, they suggested, no such conflict had to exist, because there were so many ways for the trial court to protect Simants's Sixth Amendment rights without the imposition of prior restraints on the press. As they had done repeatedly in the lower courts, the media attorneys reminded the justices of the wide assortment of alternative measures for ensuring jurors' impartiality, including extensive *voir dire* questioning of prospective jurors; isolation of defendants and witnesses from excessive public exposure; limitations on releases of information by police and prosecutors; admonitions to the jury to disregard media coverage; changing the venue of a trial; sequestration of jurors; continuance of trial until excessive publicity subsides; and, in "worst-case scenarios," the granting of new trials.

Of all these lesser restrictive measures, the petitioners devoted the most attention to the role of the voir dire process.[63] The attorneys called to the Court's attention a wide variety of surveys, studies, commission reports, and law review articles that had examined the impact of pretrial publicity on jurors' attitudes and the utility of voir dire in screening jurors for possible bias or impartiality.[64] Considered collectively, they claimed, those studies established that, even in cases where there is pervasive pretrial publicity, jurors are perfectly able, with proper instruction from the court, to render fair and impartial verdicts based entirely on the evidence presented at trial.[65] Discovering and removing potential jurors who are incapable of serving impartially, the media attorneys argued, is precisely the reason for the extensive *voir dire* process that is statutorily mandated in every state and federal trial court.

In their second line of argument, the news attorneys presented a head-on attack on the constitutionality of *any* prior restraint on the reporting of criminal proceedings under *any* circumstances. They argued that the First Amendment's prohibition of prior restraints on the press was so explicit and well established that the Court had almost never even found it necessary to enunciate the principle specifically.[66] On those rare occasions when the Court had addressed the issue, it struck down the attempted restraint every time, even in cases such as the "Pentagon Papers" decision (*New York Times v. United States* [1971]), where the majority of the Court concluded that the publication of the top-secret material at issue would in fact be harmful to the nation. The only exception to the complete ban on prior restraints that the Court had ever even hinted at, they argued, involved the "narrowest category of wartime military information." Even then, they contended, the Court had only been speculating on a hypothetical possibility—no actual prior restraint had *ever* been upheld, even in a wartime situation.[67]

Thus, the attorneys argued, "the fact that there may be a single narrow exception to an otherwise rigid rule should not allow . . . the Nebraska Supreme Court . . . to engage in a 'balancing of interests,' cavalierly carving out exceptions almost as if those made up the rule."[68] The gag orders issued by the Nebraska courts placed the Supreme Court "at the threshold of a whole new controversy over prior restraints," the brief declared, and offered the Court "a unique opportunity to stop in its tracks what could become a trend [that would be] tragically detrimental to the very first Amendment to our American Constitution."[69]

In their third line of argument, McGill, Koley, and Prettyman contended that, even if a prior restraint of news coverage might conceivably be permissible under some hypothetical extreme circumstances, the peculiarly shallow record created in the Nebraska courts did not even come close to justifying such a restraint.[70] They emphasized the paucity and speculative nature of the "evidence" upon which Judges Ruff and Stuart had based their gag orders, which consisted primarily of a few newspaper articles (most of which Judge Ruff admitted that he had never read) and the judges' generalized impressions of the impact of the crimes on the community. The brief went on to point out that even the Nebraska Supreme Court had relied on nothing more than three additional newspaper articles and the population figures for Lincoln County and the surrounding region in making its determination that Simants's Sixth Amendment rights "could be" or "might be" impaired.[71] Thus, the attorneys declared, the gag order issued by the Nebraska court was based upon "such complete generalizations, so flimsy a record, and so shifting a standard," that under no circumstances could it possibly be upheld.[72]

The media attorneys concluded their brief by urging the Court to "reassert its prior decisions and rule without equivocation" that the gag order issued by the Nebraska Supreme Court was a "direct violation of the First Amendment."[73] In accordance with Court rules, they filed forty copies of the brief with the clerk's office and served additional copies on the opposing attorneys. The respondents then had thirty days to prepare and file their briefs in response.

Three separate briefs were filed on behalf of the various respondents in the Supreme Court. Writing on behalf of Judge Hugh Stuart was Nebraska Assistant Attorney General Harold Mosher. A 1962 graduate of the University of Nebraska Law School, Mosher had spent his entire professional career with the attorney general's office. By 1975, he had become head of the office's appellate division. Although Mosher was quite experienced in appellate litigation at the state and regional levels, this would be his first appearance before the U.S. Supreme Court. The essence of Mosher's argument was that Judge Stuart possessed not only the power, but also the duty, to adopt whatever measures he felt necessary to "balance" the conflict between First and Sixth Amendment interests in his courtroom. He contended that prior restraints on publication are not per se unconstitutional, but rather must be evaluated on the basis of an examination of the specific circumstances of each case. Where a legitimate conflict between the two constitutional interests appeared, Mosher argued, "the relevant case law indicates, and quite dramatically, that . . . the balance is swung in favor of fair trial rights."[74]

In the Simants prosecution, Mosher argued, Stuart had no other realistic method to ensure a fair trial for the defendant. In support of that proposition, he sequentially rebutted all of the petitioners' claims regarding the availability of lesser restrictive alternatives such as *voir dire,* sequestration, and change of venue. As applied to the circumstances confronting Judge Stuart, the brief claimed, each of those alternatives would have been wholly ineffective.[75] Faced with such an "extraordinary" situation, Judge Stuart had adopted "the only realistic option available to him by which to fulfill his affirmative duty to provide the accused with a fair trial."[76]

By the time Mosher filed his brief in the Supreme Court on these constitutional issues, Simants had already been tried and convicted of the Kellie murders. Those circumstances offered Mosher the opportunity to bolster his argument to the Court by going "outside the record" in the case and describing an exchange that took place between Judge Stuart and the members of the jury who had convicted Simants. After the verdict had been returned and the jurors had been dismissed from their official duties, Stuart asked for a voluntary "straw vote" among the jury panel. He first asked how many of them believed that they could have been fair and impartial if they had heard or read about Simants's confession before the trial. Only one of the twelve jurors raised his hand. He then asked how many believed that they could *not* have served impartially if they had known before trial about Simants's confession. Nine of the twelve held up their hands. Stuart next asked how many could have taken an oath to be fair and impartial if they had read or heard the text of Simants's confession in the media before the trial began. Again, only one juror indicated that he could have done so. Finally, Stuart asked how many could *not* have taken an oath of impartiality if they had read or heard the text of Simants's confession in the media before the trial. This time, eleven of the twelve jurors raised their hands.[77] For Mosher, that simple, informal exchange between Judge Stuart and the Simants's jury—though not officially a part of the "record" before the high court—offered more powerful and tangible justification for what the judge had done than any elaborate case analysis could ever provide. The conclusion, he claimed, "was inescapable": the judgment of the Nebraska Supreme Court was "in all respects proper."[78]

Lincoln County Prosecutor Milton Larson prepared and filed a separate brief on behalf of the State of Nebraska, which had become a formal party to the case by virtue of its intervention in the news media's action in the Nebraska Supreme Court. Larson's brief essentially reiterated, in more elaborate terms, most of the points he had advanced in support of the gag order throughout the earlier stages of the litigation. He directed the bulk of his argument to the proposition that an absolutist view of First Amendment freedoms had never been accepted or adopted by the Court.[79] In more than twenty pages of analysis, he identified numerous examples of situations in which First Amendment values had been compelled to yield to other, equally cherished, constitutional interests. Citing cases involving issues such as national security, obscenity, fighting words, copyright, and contractual nondisclosure provisions, Larson contended that it was obvious that "the First Amendment does not take precedence over all other constitutionally secured rights."[80] The Nebraska courts' gag orders, he claimed, were not the dire threat to freedom of the press that the petitioners made them out to be, but rather were merely "narrow, limited, and temporary restrictions on publicity" designed to create "harmony" between the First and Sixth Amendments, just as the Supreme Court itself had drawn similar balances between the First Amendment and other cherished constitutional interests in dozens of previous cases.[81]

A third brief in defense of the gag order was filed by Leonard Vyhnalek and Keith Bystrom, representing Simants as a "respondent-intervenor" in the case. In contrast to the admirably competent trial work they were simultaneously providing to Simants, the brief was a weak effort, containing a number of rambling run-on sentences, non sequiturs, and sentence fragments. In defense of the attorneys, however, it should be pointed out that the brief was essentially a gratuitous endeavor on their part. By the time it was filed, their client had already been tried, convicted, and sentenced to die in Nebraska's electric chair. His conviction and death sentence were on appeal to the Nebraska Supreme Court. Vyhnalek and Bystrom simply had little further interest in the gag order controversy as a legal or practical matter. Their attention—naturally and appropriately—was focused almost entirely on saving Simants from electrocution. Indeed, the strongest section of their Supreme Court brief was devoted to the argument that the gag order issue was now completely moot and should not be entertained by the Court at all.[82]

On that issue, Vyhnalek and Bystrom's brief varied considerably from those of the other respondents. Mosher had not addressed the mootness question at all in his brief for Judge Stuart. Larson, arguing for the state, had actually agreed with the news organizations' position on that issue. He argued that, despite the expiration of the gag order and the completion of Simants's trial, the Court should proceed to decide the case in order to "provide guidance to courts, prosecutors, publishers, and broadcasters in this most difficult and confusing area."[83]

Even before the parties' briefs had been written and filed, dozens of newspapers, broadcasting companies, and media interest groups had begun offering *amicus curiae* briefs in the case. Ultimately, more than sixty such groups would join in the preparation and filings of seven separate briefs, totaling more than 400 pages of additional argument for the Court's consideration. All the *amicus* filings in the case argued in support of the media's position. No *amicus* briefs from anywhere in the country were filed in support of the respondents.

Among the groups offering their assistance as friends of the Court were many of the largest and most influential news organizations in the country, including the American Newspaper Publishers Association, the National Broadcasting Corporation, the American Broadcasting Corporation, the *Washington Post* Company, the Globe Newspaper Company, the Times-Mirror Company, *Newsday,* the Pulitzer Publishing Company, CBS, and the *New York Times* Company. All of the *amicus* briefs were authored by top-shelf attorneys and law firms, and all of them reflected exceptional research, writing, and analytical skills. For all of the *amicus* attorneys' eloquence, however, their briefs presented essentially the same legal arguments as those found in the petitioners' briefs.

The brief written and filed by renowned First Amendment attorney Floyd Abrams on behalf of NBC, the *New York Times,* the *Chicago Sun-Times,* and fifteen other news groups was representative of most of the others. Abrams forcefully contended that, whatever other considerations might come into play, the fundamental sanctity of the First Amendment in relation to reporting about judicial proceedings had always been "a given—a conclusion reached before proceeding to other more difficult issues."[84] He summarized the *amicus* briefs' collective position with the declaration that

> [A]s a matter of precedent, this case is hardly a close one. The authorities of this Court, the virtually unanimous reported decisions of both state and federal courts, and a variety of reports of bar association and judicial committees have all repeatedly concluded that

no direct prior restraints are permissible on the press with respect to its news reporting about judicial proceedings.[85]

The last brief to be presented in the case was the "reply brief" of the petitioners. Filed by McGill, Koley, and Prettyman fourteen days after the last of the respondents' briefs had been received, it represented the media attorneys' chance to offer the "last word" to the Court in written form. They took full advantage of the opportunity. Using language that was occasionally caustic and always well-crafted, the news attorneys bluntly rebutted virtually every argument advanced by the respondents. The brief contended that the state of Nebraska and Judge Stuart had either misread, misinterpreted, or misapplied virtually every precedent they had offered in support of the gag order. The attorneys argued that many of the cases relied upon by the respondents, when interpreted properly, actually supported the media's position in the case. For example, on the critical question of whether vigorous voir dire examination of potential jurors could have provided adequate protection of Simants's Sixth Amendment rights, they contended that Harold Mosher's brief for Judge Stuart cited two cases that had held that such pretrial questioning of jurors *was* an effective method of assuring the creation of an impartial jury, even in cases involving pervasive pretrial publicity, and even where the prospective jurors had read about a defendant's confession![86] The media attorneys justifiably called Mosher's reference to, and reliance on, those cases odd and inexplicable.[87]

As for the respondents' references to Judge Stuart's "straw poll" of the Simants jury after the trial, the petitioners' brief contended that those questions and answers should be completely ignored by the Court for several reasons. First, the material was not a part of the official record in the case and therefore was not properly before the court as a procedural matter. Second, they contended that the questions posed to the jurors were "so leading or confusing that the answers elicited are meaningless." Moreover, they argued that there had been no opportunity for any of the parties' attorneys to test or probe the jurors' answers. They had been elicited by Judge Stuart unilaterally and for his own purposes. Given the tone and tenor of the questions, the attorneys declared, they merely "revealed the answers the judge was seeking" and should therefore be completely disregarded.[88] Finally, in a last disparaging shot at the respondents' reasoning, they observed that it was "curious that the State and Judge Stuart rely so heavily upon the jurors' answers to the judge's informal question at the conclusion of this case and yet both respondents totally discount the value of jurors' answers to a more formal and detailed *voir dire* procedure at the outset of trials in general."[89]

With the filing of the media's reply brief, the written arguments were complete. All that remained was for the lawyers to prepare themselves for the experience that most attorneys both long for and dread—oral argument before the U.S. Supreme Court.

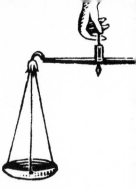

SIX
May It Please the Court

What we ask of you is nothing less than a renunciation of power—the conclusion by this Court that the Judiciary should not and indeed may not tell the press in advance what news it may print.

ATTORNEY FLOYD ABRAMS
before the U.S. Supreme Court, April 19, 1976

Oral argument is the pinnacle of Supreme Court litigation. The research has been completed, the intricate legal issues have been analyzed, and the briefs have been written and filed. All that remains is for the attorneys to appear in the high court's hearing room to present their arguments in person to the nine justices seated at the bench before them, in what can sometimes be a dramatic experience. Lawyers who participate in oral arguments before the Court almost uniformly describe the experience as both the most exhilarating and the most daunting of their professional lives, echoing the sentiment of former Chief Justice William H. Rehnquist, who once recalled that one of his own appearances before the Court left him "drenched with sweat."[1]

Of all the Court's traditional practices and procedures, oral argument is also perhaps the most ritualistic and elaborately stylized. Until recent years, all male attorneys appearing before the Court wore

United States Supreme Court Building, west façade. Photograph by Franz Jantzen, Collection of the Supreme Court of the United States.

formal striped trousers and long "cutaway" coats for their appearance (now only attorneys from the solicitor general's office arguing on behalf of the federal government follow the custom). White quill pens are provided at the counsel table for the use of the attorneys and are kept as treasured mementos of the occasion. Prior to taking the bench, the members of the Court exchange solemn handshakes among themselves, and once the Court is in session all of the participants conduct themselves with the utmost of decorum, reflecting the Court's lofty position and seminal role in American society.[2]

Even the justices' seating arrangement on the bench is dictated by tradition and protocol. The chief justice occupies the center position, with the senior associate justice at his immediate right and the next most senior associate to his left. The other six justices take their seats on the bench alternately based on their tenure with the Court. Thus, the most recently appointed justice is in the farthest seat to the left of the chief, and the second most junior appointee is at the chief's far right.[3]

In the spring of 1976, when the Court heard arguments in *Nebraska Press Association v. Stuart*, Warren E. Burger occupied the center seat. Born, raised, and educated in Minnesota, Burger had graduated with honors from the St. Paul College of Law in 1931 and quickly devel-

United States Supreme Court courtroom. Photograph by Franz Jantzen, Collection of the Supreme Court of the United States.

oped a reputation as an able and civic-minded young practitioner.[4] He also began to play an active role in partisan politics, both locally and nationally. A founder of the Minnesota Young Republican organization, Burger briefly served as a manager of Harold Stassen's run for the GOP presidential nomination in 1952, before shifting his support to Dwight Eisenhower. In 1953, Eisenhower appointed Burger head of the Justice Department's civil division, with responsibility for supervision of most of the department's civil litigation. Three years later, he was rewarded for his work in the Justice Department with a judicial appointment to the U.S. Court of Appeals for the District of Columbia Circuit, where he served for the next thirteen years.[5]

In 1969, President Richard Nixon appointed Burger chief justice of the Supreme Court. He came to the high court with a reputation as a constitutional strict constructionist and an opponent of what Nixon and many others viewed as the liberal activism of Burger's predecessor, Earl Warren.[6] Though he proved to be an able, if not particularly gifted, judicial craftsman, the consensus among court scholars today is that Burger was considerably less influential as a shaper of his Court's jurisprudence than many of his predecessors, especially Warren.[7] While his voting record remained consistent with his conservative reputation, Burger was relatively ineffectual in managing the justices' conferences to achieve unanimity within the Court on many of the most delicate and controversial issues that came before the justices during his tenure, including gender discrimination, abortion, affirmative action, and welfare rights. As a result, the Burger Court came to be known for the proliferation of individual opinions issued by the justices in many of its most important cases, with concurring and dissenting opinions published in quantities not seen for generations.[8]

On First Amendment issues, Burger's personality and his judicial record offered little encouragement to the media as the oral arguments in the *Nebraska Press Association* case approached. Often critical of the press in his public statements, Burger also had proven to be highly sensitive to media commentary related to the Court's operations and had been a zealous protector of the privacy of the Court's inner workings.[9] More specifically, he had recently authored the Court's majority opinion in *Miller v. California* (1973), upholding government regulation of erotic literary content, and he had dissented from the majority's opinion in *New York Times v. United States* (1971), the "Pentagon Papers" case.

Miller was a 5–4 decision in which the Court upheld the conviction of a California man for violation of a state statute prohibiting the sale of obscene material through the mail.[10] In his majority opinion for the Court, Burger enunciated a new definition of obscenity and rejected the notion of a national community standard for pornography, holding that trial courts should evaluate such material pursuant to local community standards.[11]

In *New York Times,* the majority of the Court had held that the *New York Times* and *Washington Post* could not be restrained from publishing controversial documents and information related to American involvement in the Vietnam conflict.[12] Burger, however, dissented, scolding the newspapers for failing to advise Pentagon officials that they were in possession of stolen government property and criticizing his colleagues for hearing and deciding the case in what he deemed to be inappropriate haste.[13] Burger's positions in both of those recent cases suggested that the chief justice might be amenable to some types of restrictions on the press in certain situations. Burger's vote in the Nebraska gag order litigation, therefore, seemed to be very much in play.

On Burger's right sat senior associate justice William J. Brennan, Jr. Since his appointment to the Court by President Dwight Eisenhower in 1956, Brennan had become the leader and most eloquent voice of what was considered the Court's liberal wing. Using both his engaging personality and a politician's gift for strategic maneuvering, Brennan became, in the words of one commentator, a "judicial pain" to Warren Burger as a result of his remarkable ability to "cobble together majorities on a variety of issues ranging from freedom of speech to rights of the accused."[14] By 1976, Brennan had established himself as the Court's most consistent articulator of an absolutist position on First Amendment issues—tolerating almost no restrictions whatsoever on free speech or press.[15] Given his judicial record and his earlier conference vote to grant an immediate stay of the Nebraska gag order, Brennan seemed to be a guaranteed vote on the side of the news organizations in the Nebraska case.

The next most senior justice was Potter Stewart, a 1958 Eisenhower appointee. Often portrayed as a centrist or a swing justice who moved between the Court's liberal and conservative factions, Stewart liked to describe himself as a "nondoctrinal" jurist who decided issues placed before him without regard to any overriding political or legal philosophy.[16] His pragmatic approach to constitutional issues was perhaps best epitomized by an oft-quoted passage from one of his 1964 opinions in which he ruminated over the definition of "hard-core" pornography. "I can't define it," Stewart wryly acknowledged, "but I know it when I see it."[17] Like Brennan, Stewart had already voted to grant a stay of the Nebraska gag order and to hear the case on an expedited basis. Thus, he too seemed to be a safe vote for the news media as the attorneys prepared for oral argument.

After Stewart, the next most senior justice in 1976 was Byron R. White. The only appointee of President John Kennedy, White had been an All-American football player at the University of Colorado and a Rhodes Scholar. Appointed to the Court in 1962 after a brief stint as a deputy attorney general in the Kennedy administration, White arrived on the bench with a reputation as a "Kennedy liberal."[18] Like so many other justices before and since, however, White confounded expectations by forging a record over his thirty-year tenure that cannot be captured with simplistic political labels. Despite his supposed liberal pedigree, White, like Potter Stewart, espoused a pragmatic, result-oriented judicial philosophy that often placed him on the conservative side of such issues as criminal rights and abortion (for example, he dissented from the liberal majority in both *Miranda v. Arizona* [1966] and *Roe v. Wade* [1973]). Given his judicial independence and centrist tendencies, White's ultimate decision on the Nebraska gag order controversy seemed hard to predict. As the argument approached, media attorney E. Barrett Prettyman worried that White might prove to be a particularly "tough nut to crack."[19] Nevertheless, his earlier vote to grant a stay of a portion of the gag order seemed to offer some encouragement to the press.

Thurgood Marshall was the next most senior justice to hear the *Nebraska Press Association* case. When he was appointed by President Lyndon Johnson in 1967, Marshall had become the first African American justice in the Court's history.[20] Even before he ascended to the high court, however, Marshall's legal career had taken on historic significance. From 1940 to 1961, he served as head of the NAACP's Legal Defense and Education Fund, a position that brought him before the Court in 1954 as the lead counsel for the petitioners in the Court's historic *Brown v. Board of Education* desegregation decision. From 1961 to 1965 he sat on the Second Circuit Court of Appeals, and from 1965 to 1967 he served as the nation's first African American solicitor general—a post that made him the federal government's chief advocate before the Supreme Court. By the time the *Nebraska Press Association* litigation came before the Court in 1976, Marshall had established himself as a steadfast partner of William Brennan on the Court's liberal wing. Like Brennan, he espoused an absolutist position on issues such as the death penalty (he consistently opposed it), personal privacy and abortion (consistently supporting those interests), and free speech and press (consistently opposing any and all prior restraints). Along with Brennan, Marshall seemed to be a sure vote for the petitioners in the Nebraska gag order litigation.

Next in seniority on the high court was Justice Harry A. Blackmun, appointed to the Court by President Richard Nixon in 1970. Given his Minnesota background and lifelong friendship with Chief Justice Burger—he had served as best man at Burger's wedding—Blackmun came to the bench saddled with the expectation among most court observers that he would become Burger's conservative "Minnesota Twin." Blackmun, however, slowly began to carve out an independent path for himself that would eventually alienate him from Burger and lead him to the Court's more liberal wing.[21] In view of his prior involvement in the case as the presiding circuit justice, Blackmun's final disposition of the Nebraska gag order case seemed especially difficult to anticipate. His earlier procedural orders had been highly critical of the broad and ambiguous provisions of the state courts' gag orders, but his November 20 chambers opinion had actually pre-served and perpetuated some of the most troubling aspects of those very orders. For the attorneys preparing for oral argument, Blackmun seemed to be a particularly unpredictable, and crucial, prospective vote.

Lewis F. Powell, Jr., the next Nixon appointee, came to the Court in 1971 after a long and distinguished career in private practice in Richmond, Virginia.[22] A courtly gentleman born and raised in tide-water Virginia, Powell was a classic political and judicial moderate. In the 1970s and 1980s, he became the quintessential swing vote between the Court's conservative and liberal voting blocs. As early as 1976, by virtue of his centrist position on most issues, Powell had become one of the most important and influential votes in some of the Court's closest and most delicate decisions on controversial topics such as abortion and affirmative action. His was a vote that none of the parties in the Nebraska gag order litigation could ignore or take for granted.

The last and the youngest of the Nixon appointees serving on the court in 1976 was William H. Rehnquist. Since his appointment in late 1971, Rehnquist had quickly gained a reputation as one of the Court's ablest and most conservative legal minds, siding frequently with Chief Justice Burger in favor of law enforcement interests over the rights of criminal suspects and in favor of the autonomy of state and local political authorities over the power of the federal

The 1976 Burger Court. Photograph by Robert Oakes, *National Geographic*,
Courtesy of the Supreme Court of the United States.

government.[23] In 1986, Rehnquist would become just the third sitting
associate justice in history to be elevated to chief justice, when President Ronald Reagan nominated him to succeed Burger. He remained
in that position until his death in September 2005. As chief justice,
Rehnquist played a key role in fashioning a Court that became decid-
edly more conservative, with many of his forceful dissents of the
1970s becoming majority positions in the 1990s.[24] In 1976, if any of
the justices might have been expected, as a matter of states' rights
principle, to defer to the discretion of Judge Stuart and the Nebraska
Supreme Court in the gag order controversy, it would have seemed to
have been Rehnquist.

Back row, left to right: Justices Rehnquist, Blackmun, Powell, and Stevens; front row, left to right: Justices White, Brennan, Burger, Stewart, and Marshall.

The most junior associate justice on the Court in 1976 was John Paul Stevens, nominated by President Gerald Ford in December 1975. Stevens had not yet been confirmed and sworn in when the Court voted to hear the Nebraska case. Given his very recent appointment, his judicial leanings were something of an enigma for the attorneys preparing for oral argument. Reputed to be a political moderate, Stevens had sailed through his Senate confirmation hearings with minimal controversy and little illumination of the judicial record he had compiled during his five years of service on the Seventh Circuit Court of Appeals. Over time, he would fashion a legacy that generally confirmed his centrist reputation, but the attorneys preparing for the gag order arguments had almost no way of anticipating Stevens's likely position in their case.[25]

Thus, as the attorneys readied themselves for oral argument, the breakdown of likely votes among the Court panel seemed to suggest a potentially close contest. Justices Brennan, Marshall, White, and Stewart appeared to be safe votes for the news media. Justice Rehnquist and Chief Justice Burger might reasonably have been expected to support the discretionary authority of Judge Stuart and the Nebraska Supreme Court to control their own local courtrooms. The votes of Justices Blackmun, Powell, and Stevens would most likely tip the balance one way or the other, and their positions seemed the most uncertain as the arguments approached.

For the petitioners in the Nebraska gag order litigation, the selection of the lawyers to present oral argument to the Court was a delicate and difficult issue to settle. Omaha attorneys Stephen McGill and James Koley, along with their co-counsel in Lincoln and North Platte, Alan Peterson and Harold Kay, had been doing most of the heavy lifting in the case from the outset. They had lived with the litigation from its inception and had handled all of the earlier phases of the case quite competently and with considerable success. None of them, however, had ever appeared before the U.S. Supreme Court, and they, along with their clients and the dozens of national media organizations who were participating in the case as *amici,* understood quite well the dramatic importance of the case. As the briefs were written and filed, and, as the significance of the case became increasingly apparent, most of the decision makers came to the conclusion that their case would probably be better served if more experienced and better-known attorneys presented the argument to the Court. Woody Howe would later recall that "as good as [McGill, Koley, Kay, Peterson, and the rest of the Nebraska attorneys] were, we felt we needed outside help once it got past the state level."[26] Money was also a factor. As Alan Peterson would later indicate, many of the national media corporations and broadcast networks that were donating funds to support the battle did so with the implicit understanding "that they would get to choose absolute top-notch, experienced Supreme Court counsel."[27] Based on all those factors, Washington co-counsel E. Barrett Prettyman, Jr., emerged as the obvious choice to lead the oral arguments.

As previously noted, Prettyman was a well-known and extremely well-connected Supreme Court veteran—the only person in the Court's history to have served as a clerk for three separate justices. In the spring of 1976, Prettyman was fifty years old and in the prime of his career as a private appellate practitioner. He had already argued more than a dozen cases before the high court, with great distinction and success.[28] His argument in *Nebraska Press Association* would prove to be a notable addition to that record.

The petitioners also decided to allow New York attorney Floyd Abrams to argue on behalf of the dozens of *amicus* parties in the case. Abrams was then, as he remains today, one of the country's foremost advocates of First Amendment protections. A partner in the New York law firm of Cahill, Gordon & Reindel, Abrams currently serves as the William J. Brennan, Jr., Visiting Professor of First Amendment Issues at Columbia University's Graduate School of Journalism. In 1976, Abrams was just beginning to develop his reputation in the field, having begun his climb to prominence on the basis of his work for the *New York Times* in the famed "Pentagon Papers" case five years earlier. Still, he was only a "rising star" at the time of the Nebraska litigation, and the decision to allow him to argue the case along with Prettyman was not made without some reservations. Woody Howe remembers being concerned that this would be Abrams's "maiden argument" before the Court. "We wanted to help him live his dream," Howe recalled, "but we were worried about him having the burden of the whole argument."[29]

For the respondents, on the other hand, the selection of the attorneys to present oral argument was a relatively clear-cut decision. Arguing for Judge Stuart would be Harold Mosher, the chief appellate attorney in the Nebraska attorney general's office. Mosher had a wealth of experience in delivering arguments in state and lower federal appellate courts, but he had never appeared before the U.S. Supreme Court. Nevertheless, he looked forward to the experience with what appeared to all observers to be great confidence and eagerness. His colleague, Milston Larson, Lincoln County prosecutor, who would argue the case on behalf of the State of Nebraska, likewise relished the opportunity to appear before the high court. Just thirty-one years old at the time (and looking even younger), Larson had never even argued a case before the Nebraska Supreme Court until the earlier proceedings in the gag order litigation, and he knew that he might be in for a rough ride before the nation's highest court. Although he felt that the unique circumstances of the case, coupled with the *Sheppard* cautionary precedent, provided him with a tenable legal argument to make, he had no illusions about the daunting burden he and Mosher would have to bear to overcome the presumption that a prior restraint was unconstitutional.

Both sides engaged in extensive and elaborate preparation for the arguments. To be sure, all of the legal issues had been comprehensively presented at four previous stages of the litigation and had been exhaustively analyzed in no fewer than thirteen briefs, totaling more than 1,200 written pages. Still, the attorneys could not expect to simply rehash the written arguments. Court tradition holds that the justices do not want to hear the attorneys simply regurgitate the written briefs during oral argument. Indeed, one of the Court's procedural rules specifically emphasizes that "the Court looks with disfavor on any oral argument that is read from a prepared text."[30]

Moreover, even when attorneys make painstaking plans for the lines of argument they hope to pursue, they are invariably driven off course by the justices' questioning throughout oral argument. It is almost impossible to predict what particular issue will most pique the justices' interest, and some members of the Court have traditionally seemed to take almost perverse delight in interrupting an attorney's prepared presentation with questions that might lead the discourse far astray from the direction the attorney had planned or anticipated.

To try to plan for all eventualities, Prettyman and Abrams met on several occasions with McGill, Koley, and numerous other media attorneys to strategize and decide on the key points to focus upon during the hearing. They also took part in several "mock court" sessions, during which they rehearsed their arguments before their colleagues, who drilled them with every conceivable question they could think of that the justices might ask. As they shaped and reshaped their strategies, the media attorneys knew that the constitutional principles at stake were momentous ones. At the very least, they had to convince the Court that no conceivable circumstances could justify a prohibition on the publication of information derived from open court proceedings or contained in public documents. Beyond that, they hoped to achieve a significant breakthrough in First Amendment jurisprudence—a specific declaration from the Court that no prior restraint of the press could *ever* be justified in the context of pretrial publicity, given the wide range of less restrictive alternatives available to trial court judges to protect a defendant's rights. Prettyman and Abrams were relatively confident of their ability to obtain the first objective; the second was much more uncertain.[31]

In preparation for argument before the justices, Mosher and Larson also met several times to debate their strategy. They agreed to divide as equally as possible the forty-five minutes the Court had allotted to them, with Mosher speaking first. He would emphasize the extraordinary crush of media attention that confronted Judges Ruff and Stuart in the days following the Kellie murders and then move on to an analysis of the controlling legal precedents in the case. He hoped to emphasize the lack of support in the case law for the absolutist position taken by the media and to appeal to the perceived moderate and conservative members of the Court, who would be most likely to defer to Judge Stuart's attempt to find an accommodation between the First and Sixth Amendments.

Larson, who was the only one of the attorneys appearing before the Court who had been personally involved in the emotional turmoil of those first days after the Kellie murders, planned to offer the justices his own unique perspective on the environment from which the gag orders arose. On the legal issues, he hoped to focus on the lack of realistic alternatives to the gag order that were available to the trial court judges as they sought to deal with the overwhelming media onslaught. Like Mosher, Larson aimed his argument at the perceived conservative and moderate justices, who seemed most likely to be receptive to arguments about the reasonableness of the gag order and the discretionary authority of local trial judges to craft a short-term accommodation of the competing constitutional interests at stake.[32]

At 1:00 p.m. on Monday, April 19, 1976, a marshal of the U.S. Supreme Court rose in the wings of the Court's hearing room and spoke the traditional words that have for more than 150 years opened the public sessions. "Oyez, oyez, oyez," he intoned. "The honorable, the chief justice and the associate justices of the Supreme Court of the United States. All persons having business before the honorable, the Supreme Court of the United States, are admonished to draw near and give their attention, for the Court is now sitting. God save the United States and this honorable court." With that, the nine justices of the Court settled into their high-backed leather chairs arrayed behind the elevated bench at the front of the chambers. Without further ceremony, Chief Justice Warren Burger announced, "We will hear arguments next in Case No. 75–817, *Nebraska Press Association v. Stuart*. Mr. Prettyman, you may proceed."[33]

And so the litigation that had begun exactly six months before in the tiny courtroom of Lincoln County Court Judge Ronald Ruff in North Platte, Nebraska, had reached its crest in the nation's highest court. Prettyman began his presentation with the traditional opening, "May it please the Court," and then launched into a brief overview of the Kellie murders, Simants's arrest and arraignment, and the initial press coverage of those events. After responding to several immediate questions from Justice Blackmun regarding the number of media outlets in Lincoln County, Prettyman began to describe the initial gag order that Judge Ruff had placed on the press prior to the start of Simants's preliminary hearing. At that point, Chief Justice Burger asked him to discuss the various alternatives that would have been available to the judge, short of a gag order, to control the publication of potentially prejudicial information. Specifically, Burger wondered, could the trial court have simply closed the preliminary hearing entirely? Prettyman responded that, of the various alternatives available, "I would certainly hope that you would bank on the *Sheppard* type alternatives and not on closed hearings. I think a closed hearing is the handmaiden to a prior restraint."[34]

"Well," Burger persisted, "would you take the same view of an order directed at the [attorneys in a trial], that they would be held in contempt if they discussed the case publicly?"[35] Prettyman responded that such an order would have First Amendment implications of its own with respect to the attorneys' rights of free speech, but he emphasized that those concerns were qualitatively different than the ones before the court in the Nebraska situation. He contended that both the hypothetical order directed against the attorneys suggested by the chief justice and the gag order issued against the Nebraska media in the instant case were prior restraints, "but certainly if you're going to have prior restraints, the one that is worse, the one that affects the public the most, the most onerous one, is the one that is the direct prior restraint on the press."[36]

As Prettyman's discourse continued, Justice Rehnquist interrupted with a series of questions related to the mootness issue. "Why is this a live case, Mr. Prettyman?" he asked. "The orders have expired."[37] Prettyman and the other attorneys had, of course, anticipated and briefed the issue extensively. He replied that the Court had apparently already decided that the case was not moot, because it had accepted the case for review while denying the media's request to expedite the hearing of the case, knowing that the result would be the expiration of the orders before the Court decided the case. Prettyman also reminded the Court of the "capable of repetition, yet evading review" principle—a long-established exception to the mootness doctrine that applied in situations where an issue is likely to recur frequently but continually avoid appellate review.[38] Rehnquist seemed to grudgingly accept the applicability of that doctrine, saying, "[This is] just sort of an exception to Article III, then?"[39]

Prettyman then took a rather unorthodox step by offering the justices a hypothetical scenario that he hoped would convey the notion that the press was being singled out for treatment that would not conceivably be tolerated if applied to other groups or individuals. It was a gambit that he and Abrams had discussed in some detail in their preparations for the argument.[40] Suppose, he suggested, "all of the ministers, priests, and rabbis in Lincoln County, Nebraska, had gotten together and decided that Simants was absolutely guilty, that he was the embodiment of evil, and that they owed it to their congregations to publicize from their pulpits the nature of his crimes and the fact that he had confessed." Is there any doubt, Prettyman asked, that the Court would strike down a court order that attempted to restrain the clergymen from making such statements from their pulpits? "And yet," he continued, "it doesn't seem so bad to the courts . . . when they do it in regard to the press [even though] the press is the one private organization that is carved out and mentioned specifically as entitled to protection under the First Amendment."[41]

The hypothetical seemed to intrigue several of the justices. Rehnquist asked, "What if the president of the local bar association had done what you suggested at a meeting of the bar?"[42] In such a case, Prettyman responded, the speaker might be subjected to discipline under the attorneys' professional canons of ethics, but he certainly could not be restrained prior to making the statements. Justice Stevens probed for the limits of Prettyman's point. "What if your ministers had also advocated lynching the man," he asked. "Could a prior restraint be permitted then?" Prettyman stood firm, saying, "I do not believe so. No, sir."[43]

Having spoken for more than twenty of the forty-five minutes allotted to the petitioners, and wanting to save some time for rebuttal, Prettyman yielded the floor to Floyd Abrams, who represented dozens of *amicus* parties, including the *New York Times,* Associated Press, and all three major television networks. Abrams began his argument by boldly asking the court for "a ruling that would be unthinkable in any nation in the world except ours. What we would ask of you is nothing less than a renunciation of power—the conclusion by this Court that the judiciary should not and indeed may not tell the press in advance what news it may print."[44]

After a very brief pause to allow that dramatic statement to settle in, Abrams proceeded to argue that, for most of the nation's history, prior restraints on the press in the realm of pretrial publicity had been almost completely unheard of. On the very rare occasions when they were attempted, he claimed, such restraints were "easily and summarily reversed" by the appellate courts. Only in recent years, he contended, had gag orders against the press become much more commonplace. He asked, rhetorically, what factors might account for the dramatic upsurge in such restraints. It was not, he argued, that the press had become more irresponsible. Even the recent heavily publicized trial of heiress-turned-terrorist Patty Hearst, he suggested, had not produced anything like the outrageous press coverage of the Sam Sheppard or Bruno Hauptmann trials in prior decades.[45] Nor, Abrams argued, had juries suddenly become less trustworthy in their ability to disregard prejudicial pretrial publicity. Indeed, he claimed, "I can hardly think of a time in our history when juries have proved their mettle more strongly than they have within the last few years."[46]

At that point, Justice Blackmun asked Abrams to comment on Judge Stuart's informal posttrial "poll" of the Simants's jury, which had been brought to the Court's attention in Mosher's brief.[47] The question offered a rather striking indication that Blackmun (or at least his clerks) had studied the briefs well, inasmuch as that material had appeared only in Mosher's brief. After first pointing out that Stuart's questions to the jurors were actually "devoid of the record"— that is, not properly before the Court as part of the official "record" in the case—Abrams noted that the phrasing of Stuart's inquiries was "to say the least, slanted," making the entire exercise "completely unreliable."[48] Moreover, he contended, it was illogical to argue that jurors' responses to that type of informal and unsworn posttrial questioning should be believed while at the same time suggesting that jurors could not be believed "when they are asked, under oath, if they could give a fair trial in the *voir dire* prior to a trial."[49]

Shortly after that exchange, Justice Stevens asked Abrams a more pointed question. "What do you do about the problem of the inadmissible confession? Say for some reason a confession is very dramatic but yet it would be rather clear that it would not be admissible at trial. Is [the pretrial publication of such a confession] just something we have to live with; there is no way of curtailing the publication of that kind of information?"[50] To his credit, Abrams did not try to evade the difficult policy implications embedded in the question, nor did he back away from the firm absolutist position he had taken. "Yes," he replied. "It is our view that there are some such things that we do have to live with." He reminded the Court, however, that the impact of the publication of such a confession could always be mitigated by the use of jury instructions, voir dire, and "all the other *Sheppard* methods."[51]

With that, Abrams's time was up, and he yielded the podium to Nebraska Deputy Attorney General Harold Mosher. Mosher's rather unpolished presentation contrasted sharply, and not favorably, with the elegant, eloquent, and seemingly extemporaneous constitutional arguments advanced by Prettyman and Abrams. He began by reading an obviously scripted, and generally superfluous, recounting of the facts that had given rise to the controversy—the murders, the flood of media attention, the coincidental showing of the movie *The*

Deadly Tower on the North Platte television station, and the population figures for Sutherland and North Platte. Mosher even took valuable time to offer the justices such folksy and extraneous nuggets of information as the fact that the area around Sutherland and North Platte, Nebraska, was "cattle country at its very best" and that the population of Sutherland had recently experienced a slight increase due to an influx of workers building "a huge electrical generating facility nearby."[52]

After listening quietly for several minutes, the chief justice gently attempted to nudge Mosher "off script" and into a discussion of the constitutional merits of the case by asking whether he thought the local courts would have been justified in trying to prohibit the showing of the *Deadly Tower* movie about the Texas sniper in the days after the Kellie murders, if prosecutors came into court and claimed that the movie would "stir up all kinds of passion and prejudice and impede a fair trial."[53] "Oh, I doubt it very much, Your Honor," Mosher casually replied. "I doubt it. I really do." He then proceeded to declare, "When all is said and done . . . the so-called restraining order here is purely a very narrow one."[54]

That assertion prompted an immediate reaction from Justice Stevens, who asked, "Could I just question your characterization of the order as a narrow one? It does include the prohibition against publishing 'any information strongly implicative of the accused as the perpetrator of the crime.' Do you regard that as a narrow prohibition?"[55] Mosher first replied, "Certainly," and then he proceeded to commit a rather egregious breach of court protocol by deferring a full response to the question until later in his argument. "May I get to it in a moment?" Mosher asked, indicating that he wanted to "continue with some facts, if I may, because I think they are important."[56]

Perhaps because he was the newest member of the Court, Stevens seemed to take no offense at being put off, saying, "Yes, certainly. I don't want to take you out of order." Mosher then resumed his recitation of the facts for several more minutes, describing Simants's arraignment and preliminary hearing and the filing of the original motion for a restrictive order by the prosecutors and defense counsel.

Eventually, without returning to Stevens's question about the "narrowness" of the gag order, Mosher waded into a discussion of the justifications for the Nebraska Supreme Court's inability or unwillingness to deal with the constitutional issues more quickly than it had done in late November and early December 1975. Despite the fact that the issue was by now a relatively obscure one and that neither the petitioners' counsel nor the justices themselves had seemed interested in pursuing it, Mosher set out to defend the professional integrity of the Nebraska Supreme Court by arguing that the contention in the media briefs that the state court had "refused to act expeditiously" in the case "is simply unfair and contrary to fact."[57] He pointed out that the Nebraska justices were burdened by an extremely heavy docket of oral arguments scheduled at the same time that the gag order litigation appeared before them and that "there was no way to stop those other cases."[58]

Several of the justices pounced on Mosher at that point, expressing considerable skepticism at his attempted defense of the state court's handling of the case. As he argued that the Nebraska court had been laboring under "a terrible caseload for any court to carry," Justice Thurgood Marshall brusquely interjected, "Well, Mr. Attorney General, that doesn't help us in this case, does it?"[59] No, Mosher acknowledged, it didn't. Still, he insisted, the important point to emphasize was that "the courts in Nebraska were not derelict in this matter."[60]

But, persisted Justice Blackmun, "Don't we have to decide whether [this case] was a routine matter or an exceptional case? And which is your position?"[61]

"Well, I think this was an exceptional case," Mosher replied.

"Well, then, should not the Supreme Court of Nebraska have expedited it?" Blackmun asked.

"They did," Mosher insisted.

"Well, then," the justice continued, "what is the relevance of all these other cases on the docket?"

Once again, Mosher declared, there was simply no way for the state court to stop the flow of already-scheduled cases.

Well, Blackmun suggested, "maybe they just had to replace one case on the docket and hear this one first."

Perhaps that could have been done, Mosher conceded, but perhaps also there was a need for delay to allow the parties to brief the matter fully.[62]

Finally, Justice Stevens tried to end the discussion of the state court's delay by asking Mosher another pointed and telling question. "Aren't you demonstrating that one of the vices in these orders is that inevitably they will remain in effect for some period of time until the judicial process can face up to the question of whether to remove them—that this is an inevitable part of the procedure, once you enter this type of order?"[63]

"Well yes," Mosher acknowledged. "There is always a certain time lag, Your Honor, there has to be. That is just part of the system."

By the time this exchange had concluded, Mosher had spent most of his allotted time without engaging in any substantive discussion of the constitutional merits of the gag order. He attempted to address those issues by offering broad generalizations about the inherent discretionary power of state trial courts in discharging their duty of providing fair trials to criminal defendants. Trial court judges are empowered, he contended, to take whatever steps they deem reasonably necessary to protect a defendant's rights, and those steps might include a restrictive order against the press in certain cases. The media, he suggested, had taken the position that no such orders could ever be issued against them, except in cases involving national security. That position, Mosher submitted, "finds no support in the Constitution of the United States, nor does it find any support in the teachings of this Court."[64] Mosher then attempted to bolster his arguments with a number of bromides, including reminders to the Court that "America's greatest claim to its place in history is its government of the people, by the people, and for the people" and "Ours is a government of laws, not men."[65]

As his argument neared conclusion, several justices attempted to bring Mosher back to the issue of the breadth and the scope of the gag order's language. Why, they wondered, should the press be expected to attend a preliminary hearing that was open to the public and then not report on it, especially when members of the public who were at the hearing were completely free to disseminate what they saw and heard? Justice Stewart broached the subject first, asking, "So the press could hear [Simants's preliminary hearing] but they couldn't publish it?"[66]

"That's correct," Mosher replied.

"Well, I don't know how any newspaper can exist if all it does is hear," chimed in Justice Marshall—an observation that must have warmed the hearts of all the media representatives seated at the counsel table and in the gallery.[67]

But, countered Mosher, the restriction on publication existed only until a jury was seated in Simants's impending trial. After that, he said, "the press was free to let it all hang out." The gag order, he insisted, was "simply an attempt, a very sincere attempt, to balance the First Amendment and the Sixth Amendment."[68]

At that point, Justice Stevens brought Mosher back to the question he had avoided earlier. Wasn't the substantive scope of the gag order's language overly broad? "What about the restriction on information 'strongly implicative of the guilt of the accused' that I asked you about before?" he asked. "Isn't that rather broad?"[69]

"No, I don't believe so at all," Mosher replied.

Obviously unsatisfied with Mosher's response, Stevens tried a different tack. "Would you think this order was appropriate in the Watergate background?" he asked. "Would you consider it a narrow order [if it applied to that scenario]?"[70]

"I don't know the scope of your question," Mosher demurred.

"Well, I am really just directing your attention to the scope of the order, the prohibition of information tending to prove guilt," Stevens replied. "Do you really think that is a narrow order?"

To his credit, Mosher stood firm. "That is a narrow order," he insisted.[71]

By then, Mosher had spoken for considerably more than his half of the forty-five minutes allowed to him and Larson as the respondents, and so he sat down with a simple "Thank you" to the Court. Justice Lewis Powell, for one, was unimpressed with his performance. He coldly recorded an impression that might well have been shared by many of his brethren, scrawling the words "Third Rate Argument" along the margin of his notes on Mosher's argument. Powell even added a rather snide and wholly gratuitous coda—"as usual from state asst. A/G."[72] Now young Lincoln County prosecutor Milton Larson was left to try to pick up the pieces of the respondents' case and make the best of what appeared to be a rather dismal situation. He did so with considerable aplomb.

With only about ten minutes left for his portion of the argument, Larson moved quickly past most of the factual background of the case, telling the justices that he believed Mosher had "done a very good job in setting forth the [factual] situation."[73] It is both ironic and perplexing to note that Larson was the only one of the four arguing attorneys who had been personally involved in the events surrounding the murders. For that reason, he, rather than Mosher, would seem to have been the logical choice to convey to the Court the nature of the media "feeding frenzy" that took place in Sutherland and North Platte during those early days of the litigation. Nevertheless, Larson only briefly alluded to the extensive media attention he had dealt with, telling the court that when he arrived at the crime scene on the night of the murders "there was an NBC helicopter from Denver that had arrived. There were media representatives from the wire services, AP, UPI, *Omaha World-Herald,* all of the local radio stations, television. It was very apparent very early that I was going to be faced with a good deal of publicity."[74]

Larson understood that, with the minimal amount of time available to him, he had to at least attempt to address the concerns that had been repeatedly expressed by several of the justices regarding the breadth of the gag order's language, particularly Justice Stevens's persistent discomfort with the ambiguous prohibition on publication of information "strongly implicative of the accused's guilt." He immediately sought to bolster Mosher's repeated characterization of the gag order as "narrowly" drawn by emphasizing that the facts surrounding Simants's murders and the media coverage presented a "very exceptional case in the criminal arena—the sensational case, the highly publicized case."[75] The heinous nature of the crimes—the number of victims, the sexual attacks on the minors, the necrophilia—all, he argued, brought the case "within the realm of an exceptional case." The overwhelming impact of the news coverage was exacerbated by the small population and rural isolation of Sutherland and Lincoln County, "where virtually everyone knew everyone, the people in the community knew both the accused and all of the victims, they were vitally interested in it, and they were going to learn all they could [about the crimes]."[76]

Under those types of extraordinary circumstances, and with the

Sheppard scenario weighing heavily on the minds of all the participants, Larson contended that it became necessary for the local attorneys and trial court judges to take "reasonable steps to protect [Simants's] right to a fair trial."[77] The original gag orders issued by Judges Ruff and Stuart, he argued, were reasonable short-term responses to an exceptional situation. As those original orders were subsequently amended by Justice Blackmun and the Nebraska Supreme Court, the final order that emerged was indeed a narrowly drawn restraint, he contended—one that was limited almost exclusively to prohibiting the publication of confessions made by the accused.

As to the problematic language in the gag order restraining the publication of facts strongly implicative of the defendant's guilt, Larson all but conceded that those words now appeared, in hindsight, to be overly broad. He directly responded to Justice Stevens's repeated questions to Mosher on that point, saying, "Now, in addressing Justice Stevens's question, that [language] would on its face appear to be rather pervasive." But, he continued, "I would submit that it is not [overly broad] when applied to the facts of this case."[78] The reason, he argued, the strongly implicative language did not invalidate the gag order in this particular case was that Simants's confession was virtually the only evidence available to the prosecution at the time of the preliminary hearing for securing his bind-over to the district court. In other words, there simply was no other evidence strongly implicative of Simants's guilt that might have been restrained by that language in the order. Thus, Larson suggested, the troubling language was merely an irrelevant throwaway line that had no direct restraining effect on the news coverage of the preliminary hearing—a "no harm, no foul" line of reasoning.

It was a creative, but ultimately unconvincing, argument. Even if Larson's reasoning had some validity as of the time of the preliminary hearing, as the weeks went on, a good deal more forensic evidence strongly implicative of Simants's guilt did become available, including fingerprint evidence, ballistics reports, and hair and fiber analysis from the FBI laboratory in Washington, D.C. Publication of that evidence was undoubtedly restrained by the "strongly implicative" language of the gag order. Fortunately for Larson, none of the justices seemed interested in pursuing the point any longer, and he was able to return to his primary points of emphasis—the extraordinary nature of the media coverage and the absolute need to keep Simants's confession out of the newspapers.

Larson wisely redirected the Court's attention to a question posed earlier to media counsel Floyd Abrams about the problem of the inadmissible confession. He pointed out that confessions made by an accused that are offered at preliminary hearings are not always admissible at a later trial, because they have not yet been subjected to the requisite tests for voluntariness that are required for admission of confessions at trial. Such tests take the form of pretrial hearings at which the prosecution must produce evidence showing that the confession was obtained in accordance with appropriate due process procedures. It is always possible, therefore, that a confession by an accused that is introduced at a preliminary hearing, before its voluntariness has been confirmed, might subsequently be adjudged inadmissible for use at trial. In such a situation, Larson argued, the inadmissibility of the confession would be of little comfort to the defendant "if the confession had already been published and the jurors already had knowledge of it." He suggested that jurors would likely just think, "Well, the prosecutor didn't introduce the confession but I know it was made." "That type of prejudice," Larson declared, "simply cannot be overcome."[79]

With the final minute available to him, Larson attempted to reach out to the Court's conservative bloc by urging the justices not to interfere with the discretionary authority of a local trial court judge to control the environment in and around his own courtroom. "I think that the basic issue here," he reminded the Court, "is that in the exceptional case who shall govern, who shall have ultimate authority to protect the due process requirements with respect to a fair trial? Shall it be the judiciary, or shall it be the [newspaper] editor? That is really what we are talking about here—the ultimate power of the courts to control their own processes to insure that due process of law is met."[80]

With that, the young prosecutor sat down, feeling both relieved and satisfied that he had done about as well as could have been expected in the time available to him. All things considered, Larson's

Lincoln County prosecutors Milton Larson and John Murphy on the steps of the Supreme Court Building, after Larson's argument before the Supreme Court. Photo Courtesy of AP/World Wide Photos

performance was indeed impressive. At the least, he had been able to refocus the Court's attention on the dramatic exceptionality of the Simants case, and he seemed to have made significant progress in demonstrating the danger of completely unrestrained press coverage in such a case, particularly with respect to the publication of a criminal defendant's confessions. Had he known of it at the time, Larson certainly would have been gratified to learn that he had impressed at least one of the justices. In the same set of notes in which he had referred to Harold Mosher's argument as "Third Rate," Justice Powell praised Larson's performance with the words "Excellent Argument."[81]

Prettyman had about eight minutes left for rebuttal. He spent most of that time reemphasizing the point that prior restraints of the press simply don't work—that gag orders like the ones imposed on the Nebraska press result only in the proliferation of "rumor and gossip and speculation that is often far more dangerous to a defendant than factual reporting in a newspaper."[82]

His argument culminated in a brief exchange with the chief justice on the issue of the supposedly limited duration of the Nebraska gag order. Prettyman pointed out that, whereas Larson and Mosher had repeatedly suggested that the restraint had been in effect for "just a short period of time," in reality the Nebraska gag orders, in one form or another, had restrained the press for more than two and a half months. He argued that the appellate courts should not be put into the position of deciding on a case-by-case basis whether a particular gag was or was not too long in its duration. To demonstrate his point, Prettyman offered another hypothetical situation, this one involving an incumbent congressman running for reelection. Suppose, he suggested, the congressman was indicted on a criminal charge and confessed to the crime on the morning of the election and his attorneys then sought and obtained a gag order restraining the press from reporting on the arrest or the confession for just seven hours, until the polls closed, and the congressman was reelected. In such a case, Prettyman asked, "Are you going to put the courts into the position of saying, 'Well, in that case, seven hours was too long, but in some other case maybe a week is all right, or a month is all right?'"[83]

Although Prettyman had clearly framed the scenario as only a hypothetical, Burger, for one, seemed skeptical. "Has there ever been such a case?" he asked.[84] Prettyman had to acknowledge that no such bizarre factual scenario had ever been ruled upon. He recovered nicely, though, by pointing out that the Court had repeatedly held that the central thrust of the First Amendment was to protect "the contemporaneous publishing of news—the public's right immediately to news, because you cannot judge the impact that news is going to have." "There is a momentum to these things," he argued in summation. "As soon as you start saying, 'Let's just keep [news] from [the public] for a little while,' you put yourself in very serious trouble."[85]

With those final words, the argument ended at 2:33 p.m. "Thank you, gentlemen. The case is submitted," the chief justice declared. The nine justices then rose and left the bench, to begin their deliberations in the days and weeks ahead. All that remained for the participants was to wait for the Court's decision.

seven
Decision and Reaction

The press may be arrogant, tyrannical, abusive, and sensationalist, just
as it may be incisive, probing, and informative. But at least in the
context of prior restraints on publication, the decision of what,
when, and how to publish is for editors, not judges.

JUSTICE WILLIAM F. BRENNAN
concurring in *Nebraska Press Association v. Stuart*

T he most fundamental and important task performed by
the U.S. Supreme Court—the actual deciding of cases—is also
the function that is most veiled in mystery. Several days after
the oral arguments in a case have been completed, the justices meet
in conference to deliberate and cast their votes on the resolution of
the controversy. Like the oral arguments, these meetings are tightly
controlled by Court tradition and protocol. In contrast to the arguments, however, they are conducted in complete secrecy. No one
other than the justices themselves are present during the conferences and little, if any, information about the actual give-and-take
between the jurists during these sessions is made available to the
public. What little information about the court's conference debates
does make its way into the public record generally comes from conference notes and other personal memoranda recorded by the individual justices, which are sometimes made available to researchers

when the private papers of the justices are archived in various repositories, typically several years after their deaths. Even then, the notes are often cryptic or convoluted and can be difficult to analyze and interpret with any degree of certainty.

While the substantive content of any particular conference is thus largely a matter of conjecture for observers of the Court, the procedural form of the meetings is relatively well known.[1] Around 1:00 p.m. on Wednesdays and Fridays while the Court is in session, a buzzer sounds in each justice's chambers summoning him or her to convene in the Court's most private of inner sanctums, the conference room. This richly paneled and elegantly appointed room is located adjacent to the chief justice's chambers and features a long rectangular conference table surrounded by nine high-backed leather chairs. As the justices assemble, they shake hands with one another in a ritualistic show of collegiality that dates back to the 1880s and the chief then calls the meeting to order. Just as on the bench in the Court's hearing room, seating at the conference table is dictated by seniority, with the chief at the head, the senior associate at the other end, and the rest of the associates at the side chairs in order of their tenure with the Court. The most junior associate sits closest to the door, taking and delivering to his or her brethren any messages that are received from outside the room—a tradition that once prompted Justice Tom C. Clark to describe himself as "the highest paid doorkeeper in the world."[2]

With the justices assembled and settled into their assigned seats, control of the conference falls to the chief justice. He sets the agenda and begins the deliberations on each case by briefly restating the relevant facts and operative legal principles. Typically, he will then present his interpretation of the applicable law and indicate how he intends to vote. When the chief is finished with his analysis, the senior associate speaks, followed by the other justices in order of their seniority. When all the justices have expressed their views, a vote is taken in reverse order of seniority—that is, the most junior associate votes first and so on, so that the junior members of the Court will not be swayed by the votes of their senior colleagues.[3]

As many commentators have pointed out, it is in the role of leader of the conference that the chief justice may exert his most significant

Justices' Conference Room, Supreme Court of the United States. Photograph by Franz Jantzen, Collection of the Supreme Court of the United States.

influence in shaping the jurisprudence of his court. The manner in which the various chiefs have exercised this power is typically viewed as one of the best indicators of the effectiveness and success of his tenure. For example, Charles Evan Hughes and Earl Warren are often identified as among the strongest and most effectual of twentieth-century chief justices, due in large part to their skill and persuasiveness in directing the Court's conferences.[4] Hughes, who presided over the Court from 1930 to 1941, was a stickler for brevity whose ability to frame succinctly and direct tightly the course of conference discussions allowed the Court to conduct its business with an efficiency and productivity that had never been seen before and has not been matched since.[5]

Earl Warren's management of conferences during his tenure from 1954 to 1969 has been even more favorably evaluated by most Court scholars, reflecting the sentiment of Justice Potter Stewart, who once described Warren as the ideal conference head.[6] Warren presented cases to his colleagues in simple, direct terms that tended to focus the discussions on the central legal issues at stake rather than irrelevancies or technicalities, and he exhibited a remarkable deftness at tactfully but effectively leading debates among the justices in the direction he wished for them to go.[7] That skill was never more notably exemplified than when Warren led his brethren to surprising unanimity in the controversial and emotionally charged decision in *Brown v. Board of Education* in 1954.[8]

In contrast, Warren Burger, who presided over the Court's deliberations in the *Nebraska Press Association* case in the spring of 1976, has been almost universally assessed as a much less skilled conference leader than many of his predecessors, especially Hughes and Warren.[9] Described by legal historian Bernard Schwartz as "turgid and unfocused, with emphasis on irrelevancies rather than central points," Burger is generally perceived to have displayed none of Warren's political skill in molding and shaping his colleagues' thinking, nor did he exert Hughes's tight-fisted control over the flow and pace of the Court's internal debates.[10] The result was a tendency toward diffusion of leadership, with associate justices frequently taking the lead in the decision-making processes of the Burger Court, particularly in the major cases.[11]

Burger has also been criticized for his handling of another of the chief justice's most important powers—the assigning of opinions. Traditionally, the chief assigns the writing of the Court's opinion in all cases in which he has voted in the majority. In cases where the chief is in the minority, the senior associate justice voting with the majority makes that assignment. Several historians of the Court, including Kermit Hall and Bernard Schwartz, have suggested that Burger did not always follow that long-established practice. Quoting a member of the Court who did not want to be identified, Schwartz has contended that "all too often [Burger] would vote with the majority so as to assign the opinion, and then end up voting in dissent."[12]

Schwartz, Hall, and others have also pointed out that Burger would sometimes assign the writing of opinions even when he was overtly in the conference minority. For example, in an important 1971 school-busing case, *Swann v. Charlotte-Mecklenburg Board of Education,* Burger assigned the opinion to himself even though he had clearly voted in the minority during conference.[13] Similarly, in the even more prominent and controversial *Roe v. Wade* abortion decision in 1973, Burger

assigned the writing of the opinion to his close friend and then-
ideological partner, Harry Blackmun, even though the chief had not
been among the majority in the voting at the conference.[14] Burger's
manipulations in this regard created a good deal of dissension and
unrest among his colleagues and drew the particularly strong wrath of
Justice William O. Douglas, who threatened to write a scathing dissent in *Roe v. Wade* revealing the chief's misuse of the assignment
power. Douglas was convinced to restrain himself only when colleagues appealed to his duty to protect the reputation of the Court.[15]

In the *Nebraska Press Association* case, glimpses of the Court's
deliberations emerge from several sources. Some limited primary
evidence is available in the personal papers of the justices, including
most notably those of Justice Lewis F. Powell, Jr., who served on the
Court from 1971 to 1987. Powell, who died in 1998, bequeathed his
papers to the library of the Washington and Lee University School of
Law in Lexington, Virginia, where they are archived and available to
researchers today. Those records include Powell's memoranda, cor-
respondence, draft opinions, and notes from Court conferences
relating to hundreds of cases he considered during his tenure on the
Court. His notes on *Nebraska Press Association* are rather sketchy, but
they do offer some insight into the Court's deliberations. The most
comprehensive secondary account of the Court's deliberations in the
case may be found in Schwartz's *The Ascent of Pragmatism: The Burger
Court in Action* (1990). Schwartz presents a remarkably detailed
account of the justices' deliberations, including several purported
direct quotations, but he is quite vague on the matter of sources, perhaps in an attempt to preserve the confidentiality of his informants.[16]
So too journalists Bob Woodward and Scott Armstrong have offered
intriguing insights into the Court's deliberations on the case in several pages of *The Brethren* (1979), their groundbreaking and best-
selling book, although their sources enjoy even more anonymity than
those utilized by Schwartz.[17] Ultimately then, piecing together the
Court's deliberations in *Nebraska Press Association* requires a syn-
thesis of the available primary and secondary sources with a healthy
dose of "educated speculation."

Whatever Warren Burger's appropriate legacy may be in terms of
his leadership of the Court's conferences during his years as chief

justice, it is quite apparent from the available evidence that he played a dominant role in the deliberation and decision of *Nebraska Press Association*. Indeed, Woodward and Armstrong claim that Burger considered the case to be one of the most important that the Court addressed that term and that "he worked harder on it than on any other opinion."[18] Burger called the case for discussion in conference on the afternoon of Wednesday, April 21, 1976, just two days after the oral arguments had been heard. He began the deliberations by briefly reminding his colleagues of the facts of the case and the fundamental constitutional issue at stake—the free press/fair trial tension. He then proceeded to stake out a position that would ultimately become the centerpiece of the majority decision rendered by the Court. "Issuance of prior restraints may in some cases be permissible," Burger asserted, "but the circumstances facing the Nebraska judges in the Simants case did not justify the restraint imposed."[19] In fact, he suggested, "we decided this case when we decided the Pentagon Papers case."[20]

In that Pentagon Papers decision five years earlier, the Court had held that the *New York Times* and *Washington Post* could not be restrained from publishing controversial documents and information related to American involvement in the Vietnam conflict.[21] But the majority of the Court had also held that a prior restraint of the press might be allowable in certain circumstances, with a proper evidentiary showing. Burger's invocation of the Pentagon Papers decision in his initial comments during the *Nebraska Press Association* conference plainly indicated that he believed the result in the Nebraska case should be the same as the one the Court had reached in that more celebrated dispute. That is, he believed the Court should strike down the Nebraska gag order but should *not* hold that such prior restraints of the press were per se unconstitutional.

Burger's framing of the issue in those terms appears to have shaped most of the Court's subsequent debate over its ruling in *Nebraska Press Association*. All of the justices agreed that the Nebraska gag order was invalid under the circumstances surrounding the Simants prosecution, and they therefore unanimously agreed that the opinion of the Nebraska Supreme Court upholding the order should be reversed. Several of the justices wanted to go further, however, and give the media petitioners precisely what they had hoped for in bringing the case to the high court—a declaration that judicial gag orders against the press in the realm of pretrial publicity could *never* be constitutionally permissible.

The precise number of votes in the conference for that "absolutist" position is a matter of substantial uncertainty in the record. Not surprisingly, Justice William Brennan appears to have made the strongest argument in conference for a complete prohibition on all pretrial gag orders, contending that no such prior restraint could ever be harmonized with the guarantees of the First Amendment. Bernard Schwartz has indicated that, during the conference, Brennan was "supported by Justices Stewart, White, Marshall, and Stevens" in that position.[22] If Schwartz's assertion is correct, Brennan would have had the necessary five votes for his absolutist viewpoint and might have, presumably, controlled the assignment of the opinion so as to ensure that it expressed that view. In the event, however, that did not happen.

The practical realities of the Court's internal dynamics and the subtle fluidity of the justices' respective viewpoints on that critical issue appear to make the deliberations somewhat more complicated than Schwartz's analysis suggests. Justices Blackmun and Rehnquist clearly supported the chief's viewpoint—that is, that the gag order in the Nebraska case was invalid but that the possibility of such restraints in certain types of circumstances should not be foreclosed. Indeed, Blackmun stated, "I don't want to close the door completely against some restraint."[23] It is just as apparent (from their later joining in Brennan's separate concurring opinion) that Justices Marshall and Stewart supported Brennan's blanket and absolute prohibition on all such gag orders. The positions taken by Justices White, Powell, and Stevens on the "absolute ban" issue, therefore, became the critical components of the Court's ultimate conclusion, and the record on their viewpoints during the conference is regrettably murky.

Because the Court unanimously concluded that the Nebraska gag order should be rejected, and because Chief Justice Burger was therefore in the majority with respect to that disposition of the case, he took control of the assignment of the opinion. As he often did in cases he considered to be particularly important, Burger opted to write the opinion himself. Woodward and Armstrong report in *The Brethren* that Brennan "exploded" when he learned that Burger had taken the opinion for himself, believing that it should have been given to "one of the five Justices in the mainstream, someone who favored an absolute ban."[24] Nevertheless, on June 7, 1976, Burger circulated to his colleagues a draft opinion in which he sought, in the words of his covering memorandum, "to express the views of all but those who would regard prior restraint barred in all cases and for whatever reason."[25] The chief further explained, "My own reexamination of all the relevant cases suggests that [a justification for a pretrial gag order] is very difficult to make under the First Amendment as construed by the Court, but neither is it a total impossibility, as yet; and this case does not call for going that far."[26]

As the chief prepared his draft opinion, Brennan, with some misgivings, authorized his clerks to draft a counter-opinion expressing the views of what he believed to be the "real majority."[27] Immediately after Burger's draft was released, Brennan allowed his clerks to release and circulate their counter-draft, accompanied by a cover memorandum that highlighted the apparent confusion over the consensus reached among the justices at the conference. Brennan's draft held that prior restraints against pretrial publicity were "forever barred"—a conclusion that he "thought was the conference consensus."[28]

Woodward and Armstrong suggest that Burger was "insulted" and "infuriated" by Brennan's challenge, viewing it as a "premeditated attempt to steal the majority."[29] The chief responded immediately with a memorandum back to Brennan. "Dear Bill," he wrote, "If the conference consensus was as you suggest, to 'forever bar prior restraint' on pretrial publicity, I would be prepared to articulate that, but that is not my recollection."[30] Burger also circulated a memorandum to all the rest of the justices, asking for clarification of their positions on that point. Specifically, he asked "whether a majority of the conference is willing in this case 'to forever bar prior restraint on pretrial publicity.'"[31]

Justice Powell, for one, wrote back to the chief, stating, "In my view, it is not necessary to go so far—certainly in the case before us. Nor did I understand that a majority of the conference voted to hold that never, under any conceivable circumstances, would a court have the power to restrain pretrial publicity even for the briefest period of time. I have not thought that our previous decisions justify such a sweeping conclusion."[32] Meanwhile, Marshall and Stewart had almost immediately joined Brennan's competing draft. Thus, the issue fell to Justices White and Stevens. Ultimately both joined in the chief's rejection of the announcement of an absolute ban, though they both wrote their own short concurrences.

Thus, Burger's and Powell's recollections of the conference debate on that point seem to have carried the day, inasmuch as the chief justice's draft, with a few minor changes, ultimately became the dispositive opinion for six members of the Court in *Nebraska Press Association*. Whatever ambiguity may exist regarding the justices' discussions in conference or elsewhere, the Supreme Court speaks officially only through its formal opinions. In the final analysis, then, whatever goes on behind the closed doors of the justices' chambers or the conference room is relevant only academically. Both practically and legally, all that matters are the conclusions and reasoning contained in the final opinions issued by the Court, and it is to them that we now turn in the *Nebraska Press Association* litigation.

The formal announcement of Supreme Court opinions is yet another of the Court's procedures that is steeped in tradition. Until the 1930s, the members of the Court read their opinions verbatim from the bench—a practice that could be "tedious or exciting, depending on the nature of the case and the eloquence of the opinion and the style of its oral delivery."[33] In the early years of the Court's operation, the reading of opinions took up literally days of the justices' time. Beginning with the administration of Chief Justice Charles Evan Hughes in 1930, however, the announcement of opinions began to evolve toward a more streamlined procedure. Hughes encouraged his colleagues to save time by delivering only summaries of their opinions, and that practice has become the norm in recent years. Former Chief Justice William H. Rehnquist described the process as follows: "The author of the opinion will describe the case, summarize the reasoning of the Court, announce the result, and announce whatever separate or dissenting opinions have been filed."[34]

In addition to the oral reading of the decision, printed copies known as bench opinions are traditionally made available to members of the press and other interested observers in the Court gallery. At or near the same time, the Government Printing Office produces thousands of copies of the decision, known as slip opinions, for distribution to federal and state courts and agencies. Recent developments in computer technology have, of course, altered some of these traditional procedures. Today, Supreme Court decisions are almost instantaneously posted electronically and available free of charge on the Court's official website and are available on dozens of legal databases, such as *Westlaw* and *Lexis,* within minutes of their release.[35]

In the summer of 1976, however, those electronic advances were still some twenty years away, and so the decision in the *Nebraska Press Association* case emerged in the traditional manner, by oral delivery from the bench and subsequent printing and dissemination of the full opinions. On June 30, 1976, Chief Justice Warren Burger and the rest of the Court took the bench and, after dispensing with various other items of Court business, the chief announced the Court's disposition of the Nebraska gag order litigation. With little drama or fanfare, Burger announced that the gag order imposed against the Nebraska press in the Simants criminal proceedings had been deemed to be an unconstitutional violation of the First Amendment rights of the members of the press affected by it and that the decision of the Nebraska Supreme Court upholding the order was, therefore, reversed. The Nebraska Press Association and the other petitioners had won. It was not, however, quite as complete a victory as they had sought.

The opinion crafted for the Court by the chief justice runs to just more than thirty-two pages as printed in the Court's official collection of opinions, *U.S. Reports.*[36] While it serves as the official decision of the Court in the case, Burger's decision is technically only a plurality opinion, inasmuch as only three members of the Court joined it without further comment. Justices White, Powell, and Stevens each filed short concurring opinions expressing slight variations on or additions to Burger's reasoning, and Justice Brennan entered a much lengthier concurrence, joined by Justices Stewart and Marshall, expressing his desire for a complete prohibition on all gag orders on pretrial journalistic publicity. Including those separate opinions, the full report of the Court's disposition of the Nebraska case runs to some seventy-eight pages in *U.S. Reports.*

Burger's opinion for the Court began with a relatively brief recitation of the facts surrounding the murders of the Kellie family and the widespread news coverage that Simants's arrest for the crimes attracted in and around Sutherland and North Platte. The chief then provided a comprehensive overview of the complex procedural path the case had taken on its way to the high court, including the various versions of the gag order entered by Judges Ruff and Stuart in the Lincoln County courts, the modifications ordered by Justice Blackmun in his chambers opinions, and the final order entered by the Nebraska Supreme Court. He concluded this introductory portion of the opinion by noting that "we are informed by the parties that [in the time] since we granted certiorari, Simants has been convicted of murder and sentenced to death."[37]

Burger's acknowledgment that Simants's trial had already been completed during the pendency of the Supreme Court appeal provided him with a convenient and natural segue into the first legal issue taken up in his opinion—the question of mootness. As previously discussed, the respondents had argued in their briefs that the Supreme Court should not entertain the petitioners' appeal because the gag order had expired by its own terms once a jury was seated in the Simants prosecution. Therefore, the argument went, the question of the constitutionality of the order would become dormant or, in legal jargon, moot, long before the high court ruled. Burger disposed of this assertion rather quickly by referring to, and relying upon, the long-recognized exception to the mootness doctrine that had been thoroughly briefed by the parties. In cases where the controversy between the litigants is likely to be repeated, yet continually evades judicial review, the Court will decide the case in order to resolve the issue, even where the particular action that is in dispute between the immediate parties has expired or otherwise become inoperative.

Burger concluded that the Nebraska gag order controversy was capable of repetition in two senses. First, he noted that if the Nebraska Supreme Court ultimately overturned Simants's conviction for the

Kellie murders and returned the case to the district court for retrial, the question of pretrial publicity might be resurrected, and the trial court judge might be inclined to enter another gag order to address the matter.[38] Moreover, Burger added, the decision of the Nebraska Supreme Court upholding the gag order essentially authorized prosecutors and defense attorneys throughout Nebraska to seek such orders in similar cases in the future. If and when such orders were entered, their constitutionality would likely continue to escape review, because the gags were, he declared, "by [their] nature short-lived."[39] Accordingly, Burger held that the issue was not moot, and he proceeded to an analysis of the substantive constitutional issues at stake.

Burger began the next portion of his opinion with a review of the free press/fair trial tension in American constitutional history. He noted that, although the framers of the Bill of Rights had not specifically addressed or resolved the potential clash between the First and Sixth Amendments, "it is inconceivable that [they] were unaware of the potential conflicts between the right to an unbiased jury and the guarantee of freedom of the press."[40] Burger concluded that the founders deliberately left such problems for future resolution, because they wanted to leave no doubt that "their chief concern was the need for freedom of expression in the political arena and the dialogue in ideas."[41]

Nevertheless, Burger continued, the risks to Sixth Amendment rights posed by an unfettered press were not long in revealing themselves, as in the 1807 trial for treason of the then-sitting vice president, Aaron Burr. In that notorious case, Burger noted, Supreme Court Chief Justice John Marshall, serving as the trial judge, had to conduct an extensive voir dire of potential jurors to find a panel that had not been tainted by the widespread, politically charged publicity surrounding Burr's arrest. Marshall's experience in the Burr trial, Burger indicated, "makes clear that the problem is not a new one."[42]

Burger proceeded to discuss more recent judicial experiences with the free press/fair trial conflict, such as the infamous trial of Bruno Hauptmann in a small New Jersey community for the abduction and murder of Ann and Charles Lindbergh's infant child in 1935. The frenzied media coverage surrounding that trial was heavily criticized both inside and outside the legal community, with commentators uniformly pointing out that "much of [that] sorry performance could have been controlled by a vigilant trial judge."[43] Contrasting that uncontrolled environment in the Lindbergh case with the Nebraska scenario, Burger repeatedly expressed respect and admiration for Judges Ruff and Stuart, as well as the prosecutors and defense counsel in the Simants litigation, for their well-intentioned attempts to deal with the constitutional dilemma they faced. In a footnote, he stated, "The record reveals that counsel for both sides acted responsibly in this case, and there is no suggestion that either sought to use pretrial news coverage for partisan advantage."[44]

With that historical perspective as a backdrop, Burger came at last to the determinative portion of his opinion—a direct evaluation of the appropriate balance between the First and Sixth Amendment concerns presented in the Nebraska situation. He began by citing with approval a long series of Court decisions, beginning with *Near v. Minnesota* in 1931 and continuing through *New York Times Co. v. United States* in 1971, in which the Court had consistently expressed the view that prior restraints on news publication are presumptively unconstitutional—that is, they "come to this Court with a heavy presumption against [their] constitutional validity."[45] "The thread running through all of these cases," Burger stated, "is that prior restraints on speech and publication are the most serious and the least tolerable infringement on First Amendment rights."[46]

Thus, the question became whether the evidentiary record before the Court in the Nebraska case justified the use of such an extraordinary and "presumptively unconstitutional" order entered by the state court judges. Burger's analysis of that issue essentially reduced itself to three lines of inquiry: the nature, extent, and probable impact of the publicity attendant to the Kellie murders and Simants's arrest; the availability and utility of other less-restrictive measures to mitigate the impact of the pretrial publicity; and the effectiveness and practicality of the gag order as a mechanism for dealing with the problem.

On the first issue, Burger concluded that Judge Stuart had been "justified in concluding that there would be intense and pervasive pretrial publicity" surrounding Simants's prosecution.[47] Moreover,

Burger noted, Stuart could "reasonably conclude, based on common human experience, that publicity might impair the defendant's right to a fair trial."[48] Again, Burger expressed his respect for Stuart's handling of the dilemma he faced, noting that his conclusion regarding the possible impact of the publicity was "of necessity speculative, dealing as he was with factors unknown and unknowable." Stuart's actions, he declared, had been taken "responsibly, out of a legitimate concern, in an effort to protect the defendant's right to a fair trial."[49]

Still, Burger continued, the Court had repeatedly held that pretrial publicity, even in cases where it is widespread and pervasive, "cannot be regarded as leading automatically and in every kind of criminal case to an unfair trial."[50] The trial judge's most delicate and difficult task, Burger stated, was to decide what precautionary steps will suffice to mitigate the adverse effects of publicity, without unduly infringing on the press's near-sacred constitutional freedoms. On that point, Burger turned, as the parties had done in their briefs and oral arguments, to the 1966 *Sheppard v. Maxwell* decision, in which the Court had excoriated an Ohio trial court judge for his failure to protect a well-known criminal defendant, Dr. Sam Sheppard, from what the Court called the "inherently prejudicial" media uproar attendant to his trial for the murder of his wife. The *Sheppard* decision enumerated a series of measures that the Ohio trial court judge could have and should have implemented to protect Sheppard's rights, including extensive voir dire of jurors, strong jury admonitions, sequestration, change of venue, or a postponement of the trial until the tumultuous publicity dissipated.

Examining the efficacy of those types of less-restrictive measures in the environment surrounding the Simants prosecution, Burger concluded that the respondents in the case—the state of Nebraska, the Nebraska Supreme Court, and Judge Stuart himself—had failed to make an adequate showing that such alternatives would not have sufficed to protect Simants's rights. "Although the entry of the [gag] order [by Judge Stuart] might be read as a judicial determination that other measures would not suffice," Burger stated, "the trial court made no express finding to that effect . . . [and] the Nebraska Supreme Court did no more than imply that such measures might not be adequate. Moreover, the record is lacking in evidence to support such a finding."[51] In the absence of such a showing, Burger concluded, the Nebraska gag order could not overcome the presumption of unconstitutionality that attached to it.

The chief justice also addressed the practical jurisdictional problems associated with the management and enforcement of gag orders in cases like the Simants prosecution. He noted that an order which sought to control the activities of newspapers and media outlets all over the country, rather than merely restraining publication within a limited geographic area, is of very dubious effectiveness. A court trying to issue such an order could not possibly obtain the necessary personal jurisdiction over all of the media personnel it seeks to restrain. In other words, in a case that is being covered by media from around the country, a local trial court could not possibly monitor and punish transgressions of its gag order wherever they might occur, particularly when there is no way to ensure that all the national media are even aware of the order, much less legally bound by its terms.

Furthermore, Burger noted, even if a gag order did serve its intended purpose of stopping the release of information to the public via the media, "it is reasonable to assume, without any news accounts being printed or broadcast, that rumors would travel swiftly by word of mouth . . . [which] could well be more damaging than reasonably accurate news accounts."[52] Accordingly, he concluded, it was far from clear, as a practical matter, that Judge Stuart's order would have protected Simants's right to an unbiased jury even if it was otherwise constitutionally sound.

In the final portion of his opinion, Burger addressed the issues that the Nebraska media and their supporters had emphasized most vigorously in their briefs—the gag order's attempt to prohibit the publication of information (such as Simants's confession) obtained from an open preliminary hearing and the language of the order that purported to prohibit publication of information "strongly implicative of the accused as the perpetrator of the slayings." The chief justice made short work of those issues, siding squarely with the media on both points. As to the prohibition on information gleaned from open court records or from a public hearing, Burger held that the attempt to restrain the publication of such material "plainly violated settled principles."[53] Nothing in any of the Court's previous holdings, he stated, justified a restraint on the dissemination of material that was freely available in open court proceedings. With respect to the language of the order barring the publication of material "strongly implicative" of Simants's guilt, Burger was even more direct and succinct. He held that those words were simply "too vague and too broad to survive the scrutiny we have given to restraints on First Amendment rights."[54]

Thus, with respect to the constitutionality of the particular order issued in the Nebraska litigation, the Court decided clearly and unanimously in favor of the Nebraska media. Burger held that "reasonable minds can have few doubts about the gravity of the evil pretrial publicity can work, but the probability that it would do so here was not demonstrated with the degree of certainty our cases on prior restraint require."[55] Accordingly, he held, "the judgment of the Nebraska Supreme Court is reversed."[56]

Still, in light of the vagaries of the conference debate on the case, a larger and more fundamental question remained in dispute. Were there *any* conceivable circumstances under which a pretrial judicial gag on the press might be justified? In his opinion, Burger went to great lengths to emphasize that the Court was *not* ruling that a prior restraint could *never* be employed. In his penultimate paragraph, he explicitly placed himself in opposition to an absolutist position on that point, stating, "We reaffirm that the guarantees of freedom of expression are not an absolute prohibition under all circumstances, but the barriers to prior restraint remain high and the presumption against its use continues intact."[57]

Burger's opinion was joined in its entirety and without further comment by only two of his fellow justices—Blackmun and Rehnquist. Each of the remaining justices sought to express their own views on the absolutist issue, and their separate concurring opinions left that question very much in doubt when the dust finally settled on the *Nebraska Press Association* litigation.

In a one-paragraph concurrence, Justice Byron White noted that, although he joined in the chief justice's final disposition of the case, he had grave doubt whether gag orders against the press in the realm of pretrial publicity would ever be justifiable.[58] Perhaps, he suggested, the Court should wait to make a final decision on that question until it had been exposed to a "broader spectrum of cases presenting similar issues." He added, however, that if the Court's decisions in future cases turned out to be similar to this one, "we should at some point announce a more general rule and avoid the interminable litigation that our failure to do so would necessarily entail."[59]

Justice Lewis Powell weighed in with an equally brief concurring opinion, explaining that "in view of the importance of the case," he wished to "emphasize the unique burden that rests upon a party . . . who undertakes to show the necessity for prior restraint on pretrial publicity."[60] Powell proceeded to enunciate specific evidentiary standards he felt would have to be met before any such restraint could be issued, and he left the very clear impression that he believed those standards would be virtually impossible to meet under almost any circumstances.

In a much lengthier and more elaborate concurring opinion joined by Justices Potter Stewart and Thurgood Marshall, William Brennan presented an eloquent and compelling justification for an absolute ban on pretrial gag orders against the press. Three decades after its issuance, Brennan's concurrence in *Nebraska Press Association* remains one of the most direct and vigorous affirmations of the primacy of the First Amendment ever authored by a member of the Court. Brennan emphasized that the press's constitutional liberties and responsibilities were especially important in the realm of the criminal justice system, declaring that

> Commentary and reporting on the criminal justice system is at the core of First Amendment values, for the operation and integrity of that system is of crucial import to citizens concerned with the administration of justice. Secrecy of judicial action can only breed ignorance and distrust of courts and suspicion concerning the competence and impartiality of judges; free and robust reporting, criticism, and debate can contribute to public understanding of the rule of law and comprehension of the functioning of the entire criminal justice system, as well as improve the quality of that system by subjecting it to the cleansing effects of exposure and public accountability.[61]

That critical role played by the media, Brennan continued, had been recognized and protected in scores of judicial decisions handed down through the previous generations and was now so firmly established that the time was right for a clear declaration by the Court, that "there can be no prohibition on the publication by the press of any information pertaining to pending judicial proceedings . . . no matter how shabby the means by which the information is obtained."[62] Such a holding, Brennan cautioned, would not constitute a complete subordination of Sixth Amendment rights to those afforded the press under the First, "for an accused's right to a fair trial may be adequately assured through methods that do not infringe First Amendment values."[63]

In coming to that conclusion, Brennan was accepting and reiterating one of the most fundamental arguments advanced by the media petitioners in their briefs and during the oral arguments in the case several months before—that there was no need to resolve, or even deal with, a purported conflict between the First and the Sixth Amendments in these situations, because there were so many alternatives short of a gag order available to trial court judges to protect a defendant's Sixth Amendment rights. Referring once again to all the methods identified in *Sheppard v. Maxwell* and other previous decisions, including extensive voir dire, sequestration of jurors, and change of venue, Brennan concluded that "the traditional techniques approved in *Sheppard* for ensuring fair trials would have been adequate in every case in which we have found that a new trial was required due to lack of fundamental fairness to the accused."[64]

Brennan reserved some of his most forceful and memorable language for the final paragraphs of his opinion. "Although there may in some instances be tension between uninhibited and robust reporting by the press and fair trials for criminal defendants," he stated, "judges possess adequate tools short of [gag orders] for relieving that tension."[65] "It may be," he continued, "that . . . the media, in an exercise of self-restraint, would choose not to publicize [inflammatory and prejudicial] material, and not make the judicial task of safeguarding precious rights of criminal defendants more difficult."[66] Still, he concluded, "the press may be arrogant, tyrannical, abusive, and sensationalist, just as it may be incisive, probing, and informative. But at least in the context of prior restraints on publication, the decision of what, when, and how to publish is for editors, not judges."[67]

The final concurrence in the case was filed by the Court's newest member, John Paul Stevens. In his brief opinion, Stevens announced that he subscribed to most of what he called Brennan's "eloquent" reasoning.[68] Nevertheless, he wrote, he was not convinced that an absolute ban on pretrial gag orders should apply "no matter how shabby or illegal the means by which the information is obtained . . . [and] no matter how demonstrably false the information [that would be disclosed] might be."[69] Those types of situations, he suggested, required further argument and deliberation by the Court. He concluded, however, that if and when he was ever required to address those issues squarely, he "may well accept [Brennan's] ultimate conclusion."[70]

Thus, when the five separate opinions entered in the *Nebraska Press Association* litigation are considered collectively, the full import of the Court's decision becomes rather muddled. Justices Blackmun and Rehnquist unqualifiedly supported the chief's plurality opinion, which firmly struck down the Nebraska gag order, but explicitly preserved the possibility of such prior restraints in future cases. Just as clearly, Justices Marshall and Stewart supported Brennan's call for an absolute ban on all such orders in all cases. The concurring opinions of Justices White, Powell, and Stevens suggested their authors' considerable support for the Brennan position but expressed an unwillingness to announce an absolute ban under the facts of the Nebraska case.

Despite that lingering ambiguity regarding the viability of pretrial gag orders in other cases, the announcement of the *Nebraska Press Association* decision left two matters quite clear: the order entered by the Nebraska courts in the Simants litigation had been unanimously rejected by the high court, and the presumptive unconstitutionality of all such prior restraints of the press had been strongly reiterated. Under any interpretation of the justices' various opinions, the net result was a significant victory for First Amendment advocates in general and for the Nebraska media petitioners in particular. They and the rest of the national press quickly took notice of their accomplishment.

Not surprisingly, the *Omaha World-Herald* led the way in reporting the Court's action, splashing the headline "Court Rules for Press in Nebraska Gag Case" across the front page of its evening edition on the day the decision was announced, June 30, 1976. The *World-Herald*'s stories that night and in the following day's editions described the decision as a landmark victory for the First Amendment and included extensive quotations from the justices' multiple opinions. *World-Herald* president Harold Anderson hailed the decision as "a significant victory not only for 'freedom of the press,' but more importantly for the public and its right to know what goes on in public courtrooms."[71] Anderson's executive assistant and *World-Herald* Vice President Woody Howe echoed those sentiments, declaring, "It's not just a victory for the newspapers and the broadcasters. It's a victory for the people."[72]

Similarly, a representative of the Reporters Committee for Freedom of the Press (RCFP) characterized the decision as a major victory for the First Amendment.[73] A. M. Rosenthal, managing editor of the *New York Times*, described himself as obviously delighted, declaring that the decision "strengthens the First Amendment."[74] The Iowa Broadcast News Association said the decision was "a cause for joy," while Joe D. Smith, Jr., chairman of the American Newspaper Publishers Association, termed it a "proper and firm setback to secrecy."[75]

Many of the initial news accounts included reaction from some of the key participants in the litigation. In North Platte, Judge Hugh Stuart was asked whether he still felt that he had been correct in issuing the gag order and responded, "Obviously, I've been reversed. I can't be right when I've been reversed."[76] Stuart went on to indicate that he felt certain the Supreme Court's decision would "cut down on the number of gag orders that are being entered," and he sharply disagreed with Justice Brennan's concurring opinion advocating a complete ban on all such prior restraints of the press.[77] "I'm glad [Brennan's position] is not the law of the land, but a minority opinion," Stuart said.[78]

Lincoln County Court Judge Ronald Ruff, who had issued the first gag order in the Simants litigation eight months before, seemed less disturbed than Stuart with the high court's ruling, stating, "I am just glad they came down with a ruling so that courts will have some guidelines on this. In October 1975, we did not know exactly what the law was, and had to do the best we could."[79] Similarly, Lincoln County Attorney Milton Larson, one of the attorneys who had argued the case before the Supreme Court, expressed hope that "we will find definitive guidelines when we're able to read the full decision."[80] "I will be disappointed," he continued, "if all the court has done is leave us high and dry again."[81]

Major newspapers across the country reported the decision with equal emphasis and, in some cases, in even more exultant tones. The *Chicago Tribune, Los Angeles Times, Wall Street Journal, Washington Post,* and *New York Times* featured the decision on the front pages of their July 1 editions, with large and dramatic headlines such as "Court Sharply Curbs Power of Judges to Gag Press" and "Court Voids Gag Nebraska Judges Placed on Press."[82] Editorials lauding the Court's action either accompanied or quickly followed the news stories in most urban papers, with many taking note of the juxtaposition of the Court's decision with the nation's bicentennial celebration—an event that was dominating the news around the time of the *Nebraska Press Association* decision.

In a July 3 editorial titled "Freedom of the Press in 1976," the *Washington Post* declared, "It is thoroughly appropriate that on the eve of the nation's Bicentennial the Supreme Court should have confronted directly and thoughtfully a critical question having to do with the exercise of First Amendment rights. Without those rights . . . and without the staunch protection the Court has given them during most of the last 200 years, it seems safe to say we would not have much to celebrate this weekend."[83] Similarly, the *Los Angeles Times* editorialized that the Nebraska gag order had been issued "with an almost cavalier disregard of the First Amendment" and described the Court's decision as "primarily a victory for the people's right to be informed by an unintimidated and unshackled press."[84]

The *New York Times* weighed in with an editorial titled "Press Freedom Upheld," which noted that the Court had "taken a significant step toward protecting the freedom of the press against already alarming erosion."[85] The *World-Herald's* editorial comment on the decision reiterated the importance of the Court's action in "main-

Editorial cartoon by George Fischer, *Omaha World-Herald,* July 2, 1976. Reprinted with permission from the *Omaha World-Herald.*

taining the flow of information on which the workings of a free society depends" and was accompanied by a large editorial cartoon depicting the Statue of Liberty with a biblike swath of cloth around its neck, suggesting a gag that had just been removed from Lady Liberty's mouth.

Despite the generally celebratory tone of the editorials and news accounts related to the decision, most of the more-detailed assessments of the high court's action were tempered by an acknowledgment of the lingering uncertainty over the future viability of judicial gag orders in all circumstances. For example, Roderick W. Beaton, president of United Press International, characterized the result as only "90 per cent good news . . . the refusal [of the majority] to bar prior restraint entirely leaves room for overzealous judges to overreact in an attempt to muzzle the press."[86] Likewise, the elation voiced by the RCFP was mitigated by the recognition that, "unfortunately, the decision does not say—as we hoped it would—that the 1st Amendment absolutely stops judges from restraining publication of news about the courts."[87] The *Washington Post* emphasized that the chief justice's majority opinion was "something less than a full vindication of the First Amendment" and went on to suggest that the continuing uncertainty over the "completeness" of the media's victory "casts a shadow over the [First Amendment's] vital guarantees."[88]

The *World-Herald*'s Howe produced one of the most comprehensive assessments of the short-term impact of the *Nebraska Press Association* decision. In an article published in the August 1976 edition of *The Nebraska Newspaper,* a trade periodical for the state's professional journalists, Howe pondered many of the questions that remained unanswered in the immediate aftermath of the high court's action. He asked rhetorically, "Did the press win or lose? Was it worth it? Will the press be faced with more lawsuits over gag orders?"[89] After a thoughtful and measured analysis of the five separate opinions issued by the justices, Howe concluded, "This much can be said: The court's unanimous decision makes it highly unlikely that a trial judge could ever again issue a gag order directly against the press that would be viewed as constitutional. If that is true, and only time will tell, then the achievement of the Nebraska news media . . . amounts to one of the most significant First Amendment victories of the century."[90]

Howe's 1976 prediction has proven to be remarkably accurate. Time has indeed revealed the impressive breadth and the depth of the impact of the Nebraska media's accomplishment. Before moving on to a more thorough assessment of the decision's historical legacy, however, it must be noted once again that the gag order conflict was only one of the legal stories that emanated from the murders of the Kellie family on that terrible night in Sutherland, Nebraska, in the fall of 1975. The criminal prosecution of Erwin Simants for those crimes remained to be completed, and the story of those proceedings would weave a long and complex path of its own through the Nebraska state court system for many years after the constitutional litigation was over.

eIGHT

The Continuing Saga of the Simants Criminal Prosecutions and the Legacy of *Nebraska Press Association*

It is the judgment of this Court that you, Erwin Charles Simants, be put to death . . . by passing through your body a current of electricity of sufficient intensity to cause death.

LINCOLN COUNTY DISTRICT JUDGE HUGH STUART
January 29, 1976

Erwin Charles Simants eventually will go free. . . .
How soon is uncertain.

Omaha World-Herald
October 18, 1979

T here can be little dispute that the Supreme Court's decision in *Nebraska Press Association v. Stuart* has become a "landmark" opinion in constitutional history. It must be remembered, however, that it was only one of several important legal stories to emerge from the events that occurred in Sutherland, Nebraska, on that terrible evening in October 1975. Erwin Simants viciously murdered six innocent people that night, and the state of Nebraska's prosecution and punishment of Simants for those crimes is a saga that continues to reverberate throughout the state, long after most people who are not lawyers or journalists have forgotten about the complex Supreme Court litigation.

The Simants criminal proceedings plied a tortuous path through the state court system that included two full jury trials and multiple appeals to the U.S. and Nebraska Supreme Courts. The net result of all that legal maneuvering is that Simants today stands acquitted of the Kellie murders by reason of insanity. He is housed at the Regional Mental Health Center in Lincoln, Nebraska, where his mental condition is reviewed annually. It is possible, though perhaps unlikely, that he might someday walk free. The long chain of events that led to that result raises controversial and often emotional questions about many elements of the American criminal justice system, including jury trial procedures, the death penalty, and the insanity defense. It is a story that deserves to be remembered.

At the preliminary hearing on October 22, 1975, District Judge Hugh Stuart scheduled Simants's trial for the Kellie murders to begin on January 5, 1976. In the months leading up to the trial, the Nebraska media continued to abide by the terms of Stuart's existing gag order, as their appeals of its constitutionality proceeded through the higher courts. Despite that muting of the media, however, rumors and speculation about the murders continued to permeate the community, and journalists continued to question and probe the limits of what they could publish consistent with the terms of the gag order. Their uncertainty was exacerbated by the modifications that were made to the order, first by Justice Harry Blackmun of the U.S. Supreme Court and later by the Nebraska Supreme Court.[1]

The ongoing friction between the press, Judge Stuart, and the trial attorneys was reflected in several attempts by Simants's attorneys to restrict the media's coverage of the pretrial proceedings even beyond the parameters of the existing gag order. Two weeks before the trial was scheduled to begin, defense attorneys Leonard Vyhnalek and Keith Bystrom filed a motion asking Judge Stuart for an order "completely closing any and all hearings to be held on any and all motions filed . . . prior to the trial scheduled for January 5, 1976."[2] Following a hearing on December 29, Stuart entered an order in which he denied the defense's request for a blanket order closing all future pretrial proceedings, but he expressly authorized the defense attorneys to file another such motion to address specific concerns about media coverage that might arise up until the moment the gag order expired with the seating of a jury in the case.[3] Several days later, Vyhnalek and Bystrom took Stuart up on that invitation.

On the afternoon of Friday, January 2, 1976, the defense attorneys filed a motion asking that Judge Stuart bar the press from attending and reporting on the voir dire of potential jurors that would occur at the beginning of the trial.[4] In their motion, they argued that the questioning of prospective jurors might involve the disclosure of "certain information which may or may not be admissible at trial" and that the dissemination of such information could taint the impartiality of other prospective jurors before they were questioned.[5] In response to that motion, Stuart convened an unusual meeting with members of the press before beginning the jury selection process on January 5, during which he asked them to sign voluntarily an agreement promising not to report or publish certain types of information that might be disclosed during the voir dire process. Unwilling to voluntarily capitulate to that type of prior restraint, and offended at the judge's affront to their professional ethics, all of the journalists present at the meeting refused to sign the agreement and opted simply not to enter the courtroom or report on the jury selection.[6]

With all of that skirmishing as prelude, jury selection began in the Simants murder trial on the morning of January 5, 1976. More than 100 citizens of Lincoln County were called to form the jury pool, with 72 of them ultimately questioned during the voir dire process. Ironically—in light of what the Nebraska media was, at that same time, arguing in the appellate courts—the questioning of the potential jurors in the Simants trial provided a vivid illustration of the dubious efficacy of pretrial gags of the press in prominent criminal cases. According to later reports, more than a third of the prospective jurors queried by the attorneys and Judge Stuart admitted that they had already formed some opinion with respect to Simants's guilt.[7] Of that number, however, less than half identified the press coverage of the crimes as the source of their "prejudgment." Many of the others cited friendship with the Kellies, conversations with some of the witnesses, discussions at work, or other word-of-mouth sources as the key factors in the formation of their pretrial opinions. Even more ironically, four of the prospective jurors who acknowledged that they had already formed impressions of the case were ultimately accepted onto the jury despite those admissions, after declaring that they could and would weigh the testimony and evidence with an open mind.[8]

After three days of voir dire, a final panel was selected by the late afternoon of Wednesday, January 7, and the trial was set to begin on the following morning. That evening, Judge Stuart met with members of the media in yet another remarkable impromptu session. The meeting occurred as a result of Stuart's acceptance of a request for an interview from several out-of-state reporters, and it evolved into a full-scale press conference that lasted almost two hours. More than a dozen reporters, including representatives from the *Washington Post, Chicago Tribune,* and *Denver Post,* took part in the session, which was later described as a "congenial, wide-ranging discussion" in which Stuart was at all times "gracious and polite."[9]

Stuart indicated that he believed that the questioning of the prospective jurors had confirmed the necessity and effectiveness of his gag order, since a good percentage of the jury pool said they had not formed an opinion as to Simants's guilt—a result that Stuart felt would not have been possible without his restrictions on the press.[10] An equally plausible counter-interpretation, of course, might have been that the fact that so many of the prospective jurors indicated that they had formed opinions about the case based on sources *other* than the media suggested that a gag on the press was of no real utility or effect. Moreover, the fact that four jurors had been accepted for the trial despite acknowledging some prior opinions about the case seemed to confirm one of the media's recurring arguments in the litigation over the gag order—that jurors can and do serve impartially even when they have been exposed to information about a case prior to trial.

Whatever the correct interpretation of the gag order's impact might have been, at 9:00 a.m. on the morning of January 8, Judge Stuart swore into service a jury composed of seven women and five men. With that act, the existing gag order against the press expired by its own terms, and unrestricted press coverage resumed.

Simants's trial was a traumatic and wrenching experience for all the participants. Over seven grueling days, prosecutors and defense counsel presented the testimony of more than thirty-five witnesses, many of whom offered chilling insights into the details of the horrifying murders.[11] The prosecution's evidence included dozens of gruesome photographs of the victims and the carnage at the crime scene, along with articles of the victims' clothing saturated and stiffened with dried blood and forensic evidence related to hair, fiber, and fingerprint analysis, all of which strongly connected Simants to the crimes.

The distressing impact of the trial on all the participants was poignantly demonstrated on the afternoon of Saturday, January 10, when prosecutor Marvin Holscher was briefly overcome by revulsion while offering into evidence several graphic photographs of the victims. Choked with emotion, Holscher asked for and received a short recess, after which defense counsel Vyhnalek asked the court to declare a mistrial due to Holscher's action, calling it an improper "commentary" on the evidence. Holscher apologized for the incident, assuring Judge Stuart that it had not been staged for theatrical impact. Stuart agreed, and overruled the motion for mistrial.[12]

The jury also heard testimony from Simants's nephew and his parents describing his confession of his crimes to each of them. Most tellingly and excruciatingly, the jury heard the defendant's taped confession to Sheriff Gilster and the other investigators on the morning after the murders, during which he admitted the cold-blooded killing of all six victims, along with the initial sexual assault on eleven-year-old Florence and his subsequent sexual molestation of the dead bodies of Marie and Deanna.[13]

The defense did not attempt to deny that Simants had committed the murders. They claimed, however, that he was not guilty by reason of insanity. Under Nebraska law at that time, a defendant's assertion of insanity placed the burden of proof on the prosecution to prove beyond a reasonable doubt that the defendant was in fact sane at the time of the crimes—that is, the state had to prove that he was able to understand the nature and quality of his actions and was able to distinguish between right and wrong at the time of the crime.[14] In an attempt to show that Simants lacked that capacity, Vyhnalek and Bystrom presented the testimony of two expert witnesses, clinical psychologist Dr. Sam Campanella and psychiatrist Dr. Jack R. Anderson, both from the Great Plains Mental Health Center in North Platte. Campanella and Anderson testified that Simants suffered from mild mental retardation, alcoholism, and various forms of psychoses and sociopathic disabilities.[15] In light of those mental infirmities, they concluded, he had been unable to "appreciate the quality of his acts, now or then."[16]

In response to the defense claims, prosecutors Larson and Holscher offered the testimony of three experts of their own, clinical psychologist Dr. Steven Scott from Seward, Nebraska, and psychiatrists Dr. Emmitt Kenney of Omaha and Dr. Eli Chesen of Lincoln. Each testified that Simants suffered from no discernible "organic brain damage or intellectual deficiency" sufficient to be considered mentally retarded and that he functioned at a capacity that was well within Nebraska's legal definition of "sanity" for purposes of responsibility for criminal acts.[17]

On the afternoon of Friday, January 16, both the prosecution and the defense concluded their cases. Judge Stuart then spent more than an hour reading an elaborate set of instructions to the jury, describing the law of the insanity defense and other legal issues raised during the trial. He then dismissed the jurors from the courtroom, directing them to begin their deliberations immediately.

For the rest of that afternoon and into the evening, the jury met and discussed the testimony and reexamined the photographs and other physical evidence introduced at the trial. They also listened again to Simants's taped confession. Jury foreman Richard Anderson, an insurance adjuster from North Platte, later recalled that the bulk of the deliberations involved trying to apply Judge Stuart's instructions regarding the insanity defense to the testimony presented by the various "expert" witnesses. "The most complicated part was trying to understand the instructions," he said. "We thought it was kind of odd that the prosecution could come up with three expert witnesses and the defense with only two, [but we ultimately decided that] our layman's opinion was as good as theirs, after we listened to it all."[18]

The jury concluded their Friday evening deliberations with an initial 10–2 vote in favor of conviction, with the two dissenters wanting to accept Simants's claim of insanity.[19] The panel reconvened and voted again the following morning, with the same result. After listening yet again to Simants's recorded confession, the vote swung to 11–1, and after another hour of discussion, the final holdout switched her vote, bringing the unanimity required for conviction. Anderson indicated that the tension in the jury room ran quite high during these sessions, as "one juror became quite emotional because she really wasn't sure we were doing the right thing."[20] Juror Lila Davis, a telephone company employee from North Platte, told reporters later that she had not slept at all on Friday night and didn't think her fellow jurors did either. "It was the most difficult decision I've ever made in my life," she said.[21]

At 10:32 a.m. on Saturday, January 17, 1976, the jury announced its verdict, finding Simants guilty on all six counts of premeditated murder. As he stood to hear the verdict, and each individual juror's subsequent confirmation of their votes, Simants slouched slightly and shifted on his feet but betrayed no emotion.[22] His attorneys immediately asked the court to set aside the verdict on the grounds that it was not supported by the evidence, and Stuart quickly overruled the motion. Stuart announced that a sentencing hearing would be held at 1:30 p.m. on January 29, and then dismissed the exhausted jury from their troubling duties.

Under the Nebraska death penalty statute in effect at that time, a judge faced with the choice of imposing life imprisonment or capital punishment for a convicted defendant was required to consider a number of specifically enunciated aggravating or mitigating circumstances in making that critical decision.[23] In the twelve days between Simants's conviction and his sentencing, Judge Stuart reviewed the evidence produced at trial and compared it to those statutory standards. He also received and considered an investigative report prepared by state probation officials detailing Simants's life and background, as well as the written briefs and oral arguments of the prosecutors and defense counsel regarding the appropriateness of the death penalty in Simants's circumstances.

On January 29, Stuart announced his decision. Finding that "sufficient aggravating circumstances" existed to warrant the ultimate punishment, he ordered that Simants be put to death in the electric chair on April 21, 1976.[24] The aggravating circumstances cited by Stuart included the "heinous, atrocious, and exceptionally depraved nature" of the sexual assaults on at least two of the victims and the fact that five of the victims were killed in an effort to cover up the first crime, the assault and murder of eleven-year-old Florence. Stuart also took into account Simants's record of prior criminal activity, including twelve intoxication-related convictions, one conviction for contributing to the delinquency of a minor, and an apparent, though unprosecuted, act of statutory rape (evidenced by his fathering of a child by a fifteen-year-old girl).[25]

The defense attorneys had argued that Simants's sentence should be mitigated by his mental infirmities and by the fact that he had committed the murders while under the influence of alcohol. Stuart agreed that those were in fact mitigating circumstances but held that they did not overcome the aggravating factors that were otherwise present.[26]

As his fate was announced, Simants again listened impassively, while his sister, sitting near the front of the courtroom, wept quietly.[27] Having completed his duties by imposing the first death sentence he had handed down in eleven years on the bench, an emotionally drained Judge Stuart banged his gavel, adjourned the proceedings, and headed for a vacation. Prosecutors, gratified at the ruling, expressed a similar desire for rest and reflection. For those who wanted to see Erwin Simants escape the electric chair, however, there was little time to rest—the legal battles were only just beginning.

Nebraska law, then as now, provides for an automatic expedited appeal to the state supreme court in any case in which the death penalty has been imposed.[28] Pursuant to that procedure, on February 19, 1976, the Nebraska Supreme Court formally stayed Simants's execution, pending the completion of the automatic appeal.[29] After a series of delays and extensions, Simants's attorneys and the Nebraska attorney general's office filed their written briefs in the state high court on August 26 and October 26, respectively. Their legal arguments essentially centered on the constitutionality of the Nebraska death penalty statute and its application to the Simants facts.[30]

On February 2, 1977, the Nebraska Supreme Court affirmed Simants's conviction and upheld Judge Stuart's imposition of the death penalty for his crimes. In its opinion, the court confirmed that Stuart had given "careful consideration to each and every aggravating and mitigating factor pertaining to these offenses" and concluded that "he correctly found [that] the aggravating factors considerably outweigh the mitigating factors."[31] The court further held that, under its review of the trial record, the sentence of death imposed upon

Simants "was not improper or excessive" and that the Nebraska capital punishment statute "does not violate any of the provisions of the state or federal Constitutions."[32] Following that affirmance of Stuart's judgment, the Supreme Court announced a new date for Simants's execution, July 1, 1977.[33] Yet the matter was still far from over.

Two weeks before Simants's second scheduled date with the electric chair, his attorney Keith Bystrom, now aided by a new assistant public defender, Scott Helvie, filed a petition for a writ of certiorari with the U.S. Supreme Court. The request for review in the high court resulted in another stay of Simants's execution date, during the time necessary for the court to rule on Bystrom and Helvie's petition. On October 3, 1977, the Supreme Court denied the petition for certiorari.[34] The denial was entered as a one-sentence "memorandum decision" by the Court without elaboration or comment but was accompanied by a notice of dissent entered by Justices William Brennan and Thurgood Marshall. Consistent with their rulings in all death penalty appeals, those two justices wrote that "adhering to our views that the death penalty is in all circumstances cruel and unusual punishment prohibited by the Eighth and Fourteenth Amendments, . . . we would grant certiorari and vacate the death sentence in this case."[35]

After the Supreme Court rejected Simants's request, the Nebraska high court entered a new order establishing yet another date for his execution, January 21, 1978.[36] Bystrom and Helvie continued their procedural maneuvering, however, by filing a motion for rehearing with the Supreme Court. That request resulted in another temporary stay of execution, this one issued on October 26 by Justice Harry Blackmun, acting unilaterally as the presiding judge for the Eighth Circuit federal appellate court.[37] Blackmun's stay was short lived, however, as the full Supreme Court quickly entered an order denying the motion for rehearing. With that decision, the January 21 execution date was resurrected. Bystrom and Helvie appeared to be running out of options, and Simants was running out of time.

On January 5, 1978, just sixteen days before their client was scheduled to die in the electric chair, Bystrom and Helvie filed yet another procedural motion with the Nebraska Supreme Court. This one would ultimately save Erwin Simants's life.

In their new filing, the defense attorneys claimed that they had recently become aware of possible misconduct by Judge Hugh Stuart and Lincoln County Sheriff Gordon "Hop" Gilster in connection with the sequestration and supervision of the jury during Simants's trial two years before. Specifically, they alleged that, while the jury was sequestered at the Howard Johnson's Motel in North Platte, Judge Stuart made several trips to the motel and may have engaged in improper communications with members of the jury during those visits.[38] More significantly, they claimed that Sheriff Gilster, who had been a witness for the prosecution during the trial, had "conversed with and played cards with" members of the jury during their sequestration.[39] Finally, they claimed that some members of the jury had discussed the case and deliberated "long into the night while not in the jury deliberation room [at the courthouse] contrary to the expressed orders of Judge Stuart."[40] Those allegations were supported by several sworn affidavits from individuals who had witnessed some of those activities, including a statement by juror Claire Nicholas claiming that Sheriff Gilster had "conversed with and played cards with" members of the jury. A bailiff's affidavit stated that the sheriff would "sit and talk and play cards with members of the jury . . . as a matter of course."[41]

On the basis of these and other allegations, Bystrom and Helvie argued that many of Simants's constitutional rights had been violated, including the right to trial by a fair and impartial jury, and the right to due process of law. They asked the district court to issue "a writ of error *coram nobis*" setting aside Simants's conviction and death sentence, and granting him a new trial.[42]

As his attorneys had intended, the filing of this new petition (hereinafter referred to as the "*coram nobis* action") resulted in another delay of Simants's date with the electric chair. On January 9, and again on April 14, 1978, the state supreme court entered orders staying his execution until the new claims were resolved.[43] In the meantime, Bystrom and Helvie filed a motion asking Judge Stuart to disqualify himself from hearing and deciding the *coram nobis* action, inasmuch as he would have to be a witness in the upcoming hearing on their new claims.[44]

Deputy County Attorney Marvin Holscher vigorously opposed the defense's new allegations of improper jury contacts, as well as the request for disqualification of Judge Stuart. In responsive pleadings filed on January 23, Holscher lambasted Bystrom and Helvie for their tactics, calling their claims "scandalous and irrelevant" and characterizing the claims against Judge Stuart as "contrived for the sole purpose of creating an inference of unprofessional misconduct upon a respected member of our judiciary."[45] Two days later, after a brief hearing, Judge Stuart entered an order in which he ruled that "his impartiality in the case has not been reasonably questioned."[46] Nevertheless, he went on, it was important for the court to avoid even the appearance of impropriety, and he therefore withdrew from further handling of the *coram nobis* action. He appointed his colleague, District Judge Keith Windrum, to preside over future proceedings in the matter.

On May 2, a hearing on the new issues began before Judge Windrum. Many of the jurors from Simants's trial testified, as did Sheriff Gilster and Judge Stuart.[47] Stuart told the court that he had gone to the motel where the jury was being housed on two occasions during the trial, both times for the sole purpose of seeing that his sequestration orders were being properly carried out.[48] He remained at the hotel for only about ten to twenty minutes each time, conferring with his bailiffs or the hotel manager with respect to the sequestration arrangements. He testified that he had no conversations with members of the jury, except for an occasional cursory acknowledgment or polite response to a juror's greeting or comment. All other witnesses confirmed Stuart's testimony on those points.

Sheriff Gilster testified that he visited the Howard Johnson's motel on three occasions during the Simants trial.[49] He admitted that, on one of those visits, he conversed with members of the jury in one of the recreation rooms set aside for their use and, at the invitation of several jurors who were playing cards, sat in on three hands of blackjack, lasting for a period of six or seven minutes. Gilster also acknowledged that, on each of his visits to the motel, he engaged in discussions lasting from thirty minutes to an hour with members of the jury. There was conflict in the testimony regarding the content of those conversations. Gilster testified that his talks with the jurors were merely "general" in nature and said he did not recall discussing his experiences as sheriff at all. Many of the jurors, on the other hand, testified that Gilster had talked a good deal about his law enforcement experiences, with several recalling a specific conversation in which the sheriff told them about testifying at a criminal trial, during which the presiding judge had told him that "he was the only one who knew what he was talking about."[50] Others remembered Gilster demonstrating the use of the plastic handcuffs he kept in his hat, while some recalled the sheriff playing cards for more extended periods of time and occasionally demonstrating card tricks to the jurors.[51]

After two days of testimony, Judge Windrum issued his decision in the *coram nobis* action. He found that Judge Stuart's brief contacts with the jury at the motel had not been improper and did not constitute "prejudicial error."[52] He ruled that Sheriff Gilster's interactions with the jury, by contrast, were "unwarranted" and "erroneous" since he was a witness in the case. He went on to hold, however, that Gilster's contacts with the jury "did not effect [*sic*] the decision of the jury either consciously or unconsciously" and therefore the sheriff's actions "were not prejudicial to the defendant Simants."[53] Thus, Judge Windrum denied the defense's request for a new trial.

Helvie and Bystrom immediately appealed Windrum's decision to the Nebraska Supreme Court. During the next ten months, while Simants's execution remained on hold, the parties presented their written briefs and arguments. On April 3, 1979, the court issued its decision. It was one that would shock many observers.

In an opinion written by Judge Hale McCown for a 6–1 majority, the state's highest court agreed with Judge Windrum's conclusion that Judge Stuart's actions at the motel had been entirely appropriate and did not constitute improper communications with the jury.[54] As to Sheriff Gilster's activities with the jury during the trial, however, the justices reached a very different conclusion. McCown wrote that Gilster's "fraternization" with members of the jury during the trial "presents problems of constitutional dimensions."[55] He noted that the only contested issue in Simants's trial had been the defendant's sanity, upon which the expert testimony conflicted. As a close observer of Simants's actions at the time of his arrest, Gilster had been allowed to offer his nonexpert opinion on that issue for the prosecution—testimony that McCown noted "may have been the critical factor in determining the one key issue which was determinative of the defendant's guilt or innocence."[56] He went on to hold that "Sheriff Gilster had no valid reason or excuse for communicating or fraternizing with the jury. An inference may be drawn that the sheriff was attempting to enhance his credibility and reliability as a witness in the eyes of the jury."[57] Based upon that reasoning, the court ultimately held that "to condone the conduct of Sheriff Gilster in this case would violate the fundamental integrity of all that is embraced in the constitutional concept of a fair trial by a fair and impartial jury."[58] Accordingly, the court vacated Simants's conviction and death sentence and sent the case back to the Lincoln County District Court for a new trial.

Reaction to the high court's decision ranged from relief and elation among Simants's defense team to shock and outrage among most members of the community in and around North Platte. Defense attorney Keith Bystrom, reached by reporters in Arizona where he was on his honeymoon, said, "I think [the Supreme Court] did the right thing. I'm relieved by the action, but we still have a long way to go."[59] Former Sutherland Mayor Herbert Meissner, though, called the high court's ruling "an injustice" and lamented the fact that, after three years, "we [still] can't get the jury's sentence enforced." "Why," he asked, "are we able to spend so much money and time on this case when there are so many other problems that need attention?" Lowell T. Howe of North Platte, an alternate juror who had participated in some of the card-playing sessions with Sheriff Gilster, expressed similar sentiment, calling the decision disappointing and unjustified. Howe went on to declare that the Simants jury had made a "fair and reasonable decision. . . . [We] weren't swayed by the judge, the sheriff or anyone." Simants himself was reported as responding with a mere "OK, thank you" when he was informed of the decision by an official at the Nebraska Penal Complex, where he was being held.

In the weeks and months after the Supreme Court's ruling, the laborious process of preparing for a second trial got under way, with new attorneys in some of the key roles. Neither of the former defense attorneys, Leonard Vyhnalek or Keith Bystrom, was involved in the case. Vyhnalek had returned to private practice in North Platte, and

Bystrom left Nebraska to take a teaching position at the University of Oklahoma Law School. Replacing them were Scott Helvie, the new Lincoln County public defender, and David Schroeder, a veteran trial lawyer from Ogallala, Nebraska, who was appointed by the court to assist the much less-experienced Helvie. On the prosecution side, Milton Larson had left the Lincoln County attorney's post to take up private practice in 1978, and he had been replaced by recently elected George Clough. Clough handed full responsibility for the retrial to Marvin Holscher, his chief deputy, who had held the same position under Larson and had played a dominant role in the original Simants prosecution.

Judge Stuart took control of the case back from Judge Windrum and was soon presented with a motion for a change of venue filed by the defense, seeking to have the trial moved out of Lincoln County. In their motion, Helvie and Schroeder argued that, in light of all of the publicity surrounding the first trial and the ensuing appeals, it would be impossible to find and seat a jury in Lincoln County that was not "tainted" by knowledge of those previous events.[60] On August 6, Judge Stuart reluctantly agreed, issuing an order in which he lamented that "pretrial publicity is destroying our legal system."[61] Specifically, Stuart criticized North Platte television station KNOP-TV for its recent airing of a program concerning the death penalty, in which prosecutor Marvin Holscher referred to Simants as "a convicted murderer."[62] Calling the broadcast irresponsible journalism that would deny Simants his right to a "completely new trial," Stuart announced that he would try the case 250 miles away from North Platte in the capital city of Lincoln, in Lancaster County, beginning on October 1.[63]

The continuing rift between Judge Stuart and the Nebraska media was reflected in both the judge's criticism of the media in his change of venue order and the media's responses. Don Feldman, news director for KNOP, defended his station's decision to air the interview with Holscher that had so irritated Judge Stuart, saying, "It was a legitimate news story about the death penalty, not a story about Simants in particular. [Holscher] volunteered the statements to us, we did not ask him."[64] *Omaha World-Herald*'s president, Harold W. Anderson, was much more strident in his reaction to the judge's comments. "I think Judge Stuart flipped his lid," he said.[65] The judge should remember, Anderson added, that Simants received a new trial "because a public official acted improperly, not newspapers."[66]

As the new trial date approached, Stuart's chronic concern over media coverage of the proceedings remained apparent. Although he stopped short of attempting another formal gag of the media, he did instruct all of the attorneys in the case to refrain from speaking to the press, and he publicly urged journalists to "use restraint" in reporting facts about the case until the jury was seated.[67] Stuart also announced plans for an extensive voir dire of the jury pool and the complete sequestration of the jury for the duration of the trial.

On Monday, October 1, 1979, jury selection began in the second Simants murder trial. More than 150 residents of Lancaster County formed the original jury pool, with 88 of them formally questioned over four long days of voir dire. Despite the gravity of the circumstances, there were some light-hearted moments that helped to reduce some of the tension and tedium. In response to questioning about his occupation, one prospective juror said that he was associated with a recently organized rural newspaper. The new business was doing well, he reported, so much so that "we are about to join the Nebraska Press Association." With a wry grin, Judge Stuart replied, "Good for you," as attorneys and court personnel familiar with the judge's conflict with the association over the gag order burst into laughter.[68] On another occasion, Stuart teased prospective female jurors to never refer to themselves as "just a housewife." His own wife, the judge went on, considered herself a "home executive."[69]

On the morning of Friday, October 5, a final panel of eight women and four men was seated and sworn, and the trial began.[70] In his opening statement, prosecutor Marvin Holscher warned the jury that they would be presented with "the most shocking, bizarre set of facts" they could ever imagine. He said that the state would prove that Simants had viciously killed the Kellies in cold blood so as to conceal his initial sexual assault on Florence and that his actions before, during, and after the crimes showed that he fully understood that what he had done was wrong.[71]

In his opening statement for the defense, David Schroeder immediately admitted to the jury that Simants had killed the Kellies. He sought to focus the jury's attention on the insanity claim, describing his client as an alcoholic with low intelligence who had long been mentally ill.[72] "He was a time bomb that exploded," Schroeder said.[73] Having admitted their client's commission of the crimes, Helvie and Schroeder asked Judge Stuart to limit the prosecution's introduction of evidence and testimony relating to the specific details of the murders, arguing that those facts were inflammatory and irrelevant to the question of Simants's sanity, which was the only remaining contested issue before the jury.[74] The next day, Stuart ruled that Holscher could continue to present detailed evidence and testimony related to the nature of the crimes because, despite its dreadfulness, he believed the evidence may have had some probative value on the questions of Simants's sanity and the premeditated nature of his crimes.[75]

Like the first trial, the proceedings ultimately became a "battle of the experts," with both the prosecution and defense introducing psychological and psychiatric testimony regarding Simants's mental capacity and his state of mind at the time of the murders. The defense again called Drs. Sam Campanella and Jack Anderson, both of whom had testified to Simants's insanity at the first trial. Schroeder and Helvie also brought in Dr. Ronald Franks of the University of Colorado Medical Center to testify for their client. Franks described Simants as a "borderline psychotic" who could not distinguish between reality and hallucinations or voices he reported hearing.[76] He also stated that Simants suffered from a "latent schizophrenia" that was most likely connected to his "harsh and sometimes amoral upbringing" and the loss of his daughter, who had been born with a birth defect and died when she was just three years old. Anderson and Campanella generally agreed with Franks's conclusions, with Anderson attributing Simants's behavior to a "psychotic breakdown shortly before the killings."[77]

Holscher strongly challenged the defense medical testimony and offered psychiatric evidence of his own from the same doctors who had declared Simants legally sane at the first trial—clinical psychologist Dr. Steven Scott, and psychiatrists Dr. Emmitt Kenney and Eli Chesen. Again, each of them testified that Simants functioned at a capacity that was well within Nebraska's legal definition of sanity.[78] The prosecution also took every opportunity to point out to the jury the many actions taken by Simants that seemed clearly to suggest his awareness of the criminality of his acts—the confessions to his nephew and parents, his handwritten "I'm sorry" note, his attempts to conceal the bodies and wipe up blood at the crime scene, and his evasion of authorities by hiding out in the fields around Sutherland during the hours after the murders. All of those actions, Holscher argued in his summation to the jury, were those of a man who knew exactly what he was doing when he killed the six Kellies. "He wanted to have sex and he didn't care what he had to do to get it," Holscher argued. "That's the whole point of this case."[79]

In his summation for the defense, Schroeder repeatedly accused Holscher of trying to inflame the passions of the jury by accentuating the tragedy of the killings rather than Simants's mental state. Repeatedly referring to his client as "dumb" and "a sick man," he argued that the bizarre nature of the crimes, in itself, demonstrated that Simants's actions must have been precipitated by some sort of psychotic breakdown. "There's no issue that [the Kellies] are dead or that the sexual assaults occurred," he said. "But can it be legally sane for a person to sexually fondle dead people?"[80]

On the afternoon of Wednesday, October 17, after eighteen hours of agonizing deliberation over two and a half days, the jury returned its verdict. On all six counts, they found Simants innocent by reason of insanity.[81] Simants reacted to the verdict with the first overt sign of emotion observers could ever remember seeing from him, smiling slightly and turning with relief to his attorneys. Schroeder and Helvie squeezed the arms of their client and quietly congratulated him, as the eyes of all three welled with tears. Prosecutor Holscher seemed terribly shaken by the verdict, his own eyes tearing up as he told reporters in a shaking voice that he was extremely disappointed in the jury's decision.[82]

Other reactions to the verdict were equally sharp and divided. In Oklahoma, Simants's former defense attorney Keith Bystrom said that he was "happy that justice has prevailed since Herb will not be executed" and offered his compliments to Helvie and Schroeder for their success. Bystrom went on to say, "I would hope that the people of Nebraska and Lincoln County would realize how barbaric and arbitrary a system is which allows for the death penalty. This case would have been over four years ago if only the death penalty would not have been requested."[83] Simants's father, seventy-two-year-old Amos Simants, said the news of the verdict "takes quite a load off my mind. . . . Maybe I'll get to feeling better now."[84]

Back in Lincoln County, most people reacted to the news with frustration, resentment, and anger. Clyde Lindstrom, an ambulance driver and friend of the Kellies who had been one of the first to arrive at the scene of the murders, described himself to a reporter as "pretty mad about the situation. Everybody thinks he should have been convicted."[85] An unidentified farmer in Sutherland echoed Lindstrom's sentiment, saying, "It's a personal thing with everyone here. But it's not like that back in Lincoln. . . . I guess this shows you can get away with murder. . . . I hope that jury can live with themselves. The Kellies were people who didn't bother anybody in their whole life."[86] Another man lamented that "our system of justice has gone to hell in a handbasket," while other residents expressed the possibility of "retaliation" against Simants if he were to be set free.[87]

With the announcement of the jury's verdict, Judge Hugh Stuart was left with only one option regarding Simants's disposition. He ordered Sheriff Gilster to return Simants to Lincoln County, where he would be held for evaluation by the Lincoln County Board of Mental Health. Under Nebraska law, that board had the duty of deciding whether Simants was "presently a mentally ill or dangerous person."[88] If they made the determination that he was still ill or dangerous, Simants would be committed to the maximum security unit at the Lincoln Regional Center—the only mental health institution in the state with facilities for holding and treating a mentally ill criminal.

Nine days after Simants's acquittal, the Lincoln County Board made the expected decision, ruling that Simants "continues to pose a significant danger to the community."[89] He was committed to the Lincoln Regional Center, where he remains today, almost thirty years later.

Yet Simants's continuing confinement has not ended the legal conflicts that have so enveloped his life. Under Nebraska law, a person acquitted of a crime by reason of insanity is entitled to an annual assessment of his status and an evidentiary hearing to determine if he is "no longer dangerous to himself . . . or others by reason of mental illness or defect and will not be so dangerous in the fore-seeable future."[90] Over the years since his commitment in 1979, those annual reviews of Simants's status have spawned many more disputes among prosecutors, defense counsel, and public officials over his appropriate treatment and handling. On several occasions, those conflicts have included challenges to the constitutionality and proper interpretation of various laws and regulations related to Simants's confinement. In 1983, and again in 1995, those issues made their way all the way to the Nebraska Supreme Court for resolution, giving Simants the dubious distinction of being, almost certainly, the only private citizen in the state's history to have been the subject of no fewer than six separate state supreme court decisions.[91]

Each time Simants's annual review occurs, and on every anniversary of the Kellie murders, the events of 1975 are resurrected across the state in newspapers and other media outlets. Each time, old wounds are reopened in the hearts and minds of the residents of Sutherland, North Platte, and Lincoln County, as they are reminded of what Simants did to their friends and neighbors. Each time, they almost uniformly express their collective disdain for the legal system that seems to protect Simants from suitable punishment for his crimes and their desire for authorities to keep Simants locked away permanently.[92]

At the time of Simants's annual review in 1984, the lone surviving member of the Kellie family, Audrey Kellie Brown, poignantly recalled the senseless and violent deaths suffered by her family:

> Simants went into the house and killed little Florence. When Daddy came in—he was out picking corn—he shot Daddy. Mother came home next. She came in the front door on the run, I know she did. She was going to fix supper. Then my brother came in the back door with the two children. He shot them all.[93]

Eight years later, at another of Simants's assessment hearings, Mrs. Brown still struggled with the memories of the deaths of her family, and with her fear of Simants. "I am fearful for my life—I still think he is mentally ill and dangerous," she said. "I'm not the type that hates him," she continued, "[but] I'm fearful of the man."[94]

Erwin Simants at the time of his annual review hearing in 1993. Reprinted with permission from the *Omaha World-Herald*.

In recent years Simants has again been in the news, seeking greater flexibility in his supervision and treatment at the Lincoln Regional Center. Simants's current attorney, Lincoln County Public Defender Robert Lindemeier, recently reached an agreement with current Lincoln County Attorney Jeff Meyer on a new protocol that would allow Simants to leave the grounds of the Lincoln Regional Centers more frequently and with less-restrictive supervision. That agreement, now in limbo, is being challenged in the Nebraska Supreme Court by the state attorney general's office.[95] And so the saga of Erwin Simants's punishment for the Kellie murders remains today what it has been since he committed those terrible crimes almost twenty-eight years ago—a tragic and still-divisive story that illuminates and informs some of the most controversial issues in modern criminal jurisprudence, most notably the insanity defense and the death penalty.

Similarly, the constitutional litigation spawned by the Kellie murders—the Supreme Court's decision in *Nebraska Press Association v. Stuart*—continues to resonate in American legal history. As *Omaha World-Herald* executive Woody Howe and others predicted at the time the decision was announced in 1976, the ruling in *Nebraska Press Association* has achieved landmark status. Countless legal scholars, judges, attorneys, and journalists have hailed the decision as one of the most important First Amendment cases in the nation's history, and it is cited as such in nearly every current textbook, monograph, and anthology devoted to First Amendment issues.[96] The decision has been analyzed and commented upon in hundreds, perhaps thousands, of panel discussions, news reports, seminars, symposia, conferences, and Internet forums.[97] Almost unanimously, commentators have praised the parties involved on both sides of the case for the tenacity, dedication, and legal skill they brought to their respective causes.

At the most fundamental level, the *Nebraska Press Association* decision has changed the rules of the game regarding press coverage of court proceedings. While Justice Burger's opinion stopped short of imposing an absolute ban on all judicial "gag orders," the Court's reaffirmation of the heavy presumption of unconstitutionality that attaches to such orders has, as a practical matter, resulted in their virtual extinction. To this day, no court has ever again attempted to place a gag order directly on the press to prevent it from publishing information gained from open public hearings. Indeed, trial courts no longer even seem to consider issuing direct prior restraints on the press with respect to *any* kind of pretrial criminal court proceedings, even in such spectacularly notorious cases as the 1995 O. J. Simpson murder trial or the racially charged prosecution of Los Angeles police officers in 1992 for the videotaped beating of Rodney King.

To be sure, the specter of judicial gags has not disappeared entirely. In the aftermath of the 1976 decision, trial court judges began to routinely close pretrial proceedings to the press as a means of evading the ruling in *Nebraska Press Association*, until two more

Supreme Court decisions curtailed that practice.[98] More recently, courts have become enamored with the use of indirect gags—orders that prohibit participants in trials, such as attorneys, witnesses, and court personnel, from discussing their case with news reporters. Those types of orders, of course, raise unique First Amendment concerns of their own—concerns that the Supreme Court has not yet ruled upon with finality.[99] Still, indirect restraints on news gathering are certainly less destructive of First Amendment rights than the direct gag imposed on the Nebraska media in the Simants case, and the fact that courts have now turned almost exclusively to those less-restrictive measures is a direct result of *Nebraska Press Association*.

As time has passed and the impact of the decision grows clearer, the Nebraska participants in the case have not been hesitant to acknowledge and celebrate their achievement. In a special section of the *Omaha World-Herald* commemorating the bicentennial of the Bill of Rights in December 1991, the paper recounted the story of the litigation and called the high court's decision "a landmark ruling . . . that remains a pillar against prior restraint in this country."[100] At the 2001 annual meeting of the Nebraska Press Association, journalists, attorneys, and First Amendment scholars from around the country gathered to commemorate the twenty-fifth anniversary of the decision. During a symposium and panel forum featuring many of the key players in the case, the acclaim for the Nebraska media's actions was effusive. First Amendment scholar Robert O'Neil, former president of the University of Virginia and founding director of the Thomas Jefferson Center for the Protection of Free Expression, served as moderator for the session and set the tone by describing *Nebraska Press Association* as one of the most important free press decisions of all time. O'Neil lavished praise on the state's media organizations for their efforts, declaring that their perseverance had produced a remarkable opinion that remained "a beacon to freedom of the press."[101] Other speakers at the conference echoed O'Neil's sentiments, including representatives from the papers most directly involved—the *North Platte Telegraph,* the *Lincoln Journal-Star,* and the *Omaha World-Herald.*[102]

Even Judge Hugh Stuart, who was by then retired from the bench and living in Omaha, took part in the meeting as a special guest of the association. The man who had been at the center of the controversy twenty-five years before seemed at peace with his place in legal history, telling the gathering that he still believed that he had acted responsibly and appropriately in issuing his gag order. "I modified [Judge Ruff's] order because I thought it was too broad," Stuart recalled. "I was trying to achieve a balance between the First Amendment and the Sixth Amendment. . . . My main concern was to conduct a fair trial that would not be overturned because of undue publicity. . . . If you ask me if I would enter the restraint again if I had it to do over, I believe I would. I worked hard on that case and it is a part of history."[103]

Stuart went on to express his bemused acceptance of the notoriety he had gained by being one of the named parties in the case, noting, "I guess I'm the only man in the state of Nebraska to be sued directly in the Supreme Court."[104] Stuart also expressed his pride in the fact that Chief Justice Warren Burger had specifically noted in his opinion for the high court that Stuart had acted responsibly. He recounted with particular pleasure a conversation about the case he once had with noted journalist Fred Friendly. Friendly told Stuart that Burger had once told him that "that trial judge in Nebraska did the only thing a responsible judge could do in those circumstances." When Friendly asked, "Why didn't you write that in the decision," the chief justice responded, "I thought I did."[105]

Whatever Judge Stuart or anyone else may think about the propriety of his gag order in retrospect, it was nearly the last of its kind in American legal history. That fact is perhaps the most profound legacy of the extraordinary series of events that began with Erwin Simants's vicious murders of the six members of the Kellie family in 1975. As Robert O'Neil has said, "This was classically Nebraska's victory, showing that the First Amendment applies as fully to trial courts in North Platte as it does to the highest and mightiest anywhere."[106] For those who still mourn the Kellie family, such lofty words may offer little solace. They are, however, a fitting epitaph to a remarkable story in American constitutional history.

notes

Introduction

1. Fred W. Friendly, "A Crime and Its Aftershock," *New York Times Magazine* 21 (March 1976): 16. This article was later expanded and reprinted as chapter 9 of Fred W. Friendly and Martha J. H. Elliott, *The Constitution: That Delicate Balance* (New York: Random House, 1984).
2. Information relating to the historical development of Sutherland and the surrounding area may be found at the Sutherland Chamber of Commerce's website, www.ci.sutherland.ne.us/index.htm. See also Merrill J. Mattes, *The Great Platte River Road: The Covered Wagon Mainline via Fort Kearny to Fort Laramie* (Lincoln: University of Nebraska Press, 1987); and Gregory M. Franzwa, *The Lincoln Highway: Nebraska* (Tucson, Ariz.: Patrice Press, 1995).
3. For illuminating discourse on the search for a distinctive regional "legal culture" of the Great Plains, see John R. Wunder, ed., *Law and the Great Plains: Essays on the Legal History of the Heartland* (Westport, Conn.: Greenwood Press, 1996).
4. Ibid., 25.
5. The applicable Nebraska statute is Neb. Rev. Stat. sec 29-3703 (Reissue 1989), which provides that persons found not guilty of a crime by reason of insanity are entitled to an annual review of their status. If the presiding judge finds that the person is no longer dangerous to himself or others, and will not be dangerous in the foreseeable future, "the court shall order such person unconditionally released from further confinement."
6. John W. Johnson, *The Struggle for Student Rights: Tinker v. Des Moines and the 1960s* (Lawrence: University Press of Kansas, 1997), xi.
7. Holmes's phrase has been more widely disseminated and popularized as the title of historian Kermit Hall's text in American legal history, *The Magic Mirror:*

Law in American History (New York: Oxford University Press, 1989). Hall cites Oliver Wendell Holmes, Jr., *The Speeches of Oliver Wendell Holmes* (1891), 17.

One: A Trying Task to Choose

1. Leonard W. Levy, *Emergence of a Free Press* (New York: Oxford University Press, 1985), 348.
2. *Schenck v. United States,* 249 U.S. 47 (1919).
3. *Bridges v. California,* 314 U.S. 252 (1941).
4. *Nebraska Press Association v. Stuart,* 427 U.S. 539 (1976).
5. See generally, Levy, 144–154.
6. See, for example, Philip Schofield, *Essays on Constitutional Law and Equity* (New York: Oxford University Press, 1978), 521, stating that "One of the objects of the revolution was to get rid of the English common law on liberty of speech and press." Other historians, however, have persuasively argued that the available evidence, including the presence of "free press" clauses in nine of the first eleven state constitutions, does not support such a sweeping conclusion about the impact of free press concerns on the Revolution, nor did those clauses necessarily indicate a rejection of the English common law with respect to seditious libel and other free speech principles. For a comprehensive presentation of the debate, see Levy, 190–200. Perhaps one of the best indicators that such concerns were not of paramount concern to the revolutionaries is the fact that Thomas Jefferson made no mention of free speech or press issues in his long litany of grievances against George III in the Declaration of Independence.
7. "Virginia Bill of Rights," June 12, 1776, Hening, *Statutes at Large* IX, 109–112. This document is conveniently available in many other online and print sources, including Edward Dumbauld, *The Bill of Rights* (Norman: University of Oklahoma Press, 1957).
8. Robert A. Rutland, *The Birth of the Bill of Rights, 1776–1791* (New York: Collier, 1966), 78.
9. Ibid.
10. Max Farrand, ed., *The Records of the Federal Convention of 1787,* rev. ed. (New Haven, Conn.: Yale University Press, 1966), 2:618.
11. Ibid.
12. Broadus Mitchell and Louise Mitchell, *A Biography of the Constitution of the United States* (New York: Oxford University Press, 1975), 193–197.
13. The records and proceedings of the earliest Congresses are available in numerous sources, including Gales and Seaton, *Annals of Congress,* a multi-volume collection that covers the First Congress through the first session of the Eighteenth Congress, from 1789 to 1824. In addition, relevant records from the separate houses of Congress may be found in the *Journal of the House* and *Journal of the Senate,* compiled for each Congressional session. Quite

fortunately, all of these materials can be quickly and easily accessed through the website of the Library of Congress, at http://memory.loc.gov.

14. *Annals of Congress* 1789, 451.

15. Ibid., 452.

16. *Journal of the Senate* 1789, 70 (September 3, 1879).

17. Ibid.

18. Mitchell, 203–204.

19. See generally, William L. Dwyer, *In the Hands of the People: The Trial Jury's Origins, Triumphs, Troubles, and Future in American Democracy* (New York: Saint Martin's Press, 2002); and Jeffrey Abramson, *We, the Jury: The Jury System and the Ideal of Democracy* (New York: BasicBooks, 1994).

20. Dwyer, 14.

21. Ibid.

22. Abramson, 34.

23. Ibid., 37.

24. *Burr v. United States,* 25 Fed. Cas. 49, Case No. 14,692g (Circuit Ct., Va., 1807). The literature on the Burr trial is abundant. See, for example, Melton Buckner, Jr., *Aaron Burr, Conspiracy to Treason* (New York: Wiley, 2002); Roger G. Kennedy, *Burr, Hamilton, and Jefferson: A Study in Character* (New York: Oxford University Press, 2000); Thomas Abernathy, *The Burr Conspiracy* (New York: Oxford University Press, 1954); and Douglas S. Campbell, *Free Press v. Fair Trial: Supreme Court Decisions Since 1807* (Westport, Conn.: Praeger, 1994).

25. *Burr v. United States,* 25 Fed. Cas. 49, at 51.

26. Ibid.

27. *Reynolds v. United States,* 95 U.S. 145 (1878).

28. Ibid., 149.

29. Ibid., 155.

30. Ibid.

31. *Irvin v. Dowd,* 366 U.S. 717 (1961).

32. Ibid., 728. The trial court judge in *Irvin v. Dowd* had granted the defendant a change of venue, but only to an adjacent county, where the publicity about the case was still intense and pervasive. The judge rejected the defense's request for a second change, on the basis of an Indiana statute that provided that only one change of venue was allowed.

33. Ibid., 729–730, Justice Frankfurter concurring.

34. *Sheppard v. Maxwell,* 384 U.S. 333 (1966).

35. Ibid., 358, 356.

36. Ibid., 355.

37. Ibid.

38. Ibid., 358.

39. Ibid., 363.

40. Ibid., 358–363.

Two: The Crimes, the Victims, the Media

1. See Bob Greene, *Once Upon a Town: The Miracle of the North Platte Canteen* (New York: William Morrow & Co., 2002).
2. The details of Simants's early life may be gleaned from various sources, including newspaper articles published around the time of the Kellie murders and during the ensuing criminal trials. They are also available in more "official" form in the numerous psychological analyses and profiles compiled on him during his criminal trials and his confinement and treatment at the Lincoln Regional Center over the past two decades. Except where otherwise noted, the biographical information given here is from a "Report of Psychiatric Clinical Interview" conducted in 1994 by Dr. Beverly T. Mead of the University of Nebraska Medical Center. Her report appears as Exhibit 28, Case No. 71–255, Lincoln County District Court, one of the annual psychiatric status hearings held to evaluate Simants's condition and course of treatment. It will hereinafter be referred to as the "Mead Report."
3. Mead Report, 2.
4. See *State of Nebraska v. Simants,* 182 Neb. 491, 155 N.W. 2d 788 (1968).
5. Mead Report, 2.
6. The most comprehensive and authoritative account of Simants's actions on the day and night of the murders may be found in the transcripts of testimony and evidence presented in his first trial, *State of Nebraska v. Erwin Charles Simants,* Lincoln County District Court, Case No. B-2904. Those transcripts total more than 2000 pages, compiled in eleven volumes, and are presently archived at North Platte in the offices of Anita Childerston, Clerk of the District Court, Lincoln County, Nebraska. References to those transcripts in this narrative will be to "Trial Transcript," with appropriate volume and page numbers.
7. Trial Transcript, Vol. V, 1206.
8. Ibid., Vol. VII, 1731.
9. Ibid., Vol. V, 1190–1195.
10. See "Anguish, Disbelief Replace Terror," *North Platte Telegraph,* October 20, 1975, 1.
11. Trial Transcript, Vol. VI, 1307.
12. Edward C. Nicholls, "Kellie Had Loaned Suspect Simants $50 For Fine," *Lincoln Star,* October 21, 1975, 8.
13. Dean Terrill, "Sutherland Residents Wonder—Why?" *Lincoln Star,* October 20, 1975, 1.
14. "Anguish, Disbelief Replace Terror," *North Platte Telegraph,* October 20, 1975, 1.
15. Dean Terrell, "Sole Survivor Arranging Sutherland Burials," *Lincoln Star,* October 22, 1975, 25.
16. Simants's confession was accepted into evidence as State's Exhibit 12 in the first murder trial, and may be read at Trial Transcript, Vol. VII, 1728–1748.

17. Ibid., Vol. VII, 1732.
18. Ibid., 1735.
19. Ibid., 1736.
20. Ibid., 1737.
21. Ibid., 1739.
22. Ibid., 1739–1741.
23. Ibid., Vol. V, 1195–1201. The note written by Simants is Exhibit 41.
24. Ibid., Vol. IA, 100–101.
25. Ibid., Vol. V, 1197.
26. Ibid., Vol. IA, 100–101.
27. Ibid., Vol. V, 1240–1241. See also Frank Santiago, "Slaying Motive Remains Puzzle," *Omaha World-Herald*, October 20, 1975, 1.
28. Trial Transcript, Vol. IA, 108. See also Edward C. Nicholls, "Man Charged in 6 Killings," *Lincoln Star*, October 20, 1975, 1.
29. Quoted in Nicholls, "Man Charged," 1.
30. Trial Transcript, Vol. V, 1243–1245.
31. Ibid., 1246.
32. Ibid., Vol. VI, 1257–1261.
33. Quoted in "Hearing Set Wednesday in Mass Murder," *North Platte Telegraph*, October 20, 1975, 1.
34. Quoted in Fred W. Friendly, "A Crime and Its Aftershock," *New York Times Magazine*, March 21, 1976, 16. See also Friendly and Martha J. H. Elliott, *The Constitution: That Delicate Balance* (New York: Viking, 1984), 145–146.
35. Ibid., 17.
36. Whitman killed sixteen people and wounded another thirty-one, before he was finally shot and killed by Austin police. For a comprehensive account of the event, see Gary M. Lavergne, *A Sniper in the Tower: The Charles Whitman Murders* (New York: Bantam Books, 1997).
37. "Sutherland Faces Long Night With Fear," *North Platte Telegraph*, October 20, 1975, 3.
38. Ibid.
39. See Milton Larson, "Free Press vs. Fair Trial in Nebraska: A Position Paper," *Nebraska Law Review* 55, no. 4 (1976): 543–571, describing the media attention to the murders. Larson was the Lincoln County attorney responsible for prosecuting Simants.
40. "Six in Family Gunned Down At Sutherland," *Omaha World-Herald*, October 19, 1975, 1.
41. Both versions of the exchange are described in Friendly and Elliott, 150.
42. Ibid.
43. Dean Terrill, "Sutherland Residents Wonder—Why?" *Lincoln Star*, October 20, 1975, 1.
44. Trial Transcript, Vol. VII, 1727.
45. Ibid., 1728–1748, Exhibit 12.

46. Lincoln County Court Records, Case No. 28-401, "Complaint," filed October 19, 1975.

47. In Nebraska, arraignment procedures are prescribed in Neb. Rev. Stat. sec. 29-1802 et. seq. The transcript of Simants's arraignment may be found at Trial Transcript, Vol. IA, 5–22. See also "Hearing Set Wednesday in Mass Murder," *North Platte Telegraph,* October 20, 1975, 1.

48. Edward C. Nicholls, "Man Charged," 1.

49. Trial Transcript, Vol. IA, 9.

50. Ibid., 12–13.

51. Ibid., 21.

52. The procedures for preliminary hearings are prescribed in Neb. Rev. Stat. sec. 29-1606 et. seq. For the setting of Simants's preliminary hearing, see *State of Nebraska v. Erwin Charles Simants,* Lincoln County Court Records, Case No. 75-789, "Journal Entry," entered by Judge Ronald Ruff, October 19, 1975.

53. Large photos of Simants, handcuffed and clad in prisoner's clothing, were published on the front pages of the *Omaha World-Herald, Lincoln Journal-Star,* and *North Platte Telegraph,* among other newspapers, on Monday, October 20, 1975.

54. By far the most comprehensive examination of the media coverage of the Kellie murders and the Simants trials may be found in Nancy Whitmore, "Nebraska Press Association v. Stuart: An Understanding of Prior Restraint," Unpublished M.A. Thesis, Department of Communications, University of Nebraska-Omaha, 1995. Whitmore's thesis catalogs more than 220 stories and editorials about the case appearing in seven midwestern and western newspapers. Significant portions of the thesis were later published in Nancy J. Whitmore, "Nebraska Suppressed: How Gagging the News Media Intensified Pretrial Press Coverage of the Simants' Murder Case," *Journalism History* 29, no. 3 (fall 2003): 107–122. Both the thesis and the article are invaluable starting points for researchers exploring the press coverage of the Simants litigation. References hereinafter to Whitmore's 1995 work will be to "Whitmore Thesis," while references to her 2003 article will be to "Whitmore, 'Nebraska Suppressed'."

55. Trial Transcript, Exhibit 5, Vol. I, 3–4.

56. Ibid. Also quoted in Whitmore Thesis, 31.

57. Trial Transcript, Exhibit 7, Vol. I, 7–8. Also quoted in Whitmore, "Nebraska Suppressed," 109, and Friendly and Elliott, 151.

58. Trial Transcript, Exhibit 7, Vol. I, 9–10. Also quoted in Whitmore Thesis, 31, n. 16.

59. Ibid. Also quoted in Whitmore Thesis, 31, n. 17, and Friendly and Elliott, 150–151.

60. Trial Transcript, Exhibit 7, Vol. I, 10. Also in Whitmore Thesis, 32, n. 18.

61. "Six Reported Slain in Nebraska Town by Shotgun Wielder," *New York Times,* October 19, 1975, 22.

62. "Six in Family Gunned Down in Sutherland," *Omaha World-Herald,* October 19, 1975, 1.

63. *Omaha World-Herald,* October 20, 1975, 1.

64. *Lincoln Star,* October 20, 1975, 1.

65. *North Platte Telegraph,* October 20, 1975, 1.

66. See, for example, "Anguish, Disbelief Replace Terror," *North Platte Telegraph,* October 20, 1975, 1; Frank Santiago, "Suspect Stopped for Beers after Slayings," *Omaha World-Herald,* October 20, 1975; and Edward C. Nicholls, "Man Charged," 1. Also quoted in Whitmore, "Nebraska Suppressed," 109.

67. See, for example, Nicholls, "Man Charged," 1; and Santiago, "Suspect Quietly Yields," 1, containing typical language relating to Simants's appearance and demeanor at the arraignment.

68. "Mourners Fill Auditorium for Mass Funeral," *Lincoln Star,* October 23, 1975, 16.

69. See "First Murder Case for Young Attorney," *Omaha World-Herald,* October 24, 1975, 39.

70. Ibid.

71. Dean Terrill, "Judge in Murder Case Sensitive to Situation," *Lincoln Journal,* October 24, 1975, 1.

72. Dean Terrill, "Judge in Murder Case Sensitive to Situation," *Lincoln Journal,* October 24, 1975, 1. See also R. G. Dunlop, "Ruling 'Agonized' North Platte Judge," *Omaha World-Herald,* October 24, 1975, 39.

73. Ibid.

74. *State of Nebraska v. Erwin Charles Simants,* Lincoln County Court Records, Case No. 28-401, "Amended Complaint," filed October 22, 1975.

75. *State of Nebraska v. Erwin Charles Simants,* Lincoln County Court Records, Case No. 28-401, "Motion For Restrictive Order," filed October 21, 1975.

76. Ibid.

77. Whitmore, "Nebraska Suppressed," 110.

78. Ibid, 110–111.

79. Ibid.

80. Friendly and Elliott, 152.

81. Ibid.

82. Whitmore, "Nebraska Suppressed," 111.

83. Joe R. Seacrest, "Gag! Nebraska Generates Most Important Freedom of Press Case Since Pentagon Papers," *Nebraska Newspaper* 27 (December 1975): 1–9, at 2.

Three: The Initial Legal Skirmishes

1. Joe R. Seacrest, "Gag! Nebraska Generates Most Important Freedom of Press Case Since Pentagon Papers," *Nebraska Newspaper* 27 (December 1975): 1–9, at 2.

2. Quoted in Charlyne Berens, "Prior Restraint Threatens Free Speech," *NU College of Journalism & Mass Communication Alumni News* 11, no. 1 (summer 2001): 1–2. As noted in the Preface and Acknowledgements, in the years since the *Nebraska Press Association* litigation concluded, the memories of Keith Blackledge and many of the other key participants in the case have been reported in published interviews in numerous sources. Along with the previously cited work of Nancy Whitmore and Fred Friendly, a particularly useful source is Joseph Russomanno, *Speaking Our Minds: Conversations With the People Behind Landmark First Amendment Cases* (Mahwah, N.J.: Lawrence Erlbaum Associates, 2002). Russomanno devotes a chapter of his book to *Nebraska Press Association v. Stuart,* and includes a full transcript of his interviews with Blackledge and many of the other participants. For reasons explained in the Preface, many of the quotes contained herein are cited to Russomanno and other earlier sources.

3. Russomanno, 263.

4. Seacrest, 3.

5. See Russomanno, 262. Peterson would wade into the battle later.

6. Seacrest, 3.

7. Ibid.

8. Nebraska bar-press guidelines, paragraph 3, provision 6.

9. As will be discussed more fully below, forty-eight hours after this night "meeting" in the County Court, the news organizations would be back for a second attempt to prevent the entry of a gag order in the Simants case. That hearing would take place in the District Court before Judge Hugh Stuart and would include the remarkable scene of Judge Ruff himself taking the witness stand to explain and justify his actions at this initial "meeting" on the question of a gag order.

10. In 1975, Neb. Rev. Stat. sec. 24-311 provided that "All judicial proceedings of all courts established in this state must be open to the attendance of the public unless otherwise specially provided by statute." The same language is now found in Neb. Rev. Stat. sec. 24-1001.

11. Dean Terrill, "Murder Hearing Coverage Argued," *Lincoln Star,* October 22, 1975, 25.

12. Ibid.

13. Bill Eddy, "Murder Charges Amended, Judge Issues 'Gag' Order to News Media," *North Platte Telegraph,* October 22, 1975, 1.

14. Ibid.

15. Ibid.

16. Terrill, 25.

17. R. G. Dunlop, "Ruling 'Agonized' North Platte Judge," *Omaha World-Herald,* October 24, 1975, 39.

18. *State of Nebraska v. Erwin Charles Simants,* Lincoln County District Court, Case No. B-2904, Trial Transcript, Vol. IA, 23, 25. Ruff would later

acknowledge that the "strong action" he was about to announce—the imposition of a gag on the press—was motivated primarily by his determination
to avoid the kind of criticism heaped upon the trial judge in *Sheppard v.
Maxwell*.

19. Ibid., 25–28. See State of *Nebraska v. Erwin Charles Simants*, "Order of the
    Court," October 22, 1975, County Court of Lincoln County, Nebraska. This
    is the first of several different versions of the gag order that would form the
    crux of the Supreme Court litigation.
20. Russomanno, 266.
21. Ibid.
22. Editorial, "The press and the courts," *North Platte Telegraph*, October 29, 1975.
23. Nebraska bar-press guidelines, paragraph 1.
24. *Sheppard v. Maxwell*, 384 U.S. 333 (1966).
25. Trial Transcript, Vol. IA, 32.
26. Ibid.
27. "Amended Complaint," *State of Nebraska vs. Erwin Charles Simants*, Case No.
    28-401, October 22, 1975. The amended complaint was read into the record
    at Trial Transcript, Vol. IA, 33–35.
28. Trial Transcript, Vol. IA, 56.
29. Ibid., 75–82.
30. Ibid., 84.
31. Ibid., 96–97.
32. Ibid., 100–101.
33. Ibid., 102.
34. Ibid., 106.
35. Ibid., 129–130.
36. Ibid., 148.
37. Ibid., 143. Simants's transcribed statement remained sealed after the pre-
    liminary hearing. Its contents did not become public until his trial several
    months later. As noted in Chapter 2, the statement may be read in its entirety
    at Trial Transcript, Vol. VII, pp. 1728–1748.
38. Trial Transcript, Vol. IA, 143.
39. Ibid., 152.
40. Ibid., 157–158.
41. Ibid., 158. Ruff's order binding Simants over for trial and denying bail
    was subsequently memorialized and entered in the court files as "Journal
    Entry," Oct. 22, 1975, Judge Ronald Ruff, Case No. 75-789, Lincoln County
    Court.
42. Seacrest, 3.
43. Russomanno, 301.
44. Fred W. Friendly, "A Crime and Its Aftershock," *New York Times Magazine* 21
    (March 1976): 87.
45. Ibid.

46. Nancy Whitmore, *"Nebraska Press Association v. Stuart:* An Understanding of Prior Restraint," Unpublished M.A. Thesis, Department of Communications, University of Nebraska-Omaha, 1995, 40–41.

47. Seacrest, 3. The 5th Circuit decision referred to is *United States v. Dickinson,* 465 F.2d 496 (5th Cir. 1972).

48. Friendly, 88.

49. Seacrest, 3.

50. Will Norton, Jr., "Nebraska Case Crucial to Freedom of Expression," *NU College of Journalism and Mass Communication Alumni News* 11, no. 1 (summer 2001): 3–4. See also interview with media counsel Alan Peterson, in Russomanno, 259.

51. "Application of Nebraska Press Association, Omaha World-Herald Company, Journal-Star Publishing Company, Western Publishing Company, North Platte Broadcasting Co., Nebraska Broadcasters Association, Associated Press, and United Press International," October 23, 1975, District Court of Lincoln County, Nebraska, Case No. B-2904. Hereinafter cited as "Application of NPA."

52. Ibid., 2–3.

53. Stuart's version of his conversation with Ruff first appeared in his interview with Fred Friendly conducted just a few months after the event. See Friendly, 87. He later reiterated the story to Nancy Whitmore and other interviewers, and told essentially the same story to this author almost thirty years later. Hugh Stuart, interview with author, June 22, 2003. For Ruff's version of the discussion, see Chapter 2.

54. Inexplicably, the transcript of the Thursday evening hearing before Judge Stuart is missing from the Lincoln County Clerk of Court's files and records. It is available, however, as part of the "Joint Appendix" filed in January 1976 by the Nebraska Press Association and other petitioners in the United States Supreme Court after the high court agreed to review the case. References herein to that hearing will be to "Joint Appendix, Transcript of October 23 hearing," with appropriate page numbers.

55. Joint Appendix, Transcript of October 23 hearing, 31–32. See also Bill Eddy, "Judge May Alter 'Gag' Order, *North Platte Telegraph,* October 24, 1975, 1.

56. "Application of NPA," October 23, 1975, District Court of Lincoln County, Nebraska, Case No. B-2904, para.6(a).

57. Joint Appendix, Transcript of October 23 hearing, 33.

58. Bill Eddy, "Judge may alter 'gag' order," *North Platte Telegraph,* October 24, 1975, 1.

59. See "Journal Entry," February 4, 1976, *State of Nebraska vs. Erwin Charles Simants,* Case No. B-2904.

60. Hugh Stuart, interview with author, June 22, 2003.

61. Joint Appendix, Transcript of October 23 hearing, 40.

62. Ibid., 44–45.

63. Ibid., 44.

64. Ibid., 54–58.

65. Ibid., Exhibits 4-A to 4-N.

66. Ibid., 60–64.

67. Ibid., 65.

68. See, e.g., Bill Eddy, "Judge may alter 'gag' order," *North Platte Telegraph*, October 24, 1975, and R. G. Dunlop, "Judge Plans to 'Modify' Press Gag," *Omaha World-Herald*, October 24, 1975.

69. Eddy, "Judge may alter 'gag' order," *North Platte Telegraph*, October 24, 1975.

70. Ibid.

71. Ibid.

72. Editorial, "The press and the courts," *North Platte Telegraph*, October 29, 1975.

73. Lorna Hansen, "In favor of 'Ruff' judges," Letter to the Editor, *North Platte Telegraph*, October 29, 1975.

74. Wilma Wyman, "Supports Judge Ruff's ruling," Letter to the Editor, *North Platte Telegraph*, October 29, 1975.

75. Joint Appendix, Transcript of October 23 hearing, 71.

76. Ibid.

77. Ibid.

78. Ibid., 72. See also "Journal Entry," Oct. 23, 1975, Judge Hugh Stuart, Case No. B-2904, Lincoln County District Court.

79. Hugh Stuart, interview with author, June 22, 2003.

80. *Bridges v. California*, 314 U.S. 252 (1941).

81. Joint Appendix, 74.

82. Ibid.

83. Stuart's reading of the decision is at Joint Appendix, 74–76. In written form, it may be found as "Order," October 27, 1975, Judge Hugh Stuart, Case No. B-2904, Lincoln County District Court. This order will hereinafter be referred to as the "Stuart Gag Order."

84. See Russomanno, 264, where Stuart characterized the original order entered by Ruff as "very restrictive" and remembered his order as "liberalizing it considerably."

85. Stuart Gag Order, paragraphs 6 through 11.

86. "Notice of Appeal," October 31, 1975, Case No. B-2904, Lincoln County District Court. This and all other documents relating to the appeal in the Nebraska Supreme Court may be found in the official transcripts of the Nebraska Supreme Court, Docket Number 40642. The Notice of Appeal is at pages 40–41 of those transcripts.

Four: Entering the Appellate Labyrinth

1. Editorial, "Lincoln County Courts Imperil Constitutional Protections," *Lincoln Evening Journal,* October 30, 1975, 4.
2. Editorial, "A Press Gag in Nebraska Stirs Widespread Resistance," *Chicago Tribune,* November 2, 1975, Sec. 2, p. 4.
3. Editorial, "Simants Case: The Judges Err," *Omaha World-Herald,* October 29, 1975, 10.
4. As previously noted, the media groups represented in these consultations were all members of Media of Nebraska, an "umbrella" organization that included, among others, the Nebraska Press Association, the *Omaha World-Herald* Company, the *Journal-Star* Printing Co., Western Publishing Co., North Platte Broadcasting Co., Nebraska Broadcasters Association, Associated Press, United Press International, and the Nebraska Professional Chapter of the Society of Professional Journalists/Sigma Delta Chi. These entities will be referred to collectively hereafter as "the media" or "the news organizations."
5. Bill Eddy, "Judge Orders New Restrictions on Press," *North Platte Telegraph,* October 28, 1975, 1.
6. The named "Appellants" were the Nebraska Press Association, the *Omaha World-Herald* Company, the *Journal-Star* Printing Co., Western Publishing Co., North Platte Broadcasting Co., Nebraska Broadcasters Association, Associated Press, United Press International, and the Nebraska Professional Chapter of the Society of Professional Journalists/Sigma Delta Chi.
7. Because of this lack of an intermediate appellate court in the state, the Nebraska Supreme Court experienced an ever-increasing backlog of cases through much of the 1970s and '80s. The situation would begin to be alleviated in 1991 with the creation of the Nebraska Court of Appeals.
8. "Application For Leave to Docket," Nebraska Supreme Court, Case No. 40471, October 31, 1975.
9. The named "Relators" in the original Supreme Court action included all of the news organizations named as Appellants in the District Court, plus four individuals: AP reporters Kiley Armstrong and Edward Nicholls, North Platte radio broadcaster James Huttenmaier, and reporter William Eddy of the *North Platte Telegraph.*
10. "Petition," Nebraska Supreme Court, Case No. 40471, October 31, 1975, Para. 8.
11. Ibid., Para. 9.
12. Ibid., Para. 10.
13. Ibid., Para. 11.
14. Ibid.
15. Ibid.
16. In 1975, Neb. Rev. Stat. sec. 24-311 (the Nebraska "open courts" law) provided that "All judicial proceedings of all courts in this state must be open to

the attendance of the public unless otherwise specially provided by statute."
The same language is now found in Neb. Rev. Stat. sec. 24-1001.

17. Petition, Nebraska Supreme Court, Case No. 40471, October 31, 1975, Para. 20.

18. "Motion to Advance Appeal," Nebraska Supreme Court, Case No. 40445, October 31, 1975.

19. "Statement in Support of the Court's Jurisdiction," Nebraska Supreme Court, Case No. 40471, October 31, 1975.

20. *Nebraska Press Association v. Stuart*, 427 U.S. 539, 96 S. Ct. 2791 (1976).

21. See "Rules of the Supreme Court of the United States," Rule 22(3) and 23.

22. For interpretive assessments of the Burger Court and its legacy, see Bernard Schwartz, *The Ascent of Pragmatism: The Burger Court in Action* (New York: Addison-Wesley, 1990); Tinsley E. Yarbrough, *The Burger Court: Justices, Rulings, and Legacy* (Santa Barbara, Calif.: ABC-CLIO, 2000); and Bernard Schwartz, ed., *The Burger Court: Counter-Revolution or Confirmation?* (New York: Oxford University Press, 1998).

23. For a recent well-received biographical assessment of Blackmun, see Linda Greenhouse, *Becoming Justice Blackmun: Harry Blackmun's Supreme Court Journey* (New York: Times Books, 2005). Short sketches of his career may be found in many other sources, including Yarbrough, 83–89; Kermit Hall, ed., *The Oxford Companion to the Supreme Court of the United States* (New York: Oxford University Press, 1992): 75–77; Elder Witt, *The Supreme Court at Work*, 2d ed. (Washington, D.C.: Congressional Quarterly, 1997): 230–231; Elder Witt, *Guide to the U.S. Supreme Court*, 2d ed. (Washington, D.C.: Congressional Quarterly, 1990): 876–877; and Joseph Foote, "Mr. Justice Blackmun," *Harvard Law School Bulletin* 21 (June 1970): 18–21.

24. "Justice Harry Blackmun Dies; His Tenure Remembered for Its Courage," Press Release, American Civil Liberties Union, March 4, 1999.

25. *Roe v. Wade*, 410 U.S. 113, 93 S. Ct. 705 (1973).

26. *Flood v. Kuhn*, 407 U.S. 258, 92 S. Ct. 2099 (1972).

27. *New York Times Co. v. United States*, 403 U.S. 713, at 761 (1971).

28. Comprehensive assessments of the Pentagon Papers litigation are abundant. For insight from one of the key participants in that case, see Floyd Abrams, *Speaking Freely: Trials of the First Amendment* (New York: Viking, 2005). Other representative treatments include Sanford J. Ungar, *The Papers and the Papers: An Account of the Legal and Political Battle over the Pentagon Papers* (New York: Dutton, 1972); and Martin Shapiro, comp., *The Pentagon Papers and the Courts: A Study in Foreign Policy-Making and Freedom of the Press* (San Francisco: Chandler Publishing, 1972).

29. *New York Times Co. v. United States*, 403 U.S. 713, at 761, (1971) (Blackmun, J., dissenting).

30. Ibid.

31. Ibid., 403 U.S. 713, at 762, 91 S. Ct. 2140, at 2165.

32. "Application for Stay," United States Supreme Court, No A-426, November 5, 1975. See also Darwin Olofson, "U.S. High Court Asked to Set Aside Gag Order," *Omaha World-Herald,* November 6, 1975, 1.

33. "Application for Stay," United States Supreme Court, No A-426, November 5, 1975.

34. "Response of the Honorable Hugh Stuart to Application for Stay," Supreme Court of the United States, Case No. A-426, November 10, 1975.

35. Ibid. See also "3 Attorneys Oppose Order on 'Gag' Ruling," *Omaha World-Herald,* November 16, 1975, 8B.

36. "*Per Curiam* Statement," Nebraska Supreme Court, November 10, 1975, Case Nos. 40455 and 40471.

37. Ibid. See also "State High Court to Await Federal Ruling on Simants," *Omaha World-Herald,* November 11, 1975, 1.

38. Ibid.

39. Justice Harry Blackmun, in-chambers opinion, *Nebraska Press Association v. Stuart,* 423 U.S. 1319, 96 S. Ct. 236 (November 13, 1975). An "in-chambers" opinion is one issued by an individual justice, acting in his or her capacity as circuit justice. They are typically used to address procedural issues related to applications like the one at issue here.

40. Ibid., at 96 S. Ct. 240.

41. Ibid.

42. Ibid.

43. Ibid.

44. Darwin Olofson, "Justice: Act Swiftly In News Limits Case," *Omaha World-Herald,* November 14, 1975, 1.

45. "State Court Will Act," *Omaha World-Herald,* November 14, 1975, 1.

46. *New York Times Co. v. United States,* 403 U.S. 713, at 761, 91 S. Ct. 2140, at 2165 (1971) (Blackmun, J., dissenting).

47. "Docketing Order," Nebraska Supreme Court, Case No. 40471, November 18, 1975.

48. *Nebraska Press Association v. Stuart,* 423 U.S. 1327, 96 S. Ct. 251 (November 20, 1975) (Blackmun, J., in-chambers).

49. The statutory language in question was couched in 28 U.S.C. sections 2101(f) and 1257(3), which gives a circuit justice of the Supreme Court authority to issue a stay of a state court's "final judgment or decree" that is subject to review by the Supreme Court on a writ of certiorari.

50. *Nebraska Press Association v. Stuart,* 423 U.S. 1327, 96 S. Ct. 251 (November 20, 1975) (Blackmun, J., in-chambers).

51. Ibid.

52. Ibid.

53. Ibid.

54. Ibid., at 255–256.

55. Ibid.

56. Ibid.

57. Ibid.

58. Ibid.

59. Ibid., at 255.

60. Ibid.

61. Ibid., at 256.

62. Ibid.

63. Editorial, "High Drama Here Tuesday," *Lincoln Evening Journal,* November 24, 1975, 10.

64. Ibid.

65. Because oral arguments of counsel are not considered to be evidence, transcripts of such arguments are typically not produced as part of the official "record" of a case as it makes its way through the appellate process.

66. See Bob Guenther, "Attorney Points Out Alternatives To Gag Order," *Lincoln Star,* November 26, 1975, 1, and R. G. Dunlop, "High Court Promises 'Gag' Ruling by Monday," *Omaha World-Herald,* November 26, 1975, 1.

67. Ibid.

68. Ibid.

69. *State v. Simants,* 194 Neb. 783, 236 N.W.2d 794 (1975).

70. Ibid., 236 N.W.2d, at 798.

71. Ibid.

72. Generally, *estoppel* is a legal doctrine which precludes a litigant from raising a particular point, or taking a particular action, as a result of his or her own actions.

73. *State v. Simants,* 194 Neb. 783, 236 N.W.2d 794, 806 (1975).

74. Ibid., at 807.

75. Ibid.

76. Ibid.

77. Ibid.

78. Ibid.

79. See Chapter 3, *infra.*

80. *State v. Simants,* 194 Neb. 783, 236 N.W.2d 794, at 798 (1975).

81. See Chapter 3, *infra.*

82. *State v. Simants,* 194 Neb. 783, 236 N.W.2d 794, at 802 (1975).

83. Ibid.

84. *State v. Simants,* 194 Neb. 783, 236 N.W.2d 794, at 800 (1975).

85. See *Bridges v. California,* 314 U.S. 252, 62 S. Ct. 190 (1941), and *New York Times Co. v United States,* 403 U.S. 713, 91 S. Ct. 2140 (1971).

86. *State v. Simants,* 194 Neb. 783, 236 N.W.2d 794, at 800 (1975).

87. See *Branzburg v. Hayes,* 408 U.S. 665, 92 S. Ct. 2646 (1972), and *Irvin v. Dowd,* 366 U.S. 717, 81 S. Ct. 1639 (1961).

88. *Branzburg v. Hayes,* 408 U.S. 665, at 685. "Dicta" refers to language contained in a judicial opinion that is not dispositive of the case before it. It is, rather, extraneous and "advisory" in nature.

89. *State v. Simants,* 194 Neb. 783, 236 N.W.2d 794, at 801 (1975).

90. Ibid., at 802.

91. Ibid., at 803.

92. Ibid. The court even attached to its opinion a table showing the populations of the eight counties adjacent to Lincoln County, as derived from the 1970 census. The largest was Dawson County, with 19,537 residents. The smallest was McPherson County, with just 623 inhabitants. Lincoln County itself was the most populous in the area, with 29,538 residents.

93. Ibid.

94. Ibid.

95. Ibid., at 804.

96. Ibid., at 805.

97. Ibid.

98. Ibid.

Five: The Paper War in the Supreme Court

1. "Gag Order Plea Goes to Entire High Court," *Omaha World-Herald,* November 22, 1975, 1.

2. "Newsmen Differ in Reaction to Blackmun Move," *North Platte Telegraph,* November 21, 1975, 1.

3. Among the national groups voicing opposition to the Nebraska gag order decisions were the AP Managing Editors Association, the Reporters Committee for Freedom of the Press, the Inter-American Press Association, and Sigma Delta Chi, the Society of Professional Journalists. Representative editorials and columns from around the country include "Justice Blackmun vs. The Press," *Denver Post,* November 26, 1975, 20; "Press Can't be Muted for What Might Happen," *Kansas City Star,* November 26, 1975, 29; "Blackmun's Ruling May Reverberate," *Lincoln Journal,* November 27, 1975, 81; "Prior Restraint on Press a Peril," *Kansas City Times,* December 4, 1975, 11G; and "Don't Put Gag on the People," *Denver Post,* December 5, 1975, 20. For a comprehensive listing of the local, regional, and national press reaction to Blackmun's ruling, see Nancy Whitmore, "Nebraska Press Association v. Stuart: An Understanding of Prior Restraint," Unpublished M.A. Thesis, Department of Communications, University of Nebraska-Omaha, 1995.

4. "Newsmen Differ in Reaction to Blackmun Move," *North Platte Telegraph,* November 21, 1975, 1.

5. Carl T. Rowan, "Hello Gag Rule, Goodby [*sic*] Liberty," *Omaha World-Herald,* November 27, 1975, 5.

6. Ibid.

7. Tom Wicker, "Pentagon Papers Lesson and the Nebraska Case," *Omaha World-Herald,* November 29, 1975, 5.

8. Clayton Kirkpatrick, "Big Test in Nebraska," *Chicago Tribune,* November 30, 1975, 2B.

9. Ibid.

10. James J. Kilpatrick, "Right to Know Threatened," *Omaha World-Herald,* December 4, 1975, 15.

11. Ibid.

12. Anthony Lewis, "Another Point of View: Does the Press Protest Too Much?" *Omaha World Herald,* December 13, 1975, 7.

13. Ibid.

14. Ibid.

15. Ibid.

16. "Motion of Nebraska Press Association et al. for Stay," Supreme Court of the United States, Case No. A-426, November 21, 1975.

17. Ibid., See also Jack C. Landau, "Press Confrontation May Face Justices," *Omaha World-Herald,* November 23, 1975, 2.

18. For information on the history and current activities of the Reporters Committee for Freedom of the Press, see its website, http://www.rcfp.org.

19. "Gag Order Cites Function of the Press," *Omaha World-Herald,* November 1, 1975, 1.

20. Prettyman's impressive resume may be viewed at his firm's website, http://www.hhlaw.com. For more on his background and career, see "Legends in the Law: An Interview with E. Barrett Prettyman, Jr.," *D.C. Bar Report* (April/May, 1997), available online at http://prettyman.ourfamily.com/people/ebarrettjr/ebarrettjr.htm.

21. For details of "amicus" procedures, see Rule 37, Rules of the Supreme Court of the United States.

22. "Amicus Memorandum of Reporters Committee For Freedom of the Press in Support of Motion for Stay," Supreme Court of the United States, Case No. A-426, November 21, 1975.

23. Ibid.

24. "Motion of Nebraska Press Association, et al. for Stay," Supreme Court of the United States, Case No. A-513, December 4, 1975.

25. "Motion of Nebraska Press Association, et al. for Expedited Hearing," Supreme Court of the United States, Case No. A-513, December 4, 1975.

26. "Motion of Nebraska Press Association, et al. to Treat All Previously-Filed Papers as Petition for Writ of Certiorari," Supreme Court of the United States, Case No. A-513, December 4, 1975.

27. For insight into the Supreme Court's operational patterns and procedures, see Kermit L. Hall, ed., *The Oxford Companion to the Supreme Court of the United States* (New York: Oxford University Press, 1992). Similarly useful reference works include Joan Biskupic and Elder Witt, *The Supreme Court at Work,* 2d ed.

(Washington, D.C.: Congressional Quarterly, 1997), and Elder Witt, *Guide to the U.S. Supreme Court,* 2d ed. (Washington, D.C.: Congressional Quarterly, 1990).

28. Hall, 132.

29. Rules of the Supreme Court of the United States, Rule 10.

30. Ibid.

31. See Hall, 132, where H. W. Perry, Jr., asserts that "the rule [governing the granting of certiorari] is almost a tautology: cases are important enough to be reviewed by the justices when the justices think they are important." See also John W. Johnson, *The Struggle for Student Rights: Tinker v. Des Moines and the 1960s* (Lawrence: University Press of Kansas, 1997), 122, making precisely the same point.

32. Lee Epstein et al., eds., *The Supreme Court Compendium: Data, Decisions, and Developments* (Washington, D.C.: Congressional Quarterly, 1994), 70.

33. Hall, 133.

34. Individual justices often record their thoughts and observations in notes recorded during the conferences, and those notes typically make their way into the collections of the personal papers of the justices after their retirement and/or death. Such collections, however, are often not made available for examination until some years after the justice's death, or have other restrictions attached to them. The papers of Warren Burger, for example, are held by the Library of the College of William and Mary, but will not be made available to researchers until 2026. Justice Harry Blackmun's papers have been bequeathed to the Library of Congress, but only became available to researchers in 2004.

35. The Court's December 8 procedural order is reported at *Nebraska Press Association v. Stuart,* 423 U.S. 1011, 96 S. Ct. 442 (1975).

36. Ibid.

37. "Response of State of Nebraska," and "Response of the Honorable Hugh Stuart," Supreme Court of the United States, Case No. A-513, December 8, 1975.

38. Ibid.

39. Ibid.

40. This order is reported at *Nebraska Press Association v. Stuart,* 423 U.S. 1027, 96 S. Ct. 557 (1975).

41. The Court's votes on the cert question, and Justice Powell's handwritten notes on the conference sessions, may be found in the archival collection of his judicial papers, housed in the Library of the Washington and Lee University School of Law in Lexington, Virginia. See Lewis Powell, internal memoranda and notes, April 19, 1976. Lewis F. Powell, Jr., Papers, File No. 75-817, Powell Archives, Washington and Lee University School of Law.

42. Ibid.

43. *Nebraska Press Association v. Stuart,* 423 U.S. 1027, 96 S. Ct. 557 (1975).

44. Ibid.

45. Ibid.

46. Rules of the Supreme Court of the United States, Rule 16(2).

47. Ibid., Rule 26.

48. Ibid., Rule 26(1).

49. Generally, Rules 24 and 25 provide the "content requirements" for Supreme Court briefs, while formatting, page limitations, cover colors, and other "mechanical" requirements are set out in Rule 33.

50. For more on the mootness doctrine, see Hall, *The Oxford Companion*, 562.

51. *Southern Pacific Terminal Co. v. Interstate Commerce Commission*, 219 U.S. 498, 515 (1911). See also *Sosna v. Iowa*, 419 U.S. 393 (1975); and *Storer v. Brown*, 415 U.S. 724, 737 n.8 (1974).

52. "Brief of Petitioners," Supreme Court of the United States, Case No. 75–817, 21.

53. Ibid., 22.

54. Ibid.

55. *Craig v. Harney*, 331 U.S. 367, 374 (1947).

56. *Estes v. Texas*, 381 U.S. 532, 541–542 (1965).

57. *Cox Broadcasting Corp. v. Cohn*, 420 U.S. 469, 496 (1975).

58. "Brief of Petitioners," Supreme Court of the United States, Case No. 75–817, 28.

59. See Russomanno, 284–285, where Floyd Abrams recalls the attorneys' strategizing over how best to deal with the *Branzburg* language that the state court had relied upon.

60. "Brief of Petitioners," Supreme Court of the United States, Case No. 75–817, 54.

61. Ibid., 28.

62. Ibid., 29.

63. "Voir dire" is a French phrase that has made its way into common usage in American trial procedure. It means "to speak the truth," and refers to the process of questioning potential jurors about their background, experience, education, and knowledge of a particular case, before they are seated on a jury. Prospective jurors who reveal bias or who are otherwise unable to serve with impartiality will be removed from the jury pool for cause. In most jurisdictions, each side in a trial will have the opportunity to dismiss a certain number of prospective jurors peremptorily as well—that is, without having to identify or prove any specific reason for doing so.

64. "Brief of Petitioners," Supreme Court of the United States, Case No. 75–817, 29–44, and sources cited therein.

65. Ironically, that is precisely what had occurred at Simants's trial in North Platte earlier in the year. At least four members of the jury that convicted Simants acknowledged during voir dire that they had formed some pretrial opinions about the case, but they were seated on the jury anyway, because they vowed that they could listen to the evidence impartially, and would

render a verdict solely on the basis of the evidence they heard at trial. See Chapter 8, *infra*.

66. "Brief of Petitioners," 44–45.

67. Ibid., 46. The possible "exception" for certain wartime information was first mentioned in *dictum* in Chief Justice Charles Evan Hughes's opinion in *Near v. Minnesota*, 283 U.S. 697 (1931). For more on that important First Amendment decision, see Fred W. Friendly, *Minnesota Rag: The Dramatic Story of the Landmark Case That Gave New Meaning to Freedom of the Press* (New York: Random House, 1981).

68. Ibid., 48.

69. Ibid., 60–61.

70. Ibid., 61–67.

71. Ibid., 65.

72. Ibid., 67.

73. Ibid., 68.

74. "Brief of Respondent Hugh Stuart," Supreme Court of the United States, Case No. 75-817, 6.

75. Ibid., 44–46.

76. Ibid., 38.

77. Ibid., 50–51.

78. Ibid., 51.

79. "Brief of Respondent, State of Nebraska," Supreme Court of the United States, Case No. 75-817, 9.

80. Ibid., 19.

81. Ibid., 11.

82. "Brief of Respondent-Intervenor, Erwin Charles Simants," Supreme Court of the United States, Case No. 75-817, 26–29.

83. "Brief of Respondent, State of Nebraska," Supreme Court of the United States, Case No. 75-817, 41.

84. "Brief of National Broadcasting Company, et al. as *Amici Curiae*," Supreme Court of the United States, Case No. 75-817, 14.

85. Ibid.

86. See "Reply Brief of Petitioners," Supreme Court of the United States, Case No. 75-817. The cases in question were *United States v. Liddy*, 509 F.2d 428 (D.C. Cir. 1974) and *State v. Van Duyne*, 43 N.J. 369, 204 A.2d 841 (N.J. 1964).

87. "Reply Brief of Petitioners," 7–8.

88. Ibid., 14–15.

89. Ibid., 15.

Six: May It Please the Court

1. William H. Rehnquist, *The Supreme Court* (New York: Alfred A. Knopf, 2001), 250.

2. For a thorough discussion of the Court's procedural traditions and practices with respect to oral argument, see Kermit Hall, ed., *The Oxford Companion to the Supreme Court of the United States* (New York: Oxford University Press, 1992). Similarly useful sources include Joan Biskupic and Elder Witt, *The Supreme Court at Work*, 2d ed. (Washington, D.C.: Congressional Quarterly, 1997), and Elder Witt, *Guide to the U.S. Supreme Court*, 2d ed. (Washington, D.C.: Congressional Quarterly, 1990).

3. Hall, 989.

4. Tinsley E. Yarbrough, *The Burger Court: Justices, Rulings, and Legacy* (Santa Barbara, Calif.: ABC-CLIO, 2000), 78.

5. Ibid., 80.

6. Hall, 104–105. Brief biographical sketches of all the justices on the *Nebraska Press Association* Court are available in Hall and many other reference works, including Rehnquist and Biskupic and Witt, *supra*. See also Leon Friedman and Fred L. Israel, eds., *The Justices of the United States Supreme Court, 1798–1978* (New York: Chelsea House, 1978), and Charles M. Lamb and Stephen C. Halpern, eds., *The Burger Court: Political and Judicial Profiles* (Chicago: University of Illinois Press, 1991).

7. For assessments of Burger's record as chief justice, see Bernard Schwartz, *The Ascent of Pragmatism: The Burger Court in Action* (New York: Addison-Wesley, 1990); Yarbrough; and Bernard Schwartz, ed., *The Burger Court: Counter-Revolution or Confirmation?* (New York: Oxford University Press, 1998).

8. Hall, 105.

9. Ibid. See also Yarbrough, 82–83.

10. *Miller v. California*, 413 U.S. 15 (1973).

11. Ibid., 24.

12. *New York Times Co. v. United States*, 403 U.S. 713 (1971).

13. Ibid., Chief Justice Burger dissenting.

14. Melvin I. Urofsky, *Affirmative Action on Trial: Sex Discrimination in Johnson v. Santa Clara* (Lawrence: University Press of Kansas, 1997): 130.

15. For more on Brennan's career and judicial legacy, see K. I. Eisler, *A Justice for All: William J. Brennan, Jr.* (New York: Simon & Schuster, 1994).

16. Schwartz, *The Ascent of Pragmatism*, 22–23. See also R. S. Marsell, "The Constitutional Jurisprudence of Justice Potter Stewart," *Tennessee Law Review* 55 (1987): 1.

17. *Jacobellis v. Ohio*, 378 U.S. 184, 197 (1964).

18. See Yarbrough, 65–71. For more on White's background and pre-Court career, see Dennis J. Hutchinson, *The Man Who Once Was Whizzer White: A Portrait of Justice Byron R. White* (New York: Free Press, 1998).

19. Russomanno, 285.

20. See Biskupic and Witt, 228. Marshall's career has been the subject of a good deal of academic scrutiny and comment. See, for example, Mark V. Tushnet,

Making Constitutional Law: Thurgood Marshall and the Supreme Court, 1961–1991 (New York: Oxford University Press, 1997).

21. The evolution of Blackmun's judicial philosophy and the deterioration of his relationship with Burger are thoroughly detailed in Linda Greenhouse, *Becoming Justice Blackmun: Harry Blackmun's Supreme Court Journey* (New York: Times Books, 2005).

22. See Biskupic and Witt, 231–232, and Urofsky, 131. For more on Powell's life and judicial career, see John C. Jeffries, Jr., *Justice Lewis F. Powell, Jr.* (New York: Scribner's, 1994).

23. Rehnquist's legacy as an associate justice is thoroughly analyzed in Sue Davis, *Justice Rehnquist and the Constitution* (Princeton, N.J.: Princeton University Press, 1989).

24. For more on the transition in constitutional interpretation from the Burger to the Rehnquist era, see Tinsley Yarbrough, *The Rehnquist Court and the Constitution* (New York: Oxford University Press, 2000).

25. For analysis of Stevens's constitutional interpretations, see R. J. Sickles, *John Paul Stevens and the Constitution* (State College: Pennsylvania State University Press, 1988).

26. Russomanno, 272.

27. Ibid.

28. For more on Prettyman's background, see Chapter 5 *infra.*

29. Russomanno, 276.

30. Rule 38(1), Rules of the Supreme Court of the United States.

31. Russomanno, 281–283.

32. Ibid.

33. Transcripts and audio recordings of Supreme Court oral arguments are available from numerous commercial, academic, and online sources. With a few clicks of a computer mouse, interested persons can listen to the arguments presented in *Nebraska Press* and other Supreme Court cases by going to www.oyez.org. Quotations contained herein are from Information Handling Services, "U.S. Supreme Court Records and Briefs," Microfiche collection, Schmid Law Library, University of Nebraska-Lincoln. Reference hereafter will be to "Transcript, Oral Argument," with appropriate page references.

34. Transcript, Oral Argument, 8.

35. Ibid., 9.

36. Ibid., 10.

37. Ibid., 14.

38. For more on the mootness doctrine and the "capable of repetition, yet evading review" exception, see Chapter 5 *infra.*

39. Transcript, Oral Argument, 16.

40. Recognizing that it was only the justices who typically posed hypotheticals during oral arguments, Prettyman understood that it was an unusual and

potentially dangerous tactic to offer one himself. Nevertheless, he took the risk, because he felt so strongly about the point he was making. See Russomanno, 282–283.

41. Transcript, Oral Argument, 17–18.
42. Ibid., 18.
43. Ibid., 18–19.
44. Ibid., 26.
45. The 1935 trial of Bruno Hauptmann for the kidnapping and murder of Anne and Charles Lindbergh's infant child has become notorious for the frenzied media coverage it produced. See *Hauptmann v. New Jersey*, 115 N.J.L. 412, 180 A. 809 (1935). The 1954 trial of Cleveland surgeon Sam Sheppard for the murder of his wife exceeded even the Hauptmann proceedings in that regard. For more on *Sheppard*, see Chapter 1 *infra*., and *Sheppard v. Maxwell*, 384 U.S. 333 (1966).
46. Transcript, Oral Argument, 28.
47. As discussed in Chapter 5 *infra*, after Simants's trial and conviction in January 1976 (several months before the Supreme Court arguments), Judge Stuart informally asked the jurors a series of questions about the impact of press coverage of the murders on their deliberations. Generally, the jurors indicated that, if they had known about Simants's confession, they would not have been able to serve "impartially" at his trial. See Chapter 5 *infra*.
48. Transcript, Oral Argument, 29.
49. Ibid.
50. Ibid., 32.
51. Ibid., 33.
52. Ibid., 34.
53. Ibid., 35.
54. Ibid.
55. Ibid., 36.
56. Ibid.
57. Ibid., 44.
58. Ibid.
59. Ibid., 45.
60. Ibid., 46.
61. Ibid.
62. Ibid., 47.
63. Ibid.
64. Ibid., 49.
65. Ibid., 49–50.
66. Ibid., 53.
67. Ibid., 54.
68. Ibid.
69. Ibid.

70. Ibid., 55.

71. Ibid., 56.

72. Lewis Powell, internal memoranda and notes, April 19, 1976. Lewis F. Powell, Jr., Papers, File No. 75-817, Powell Archives, Washington and Lee University School of Law (Hereinafter cited as "Powell Papers").

73. Transcript, Oral Argument, 57.

74. Ibid., 58.

75. Ibid.

76. Ibid.

77. Ibid., 59.

78. Ibid., 61.

79. Ibid., 65.

80. Ibid., 66.

81. Lewis Powell, internal memoranda and notes, April 19, 1976. Powell Papers.

82. Transcript, Oral Argument, 66.

83. Ibid., 71–72.

84. Ibid., 72.

85. Ibid.

Seven: Decision and Reaction

1. Details regarding the Court's procedural traditions and protocol during conferences are available in numerous sources. See especially Kermit Hall, ed., *The Oxford Companion to the Supreme Court of the United States* (New York: Oxford University Press, 1992); Joan Biskupic and Elder Witt, *The Supreme Court at Work,* 2d ed. (Washington, D.C.: Congressional Quarterly, 1997); William H. Rehnquist, *The Supreme Court* (New York: Alfred A. Knopf, 2001); Bernard Schwartz, *The Ascent of Pragmatism: The Burger Court in Action* (New York: Addison-Wesley, 1990); John W. Johnson, *The Struggle for Student Rights: Tinker v. Des Moines and the 1960s* (Lawrence: University Press of Kansas, 1997); and Melvin I. Urofsky, *Affirmative Action on Trial: Sex Discrimination in Johnson v. Santa Clara* (Lawrence: University Press of Kansas, 1997).

2. Quoted in Biskupic and Elder, 78.

3. Johnson, 164.

4. See Rehnquist, 255–257.

5. Biskupic and Witt, 78.

6. Quoted in Schwartz, 12.

7. Biskupic and Witt, 78.

8. Tangible evidence of Warren's leadership in *Brown* is dramatically accessible at the Library of Congress' "American Memory" website. In its "Earl Warren Papers" collection, the LOC provides digitized copies of handwritten notes to Warren from Justices William Douglas, Harold Burton, and Felix Frankfurter, all congratulating him for his persuasive diplomacy in forging the Court's

unanimous opinion in the case. See http://memory.loc.gov. For more on Warren's career, see G. Edward White, *Earl Warren: A Public Life* (New York: Oxford University Press, 1987), and Ed Cray, *Chief Justice: A Biography of Earl Warren* (New York: Simon & Schuster, 1997).

9. See, for example, Hall, 105, and Urofsky, 147–148.

10. Schwartz, 12.

11. Ibid.

12. Ibid., 14. For similar criticism of Burger in this regard, see Hall, 105.

13. *Swann v. Charlotte-Mecklenburg Board of Education,* 402 U.S. 1 (1971).

14. *Roe v. Wade,* 410 U.S. 113 (1973).

15. Biskupic and Witt, 79.

16. See Schwartz, 171–173.

17. Bob Woodward and Scott Armstrong, *The Brethren: Inside the Supreme Court* (New York: Simon & Schuster, 1979).

18. Ibid., 422.

19. Quoted in Schwartz, 171.

20. Ibid.

21. *New York Times Co. v. United States,* 403 U.S. 713 (1971).

22. Schwartz, 171.

23. Ibid., 172.

24. Woodward and Armstrong, 421.

25. Schwartz, 172.

26. Ibid.

27. Woodward and Armstrong, 421–422.

28. Schwartz, 172.

29. Woodward and Armstrong, 422.

30. Schwartz, 172.

31. Quoted in Schwartz, 171.

32. Ibid. Powell's position is also reflected in numerous notes and memoranda in his personal papers. See Lewis F. Powell, Jr., Papers, File No. 75-817, Powell Archives, Washington and Lee University School of Law.

33. Biskupic and Witt, 82.

34. Rehnquist, 266.

35. See generally Biskupic and Witt, 82–83.

36. *Nebraska Press Association v. Stuart,* 427 U.S. 539 (1976).

37. Ibid., 547.

38. Ultimately, the Nebraska Supreme Court did in fact reverse Simants's conviction, though the reversal had nothing to do with pretrial publicity. See chapter 8 *infra.*

39. *Nebraska Press Association v. Stuart,* 427 U.S. 539 (1976), 548.

40. Ibid.

41. Ibid.

42. Ibid., 549.

43. Ibid., 550.

44. Ibid., 556, n.4.

45. Ibid., 559, quoting from *Carroll v. Princess Anne,* 393 U.S. 175, 181 (1968). See also *Near v. Minnesota,* 283 U.S. 697 (1931), and *New York Times Co. v. United States,* 403 U.S. 713 (1971). In *Near,* Chief Justice Charles Evan Hughes held, for a 5–4 majority, that a Minnesota statute purporting to prohibit the publication of "malicious, scandalous, or defamatory" material constituted an unconstitutional "prior restraint" of the press, in violation of the First Amendment.

46. Ibid., 560.

47. Ibid., 563.

48. Ibid., 564.

49. Ibid.

50. Ibid., 566.

51. Ibid., 564–566.

52. Ibid., 568.

53. Ibid., 569.

54. Ibid.

55. Ibid., 570.

56. Ibid., 571.

57. Ibid.

58. Ibid., 572, Justice White concurring.

59. Ibid.

60. Ibid., Justice Powell concurring.

61. Ibid., 588, Justice Brennan concurring.

62. Ibid., 589.

63. Ibid.

64. Ibid., 605.

65. Ibid., 613.

66. Ibid.

67. Ibid., 614.

68. Ibid., 618, Justice Stevens concurring.

69. Ibid.

70. Ibid.

71. "Court Rules for Press in Nebraska Gag Case," *Omaha World-Herald,* June 30, 1976, 1.

72. Ibid. See also "State News Group Head, Local Attorney Pleased," *Lincoln Star,* July 1, 1976, 3.

73. "Reporters Committee Says Ruling 'Victory,'" *Omaha World-Herald,* July 1, 1976, 4.

74. Ibid.

75. Ibid.

76. "Falloff 'Certain' In Gag Orders," *Omaha World-Herald,* July 1, 1976, 1.

77. Ibid.

78. Ibid. See also Dean Terrill, "Minority Opinion Disturbs Judge Stuart," *Lincoln Star,* July 1, 1976, 3.

79. "Court Rules for Press in Nebraska Gag Case," *Omaha World-Herald,* June 30, 1976, 1.

80. Quoted in Terrill, 3.

81. Ibid.

82. See Glen Elsasser, "High Court Strikes Down Nebraska Press Gag, 9–0," *Chicago Tribune,* July 1, 1976, 1; Linda Mathews, "Court Sharply Curbs Power of Judges to Gag Press," *Los Angeles Times,* July 1, 1976, 1; Wayne Green, "Justices Limit Courts' Authority to Restrict Press," *Wall Street Journal,* July 1, 1976, 2; Leslie Oelsner, "High Court Rules Judges May Not, In General, Gag Press in Criminal Cases," *New York Times,* July 1, 1976, 1; and John P. MacKenzie, "Court Voids Gag Nebraska Judge Placed on Press," *Washington Post,* July 1, 1976, 1.

83. Editorial, "Freedom of the Press in 1976," *Washington Post,* July 3, 1976, A12.

84. Editorial, "Pulling Out the Gag," *Los Angeles Times,* July 1, 1976, Pt. II, 4.

85. Editorial, "Press Freedom Upheld," *New York Times,* July 1, 1976, 28.

86. "Reporters Committee Says Ruling 'Victory,'" *Omaha World-Herald,* July 1, 1976, 4.

87. Ibid.

88. Editorial, "Freedom of the Press in 1976," *Washington Post,* July 3, 1976, A12.

89. G. Woodson Howe, "Fair Trial vs. Free Press: Who Won?" *The Nebraska Newspaper* 34 (August 1976): 1.

90. Ibid.

Eight: The Continuing Saga of the Simants Criminal Prosecutions and the Legacy of *Nebraska Press Association*

1. For more on the various versions of the gag order, see chapters 3 and 4, *infra.*

2. "Motion to Close Pre-Trial Proceedings," December 23, 1975, *State of Nebraska vs. Erwin Charles Simants,* Lincoln County District Court, Case No. B-2904. The pleadings, motions, memoranda, testimony, evidence, and other documents entered in Simants's trial are compiled in eleven volumes of records, which are presently archived at North Platte in the offices of Anita Childerston, Clerk of the District Court, Lincoln County, Nebraska. References herein to documents culled from those records will be by title and date, where available.

3. Judge Hugh Stuart, "Journal Entry," December 29, 1975, *State of Nebraska vs. Erwin Charles Simants,* Lincoln County District Court, Case No. B-2904. In this same order, Stuart also denied the defense's request for a change of venue, granted the request of both the defense and the prosecution for sequestration of the jury, and held that Simants's taped confession had been given voluntarily, and would therefore be admissible at trial. The latter ruling

came only after Stuart had cleared the courtroom of all spectators and heard evidence in a closed setting.

4. "Motion to Close Pre-Trial Proceedings," January 2, 1976, *State of Nebraska vs. Erwin Charles Simants*, Lincoln County District Court, Case No. B-2904. As previously noted *infra*, "voir dire" refers to the process of questioning potential jurors about their background, experience, education, and knowledge of a particular case, before they are seated on a jury. Prospective jurors who reveal bias or who are otherwise unable to serve with impartiality will be removed from the jury pool "for cause." Each side in a trial will typically have the opportunity to dismiss a certain number of prospective jurors "peremptorily" as well—that is, without having to identify or prove any specific reason for doing so.

5. Ibid., "Motion to Close."

6. R. G. Dunlop, "Jury is Half-Picked; Media Stays Outside," *Omaha World-Herald,* January 7, 1976, 1. See also "Press Rejects Rules, Skips Jury Selection," *Lincoln Journal,* January 6, 1976, 1; "Stuart Closes Jury Selection," *North Platte Telegraph,* January 5, 1976, 1; and "Court Reopens, But Reporters Decline Judge's Limitations," *North Platte Telegraph,* January 6, 1976, 1.

7. Fred W. Friendly, "A Crime and Its Aftershock," *New York Times Magazine,* March 21, 1976, 94.

8. Ibid.

9. Dean Terrill, "Jury Panel Chosen in Simants Trial," *Lincoln Journal-Star,* January 8, 1976, 1. See also R. G. Dunlop, "Curbs on Press Likely to Grow," *Omaha World-Herald,* January 8, 1976, 1.

10. Ibid.

11. The transcripts of the testimony of the prosecution witnesses may be found in Volumes V, VI, and VII of the trial records. See note 2 above.

12. Trial Transcript, Vol. VI, 1389–1390.

13. Simants's confession to law enforcement officials was accepted into evidence as State's Exhibit 12, and may be read at Trial Transcript, Vol. VII, 1728–1748. See also R. G. Dunlop, "Killings Recalled on Simants Tape," *Omaha World-Herald,* January 14, 1976, 2.

14. Neb. Rev. Stat. sec. 29-2303. See, e.g., *State v. Jacobs,* 190 Neb. 4, 205 N.W.2d 662, *cert. denied,* 414 U.S. 860 (1973). During the 1980s, the Nebraska statute was amended several times, and it now requires a defendant asserting an insanity defense to affirmatively prove his incapacity by a preponderance of the evidence. The standards for such a showing remain essentially the same— only the party who bears the burden of proof has been changed. See, e.g., *State v. Carr,* 231 Neb. 127, 435 N.W.2d 194 (1989) and *Tulloch v. State,* 237 Neb. 138, 465 N.W.2d 448 (1991).

15. Inexplicably, Volumes VIII, IX, and X of the records of Simants's trial are missing from the clerk's office. Those volumes would contain the transcripts of testimony from the defense's medical witnesses, and the prosecution's

rebuttal witnesses on the insanity issue. Accounts of that testimony given here are from contemporaneous newspaper stories.

16. R. G. Dunlop, "Simants Actions Called Unfeeling, Schizophrenic," *Omaha World-Herald,* January 15, 1976, 1.

17. R. G. Dunlop, "Tests Called No Evidence of Insanity," *Omaha World-Herald,* January 16, 1976, 2; and R. G. Dunlop, "Jurors Try Again Today on Simants," *Omaha World-Herald,* January 17, 1976, 1.

18. Quoted in Laura Poland, "Jury Says Simants Guilty, Sentence Hearing Jan. 29," *North Platte Telegraph,* January 19, 1976, 1.

19. Ibid.

20. Ibid.

21. Quoted in R. G. Dunlop, "Simants Fate Will Be Told January 29," *Omaha World-Herald,* January 18, 1976, 1.

22. Ibid.

23. Neb. Rev. Stat. sec. 29-2523. Included among the eight "aggravating" circumstances listed in the statute are the defendant's prior criminal history, the "atrocious or particularly heinous" nature of the crime, and the commission of murder in an attempt to conceal other crimes.

24. "Order," Judge Hugh Stuart, January 29, 1976, *State of Nebraska vs. Erwin Charles Simants,* Lincoln County District Court, Case No. B-2904. The dispositive language of the order reads, in full, "It is the judgment of this Court that you, Erwin Charles Simants be put to death on Wednesday April 21, 1976, at 11:00 o'clock in the morning of that day by the proper person or persons authorized by the Statutes of the State of Nebraska by causing to be passed through your body a current of electricity of sufficient intensity to cause death; and the application of such current shall be continued until you, Erwin Charles Simants, are dead."

25. Ibid.

26. Ibid. See also R. G. Dunlop, "'Atrocious' Acts Convince Judge," *Omaha World-Herald,* January 30, 1976, 1.

27. Laura Poland, "Simants Sentenced to Die, but Appeal Is Automatic," *North Platte Telegraph,* January 30, 1976, 1.

28. Neb. Rev. Stat. sec. 29-2525. Simants's automatic appeal from his conviction and death sentence was docketed in the Nebraska Supreme Court as Case No. 40642, and the records related to those proceedings are archived in the office of the Clerk of the Nebraska Supreme Court.

29. "Writ of Error," Nebraska Supreme Court, Case No. 40642, February 23, 1976.

30. See "Brief of Appellant," Nebraska Supreme Court, Case No. 40642, August 26, 1976; and "Brief of Appellee," Nebraska Supreme Court, Case No. 40642, October 26, 1976.

31. *State of Nebraska v. Erwin Charles Simants,* 197 Neb. 549, 571, 250 N.W. 2d 881, 894 (1977).

32. Ibid.

33. "Order for Execution of Sentence," Nebraska Supreme Court, Case No. 40642, March 18, 1977. See also "Death Dates For 3 Killers Set by Court," *Omaha World-Herald,* March 19, 1977, 1.

34. *Erwin Charles Simants v. State of Nebraska,* 434 U.S. 878 (1977).

35. Ibid.

36. "Order for Execution of Sentence," Nebraska Supreme Court, Case No. 40642, October 12, 1977.

37. Justice Harry Blackmun, "Order," United States Supreme Court, Case No. A-373, October 26, 1977.

38. "Petition for Writ of Error *Coram Nobis,*" Lincoln County District Court, Case No. 75-201, January 5, 1978.

39. Ibid.

40. Ibid.

41. "Affidavit of Claire Nicholas" and "Affidavit of Eugene Larson," Exhibits "C" and "D," respectively, attached to "Petition for Writ of Error *Coram Nobis,*" Lincoln County District Court, Case No. 75–201, January 5, 1978.

42. The "writ of error coram nobis" is an ancient and seldom-used procedural mechanism by which a party can seek to correct a judgment rendered by a court, on the basis of new factual matters or errors in the proceeding that were not apparent or available at the time of the original judgment. The party seeking such a writ must show that, if the new facts had been known at the time of the original judgment, they would have prevented the entry of that judgment. See "Writ of Error Coram Nobis," *Black's Law Dictionary,* 4th ed. (St. Paul, Minn.: West Publishing, 1968), 1785; and *State v. Turner,* 194 Neb. 252, 231 N.W.2d 345 (1975).

43. "Court Grants Three Stays of Execution," *Omaha World-Herald,* January 10, 1978, 1; and "Court Orders Delay in Three Executions," *Omaha World-Herald,* April 15, 1978, 1.

44. "Motion to Disqualify District Judge Hugh Stuart," Lincoln County District Court, Case No. 75-201, January 18, 1978.

45. "Motion to Strike Affidavit of Counsel, Keith N. Bystrom," and "Objections and Response to Motion to Disqualify District Judge Hugh Stuart," Lincoln County District Court, Case No. 75-201, January 23, 1978.

46. "Journal Entry," Judge Hugh Stuart, Lincoln County District Court, Case No. 75-201, January 25, 1978.

47. The transcripts of the testimony and evidence presented in the District Court during the *coram nobis* proceedings are available as part of the "Bill of Exceptions" filed later in the Nebraska Supreme Court, Docket Number 42206. They will be cited hereinafter as "*Coram Nobis* transcript," with appropriate volume and page references.

48. *Coram Nobis* transcript, Vol. I, 168–175.

49. Ibid., Vol. II, 196–247.

50. Ibid., 322.

51. Ibid., 209, 268, 343, and 405.

52. "Judgment," Judge Keith Windrum, Lincoln County District Court, Case No. 75-201, May 15, 1978.

53. Ibid.

54. *Erwin Charles Simants v. State of Nebraska,* 202 Neb. 828, 277 N.W.2d 217 (1979).

55. Ibid., 834.

56. Ibid., 835.

57. Ibid.

58. Ibid., 839.

59. Quoted in Frank Santiago, "New Trial for Simants Likely Soon," *Omaha World-Herald,* April 3, 1979, 1.

60. "Motion for Change of Venue," Lincoln County District Court, Case No. 75-201, July 12, 1978.

61. "Order," Lincoln County District Court, Case No. 75-201, August 6, 1978.

62. Ibid.

63. At the time of Simants's first trial in January 1976, Nebraska law provided that changes of venue in criminal proceedings could only be granted to counties directly adjacent to the one in which the crime occurred. That law was changed in 1978, allowing Judge Stuart to shift the site of the second trial to Lincoln. See Neb. Rev. Stat. sec. 29-1301.

64. Michael Kelly, "W-H Chief: Judge Spoke Irresponsibly," *Omaha World-Herald,* August 8, 1979, 5.

65. Ibid.

66. Ibid.

67. "Juror Pool Will Form Next Week," *Omaha World-Herald,* August 9, 1979, 18.

68. Frank Partsch, "Simants Murder Trial Has Light Moments," *Omaha World-Herald,* October 4, 1979, 4.

69. Ibid.

70. Paula Dittrick, "Selection of Jury For Simants Retrial Is Under Way," *Lincoln Star,* October 2, 1979, 25. See also Frank Partsch, "Judge Seats Simants Jurors; Motel Now Their Home," *Omaha World-Herald,* October 5, 1979, 6. Because no appeal was taken from the result of Simants's second trial, there is no existing transcript of the testimony and evidence introduced at trial. (Such transcripts, being quite lengthy and expensive to produce, are typically only created when a party appeals from a trial court judgment.) Therefore, the brief account of the second trial given here is derived largely from contemporary newspaper reports.

71. Frank Partsch, "Simants' Sanity Trial Focus; Killings, Assaults Admitted," *Omaha World-Herald,* October 6, 1979, 16.

72. Ibid.

73. Ibid.

74. Ibid.

75. Frank Partsch, "Judge Allows Testimony at Simants' Trial," *Omaha World-Herald,* October 7, 1979, 9-B.

76. Paula Dittrick, "Psychiatrists Believe Simants Was Insane," *Lincoln Star,* October 12, 1979, 12. See also Frank Partsch, "Witness: Simants Brooded Over Death," *Omaha World-Herald,* October 12, 1979, 20.

77. Ibid.

78. Frank Partsch, "State's Doctors Say Simants Sane," *Omaha World-Herald,* October 13, 1979, 12.

79. Paula Dittrick, "Jury Deliberates Simants Decision," *Lincoln Star,* October 16, 1979, 1.

80. Ibid.

81. The jury deliberations in Simants's second trial became quite controversial in the days after the verdict was announced. Some of the jurors alleged that one particular member had exercised an inordinate degree of influence and "coercion" over the rest of the panel, because of his background and training in psychology. See "Juror Thinks Some Coerced," *Omaha World-Herald,* October 18, 1979, 3.

82. Frank Partsch, "'Mad, Not Bad' Simants Grins after Trial Finds Him Insane," *Omaha World-Herald,* October 18, 1979, 1.

83. Paula Dittrick, "Lancaster County Jury Finds Simants Innocent," *Lincoln Star,* 18 October 1979, 1.

84. "Simants' Father: Verdict Takes Load Off My Mind," *Omaha World-Herald,* October 18, 1979, 4.

85. "Simants Acquittal Upsets Town," *Lincoln Star,* October 18, 1979, 18.

86. Ibid.

87. Ibid. See also Sally Schull, "Verdict Upsets Kellies' Town," *Omaha World-Herald,* October 18, 1979, 4; "Insanity Ruling Rankles '76 Jurors," *Omaha World-Herald,* October 18, 1979, 4; John Taylor, "Dismay and Surprise Greet Verdict," *Omaha World-Herald,* October 18, 1979, 4.

88. Neb. Rev. Stat. sec. 29-3701.

89. "Simants Committed To Lincoln Regional Center," *North Platte Telegraph,* October 27, 1979, 1.

90. Neb. Rev. Stat. sec. 29-3703.

91. *State of Nebraska v. Erwin Charles Simants,* 213 Neb. 638, 330 N.W.2d 910 (1983), and *State of Nebraska v. Erwin Charles Simants,* 248 Neb. 581, 537 N.W. 2d 346 (1995). The other cases, all discussed in previous chapters *infra,* were *State v. Simants,* 182 Neb. 491, 155 N.W.2d 788 (1968) (involving his prior conviction for contributing to the delinquency of a minor); *State v. Simants,* 194 Neb. 783, 236 N.W.2d 794 (1975) (involving the constitutionality of the gag order); *State v. Simants,* 197 Neb. 549, 250 N.W. 2d 881 (1977) (affirming his original conviction and death sentence); and *Simants v. State,* 202 Neb. 828, 277 N.W.2d 217 (1979) (reversing his conviction and ordering a new trial).

92. See, for example, Dan Day, "Recluse Simants' Night of Terror Shocked Town 10 Years Ago Today," *Omaha World-Herald,* October 18, 1985, 13; Paul Hamel, "Supervision of Simants is Debated," *Omaha World-Herald,* August 24, 1994, 13; Editorial, "Horrors of the Past Lose Sharpness as Distortions Creep Into the Story," *Omaha World-Herald,* September 5, 1994; Paul Hamel, "Court Weighs Mental Help for Simants," *Omaha World-Herald,* September 5, 1995, 11; "Simants' Appeal on Supervision Rejected," *Omaha World-Herald,* September 22, 1995, 14; "Limits Eased On Simants," *Omaha World-Herald,* October 23, 1999, 61; "Simants' Status Is Unchanged after Review," *Omaha World-Herald,* May 24, 2000, 20.

93. Quoted in Editorial, "Whether to Ease Limits on Simants Is Mainly a Public Safety Concern," *Omaha World-Herald,* August 26, 1984, 20.

94. Lisa Johns, "Kellie Relative Still Fears Simants," *Lincoln Journal,* June 13, 1992, 12.

95. See Robynn Tysver, "Supervision on Outings is Loosened for Simants," *Omaha World-Herald,* January 8, 2003, 4B; and "Simants May Lose Deal Allowing Outings," *Omaha World-Herald,* January 30, 2003, 3B.

96. For examples of typical textbook and monographic treatments of *Nebraska Press Association v. Stuart,* see Douglas S. Campbell, *Free Press v. Fair Trial: Supreme Court Decisions Since 1807* (Westport, Conn.: Praeger, 1994); Richard Davis, *Decisions and Images: The Supreme Court and the Press* (Englewood Cliffs, N.J.: Prentice-Hall, 1994); Donald E. Lively et al., *First Amendment Anthology* (Cincinnati: Anderson Publishing, 1994); James V. Calvi and Susan Coleman, *Cases in Constitutional Law* (Englewood Cliffs, N.J.: Prentice-Hall, 1994), and Alfred H. Kelly, Winfred A. Harbison, and Herman Belz, *The American Constitution: Its Origins and Development,* Vol. II (7th ed.) (New York: Norton, 1991).

97. In addition to the voluminous news reports and commentary on the case cited elsewhere herein, the scholarly assessments of *Nebraska Press Association v. Stuart* include Thomas G. Abbey, "Constitutional Law—Judicial Restraint of the Press—*Nebraska Press Association v. Stuart,*" *Creighton Law Review* 9 (1976): 693–716; Glenn H. Alberich, "*Nebraska Press Association v. Stuart:* Balancing Freedom of the Press Against the Right to a Fair Trial," *New England Law Review* 12 (winter 1977): 763–788; William H. Erickson, "Fair Trial and Free Press: The Practical Dilemma," *Stanford Law Review* 29 (February 1977): 485–496; James C. Goodale, "The Press Ungagged: The Practical Effect on Gag Order Litigation of *Nebraska Press Association v. Stuart,*" *Stanford Law Review* 29 (February 1977): 497–514; Milton R. Larson, "Free Press v. Fair Trial in Nebraska: A Position Paper," *Nebraska Law Review* 55 (1976): 543–571; Milton R. Larson and John P. Murphy, "*Nebraska Press Association v. Stuart*—A Prosecutor's View of Pre-Trial Restraints on the Press," *DePaul Law Review* 26 (spring 1977): 417–446; Cynthia M. Nakao, "Constitutional Law: Gag Me with a Prior Restraint: A Chilling Effect that Sends Shivers Down

the Spines of Attorneys and the Media," *Loyola Entertainment Law Journal* 7 (1987): 353–369; Sheldon Portman, "The Defense of Fair Trial from Sheppard to Nebraska Press Association: Benign Neglect to Affirmative Action and Beyond," *Stanford Law Review* 29 (February 1977): 393–410; and D. Grier Stephenson, Jr., "Fair Trial—Free Press: Rights in Continuing Conflict," *Brooklyn Law Review* 46 (fall 1979): 39–66.

98. *Richmond Newspapers Inc v. Virginia,* 448 U.S. 555 (1980), and *Globe Newspapers Co. v. Superior Court,* 457 U.S. 596 (1982).

99. For commentary on the increasing prevalence of "indirect" gag orders, see Sheryl A. Bjork, "Indirect Gag Orders and the Doctrine of Prior Restraint," *University of Miami Law Review* 44 (September 1989): 165–195; See also Editorial, "The News Media Must Keep Fighting the 'Gag Instinct'," *News Media and the Law* 24, no. 2 (May 2000): 2, lamenting "a nationwide epidemic" of indirect gag orders, and urging media outlets to challenge them regularly and vigorously. The *Omaha World-Herald,* along with many other major newspapers, has been doing just that. See Paul Hammel, "World-Herald Plans to Fight Gag Order in Homicide Probe," *Omaha World-Herald,* December 23, 2000, 43, describing the paper's intention to challenge an order issued by a judge in Gage County, Nebraska, purporting to prohibit reporters from interviewing grand jurors or witnesses in a homicide investigation.

100. Robert Dorr, "Nebraska Press Case Brought Landmark Ruling," *Omaha World-Herald,* December 11, 1991, 13.

101. Quoted in Charlyne Berens, "Prior Restraint Threatens Free Speech," *NU College of Journalism and Mass Communications Alumni News,* 11, no. 1 (summer 2001): 1.

102. Tammy Skrdlant, "Nebraska Court Case Held Vital Free Press Role," *Omaha World-Herald,* April 28, 2001, 17. See also John R. Bender, "Nebraska Case Guaranteed Our Right to Information," *Lincoln Journal-Star,* June 30, 2006, 9B, commemorating the thirtieth anniversary of the decision.

103. Berens, 3.

104. Ibid.

105. The same story is told in various other sources, including Joseph Russomanno, *Speaking Our Minds: Conversations with the People behind Landmark First Amendment Cases* (Mahwah, N.J.: Lawrence Erlbaum Associates, 2002); and Nancy Whitmore, *"Nebraska Press Association v. Stuart:* An Understanding of Prior Restraint," Unpublished M.A. Thesis, University of Nebraska at Omaha, 1995. Judge Stuart died on April 3, 2006, at age 84. The *Omaha World-Herald* eulogized him as a "dignified, precise jurist" and a "courtly gentleman" who not only left his name on the famous court ruling "but also gave the people of Nebraska many years of dedicated service." "Hugh Stuart," *Omaha World-Herald,* April 5, 2006, 6B.

106. Berens, 8.

BIBLIOGraPHY

Manuscripts and Archival Materials

Pleadings, Motions, Briefs, Transcripts of Arguments, and related documents contained in the following Court Files:

In the offices of the Clerk of the Lincoln County District Court,
North Platte, Nebraska:

State of Nebraska v. Erwin Charles Simants, Lincoln County Court, Docket No. 28-401.

State of Nebraska v. Erwin Charles Simants, Lincoln County District Court, Docket No. 75-201.

State of Nebraska v. Edwin Charles Simants, Lincoln County District Court, Docket No. B-2904.

In the offices of the Clerk, Supreme Court of the State of Nebraska,
Lincoln, Nebraska:

State v. Simants, Docket No. 36663.

State v. Simants, Docket No. 40445, 40471.

State v. Simants, Docket No. 40642.

Simants v. State, Docket No. 42206.

State v. Simants, Docket No. 82–903.

State v. Simants, Docket No. S-93–684.

State v. Simants, Docket No. S-94–943.

In the offices of the Clerk, United States Supreme Court, Washington, D.C.:

Nebraska Press Association v. Stuart, Docket No. A-426.

Nebraska Press Association v. Stuart, Docket No. A-513.

Nebraska Press Association v. Stuart, Docket No. 75–817.

Papers of William F. Brennan, Jr., Library of Congress, Washington, D.C.

Papers of Thurgood Marshall, Library of Congress, Washington, D.C.

Papers of Lewis F. Powell, Jr., Powell Archives, Washington and Lee University School of Law, Lexington, Va.

Papers of Byron R. White, Library of Congress, Washington, D.C.

Published Judicial Opinions

Bridges v. California, 314 U.S. 252 (1941).
Branzburg v. Hayes, 408 U.S. 665 (1972).
Burr v. United States, 25 Fed. Cas. 49, Case No.14,692g (Circuit Ct., Va., 1807).
Cox Broadcasting Corp. v. Cohn, 420 U.S. 469 (1975).
Craig v. Harney, 331 U.S. 367 (1975).
Estes v. Texas, 381 U.S. 532 (1965).
Flood v. Kuhn, 407 U.S. 258 (1972).
Globe Newspapers Co. v. Superior Court, 457 U.S. 596 (1982).
Hauptmann v. New Jersey, 115 N.J.L. 412, 180 A. 809 (1935).
Irvin v. Dowd, 366 U.S. 717 (1961).
Jacobellis v. Ohio, 378 U.S. 184 (1964).
Miller v. California, 413 U.S. 15 (1973).
Near v. Minnesota, 283 U.S. 697 (1931).
Nebraska Press Association v. Stuart, 423 U.S. 1027 (1975).
Nebraska Press Association v. Stuart, 423 U.S. 1319 (1975).
Nebraska Press Association v. Stuart, 423 U.S. 1327 (1975).
Nebraska Press Association v. Stuart, 427 U.S. 539 (1976).
New York Times Co. v. United States, 403 U.S. 713 (1971).
Reynolds v. United States, 95 U.S. 145 (1878).
Richmond Newspapers Inc. v. Virginia, 448 U.S. 555 (1980).
Roe v. Wade, 410 U.S. 113 (1973).
Schenck v. United States, 249 U.S. 47 (1919).
Sheppard v. Maxwell, 384 U.S. 333 (1966).
Simants v. State of Nebraska, 434 U.S. 878 (1977).
Simants v. State of Nebraska, 202 Neb. 828, 277 N.W.2d 217 (1979).
Sosna v. Iowa, 419 U.S. 393 (1975).
Southern Pacific Terminal v. Interstate Commerce Commission, 219 U.S. 498 (1911).
State v. Carr, 231 Neb. 127, 435 N.W.2d 194 (1989).
State v. Jacobs, 190 Neb. 4, 205 N.W.2d 662, cert. denied, 414 U.S. 860 (1973).
State v. Simants, 182 Neb. 491, 155 N.W.2d 788 (1968).
State v. Simants, 194 Neb. 783, 236 N.W.2d 794 (1975).
State v. Simants, 197 Neb. 549, 250 N.W.2d 881 (1977).
State v. Simants, 213 Neb. 638, 330 N.W.2d 910 (1983).

State v. Simants, 248 Neb. 581, 537 N.W. 2d 346 (1995).

State v. Turner, 194 Neb. 252, 231 N.W.2d 345 (1975).

State v. Van Duyne, 43 N.J. 369, 204 A.2d 841 (N.J. 1964).

Storer v. Brown, 415 U.S. 724 (1974).

Swann v. Charlotte-Mecklenburg Board of Education, 402 U.S. 1 (1971).

Tulloch v. State, 237 Neb. 138, 465 N.W.2d 448 (1991).

United States v. Dickinson, 465 F.2d 496 (5ᵗʰ Cir. 1972).

United States v. Liddy, 509 F.2d 428 (D.C. Cir. 1974).

Statutes, Procedural Rules, and Miscellaneous Primary Sources

Nebraska. *Nebraska Revised Statutes.* Sections 24–311; 24–1001; 29–1606; 29–1802; 29–2303; 29–2523; 29–2525; 29–3701; 29–3703.

Supreme Court of the United States. *Rules of Procedure* 10, 16, 22, 23, 24, 25, 33, 37.

United States Code. Title 28, sections 2101(f) and 1257(3).

U.S. Congress. *Annals of Congress.* (Gales and Seaton, 1789–1824).

Virginia. *Virginia Bill of Rights. Statutes at Large* Vol. IX (Hening, 1776).

Books

Abernathy, Thomas. *The Burr Conspiracy.* New York: Oxford University Press, 1954.

Abrams, Floyd. *Speaking Freely: Trials of the First Amendment.* New York: Viking, 2005.

Abramson, Jeffrey. *We, the Jury: The Jury System and the Ideal of Democracy.* New York: BasicBooks, 1994.

Biskupic, Joan, and Elder Witt. *The Supreme Court at Work, 2d ed.* Washington, D.C.: Congressional Quarterly, 1997.

Black's Law Dictionary. St. Paul, Minn.: West Publishing, 1968.

Buckner, Melton, Jr. *Aaron Burr, Conspiracy to Treason.* New York: Wiley, 2002.

Calvi, James V., and Susan Coleman. *Cases in Constitutional Law.* Englewood Cliffs, N.J.: Prentice-Hall, 1994.

Campbell, Douglas S. *Free Press v. Fair Trial: Supreme Court Decisions since 1807.* Westport, Conn.: Praeger, 1994.

Cray, Ed. *Chief Justice: A Biography of Earl Warren.* New York: Simon & Schuster, 1997.

Davis, Richard. *Decisions and Images: The Supreme Court and the Press.* Englewood Cliffs, N.J.: Prentice-Hall, 1994.

Davis, Sue. *Justice Rehnquist and the Constitution.* Princeton, N.J.: Princeton University Press, 1989.

Devol, Kenneth S., ed. *Mass Media and the Supreme Court: The Legacy of the Warrren Years.* Mamaroneck, N.Y.: Hastings House, 1990.

Dumbauld, Edward. *The Bill of Rights.* Norman: University of Oklahoma Press, 1957.

Dwyer, William L. *In the Hands of the People: The Trial Jury's Origins, Triumphs, Troubles, and Future in American Democracy.* New York: Saint Martin's, 2002.

Eisler, K. I. *A Justice for All: William J. Brennan, Jr., and the Decisions that Transformed America.* New York: Simon & Schuster, 1994.

Epstein, Lee, Jeffrey A. Segal, Harold J. Sparta, and Thomas G. Walker, eds. *The Supreme Court Compendium: Data, Decisions, and Developments.* Washington, D.C.: Congressional Quarterly, 2002.

Farrand, Max, ed. *The Records of the Federal Convention of 1787.* New Haven, Conn.: Yale University Press, 1966.

Franzwa, Gregory M. *The Lincoln Highway: Nebraska.* Tucson: Patrice Press, 1995.

Friedman, Leon, and Fred L. Israel, eds. *The Justices of the United States Supreme Court, 1798–1978.* New York: Chelsea House, 1978.

Friendly, Fred W. *Minnesota Rag: The Dramatic Story of the Landmark Case That Gave New Meaning to Freedom of the Press.* New York: Random House, 1981.

Friendly, Fred W., and Martha J. H. Elliott. *The Constitution: That Delicate Balance.* New York: Random House, 1984.

Gillmor, Donald M. *Free Press and Fair Trial.* New York: Public Affairs Press, 1966.

Greene, Bob. *Once Upon a Town: The Miracle of the North Platte Canteen.* New York: William Morrow, 2002.

Greenhouse, Linda. *Becoming Justice Blackmun: Harry Blackmun's Supreme Court Journey.* New York: Times Books, 2005.

Hall, Kermit, ed. *The Oxford Companion to the Supreme Court of the United States.* New York: Oxford University Press, 1992.

———. *The Magic Mirror: Law in American History.* New York: Oxford University Press, 1989.

Hutchinson, Dennis J. *The Man Who Once Was Whizzer White: A Portrait of Justice Byron R. White.* New York: Free Press, 1998.

Jeffries, John C., Jr. *Justice Lewis F. Powell, Jr.* New York: Scribner's, 1994.

Johnson, John. *The Struggle for Student Rights: Tinker v. Des Moines and the 1960s.* Lawrence: University Press of Kansas, 1997.

Kelly, Alfred H., Winfred A. Harbison, and Herman Belz. *The American Constitution: Its Origins and Development.* 7th ed. New York: Norton, 1991.

Kennedy, Roger G. *Burr, Hamilton, and Jefferson: A Study in Character.* New York: Oxford University Press, 2000.

Lamb, Charles M., and Stephen C. Halpern, eds. *The Burger Court: Political and Judicial Profiles.* Chicago: University of Illinois Press, 1991.

Lavergne, Gary M. *A Sniper in the Tower: The Charles Whitman Murders.* New York: Bantam Books, 1997.

Levy, Leonard W. *Emergence of a Free Press.* New York: Oxford University Press, 1985.

Lively, Donald E., Dorothy E. Roberts, and Russell L. Weaver, *First Amendment Anthology.* Cincinnati: Anderson, 1994.

Mattes, Merrill J. *The Great Platte River Road: The Covered Wagon Mainline via Fort Kearny to Fort Laramie.* Lincoln: University of Nebraska Press, 1987.

Mitchell, Broadus, and Louise Mitchell. *A Biography of the Constitution of the United States*. New York: Oxford University Press, 1975.

Rehnquist, William H. *The Supreme Court*. New York: Alfred A. Knopf, 2001.

Russomanno, Joseph. *Speaking Our Minds: Conversations with the People behind Landmark First Amendment Cases*. Mahwah, N.J.: Lawrence Erlbaum Associates, 2002.

Rutland, Robert A. *The Birth of the Bill of Rights, 1776–1791*. New York: Collier, 1966.

Scholfield, Philip. *Essays on Constitutional Law and Equity*. New York: Oxford University Press, 1978.

Schwartz, Bernard. *The Ascent of Pragmatism: The Burger Court in Action*. New York: Addison-Wesley, 1990.

———, ed. *The Burger Court: Counter-Revolution or Confirmation?* New York: Oxford University Press, 1998.

Shapiro, Martin, comp. *The Pentagon Papers and the Courts: A Study in Foreign Policy-Making and Freedom of the Press*. San Francisco: Chandler Publishing, 1972.

Sickles, R. J. *John Paul Stevens and the Constitution*. State College: Pennsylvania State University Press, 1988.

Taylor, Telford. *Two Studies in Constitutional Interpretation: Search, Seizure, and Surveillance and Fair Trial and Free Press*. Columbus: Ohio State University Press, 1969.

Tushnet, Mark V. *Making Constitutional Law: Thurgood Marshall and the Supreme Court, 1961–1991*. New York: Oxford University Press, 1997.

Twentieth-Century Task Force on Justice, Publicity, and the First Amendment. *Rights in Conflict*. New York: McGraw-Hill, 1976.

Ungar, Sanford J. *The Papers and the Papers: An Account of the Legal and Political Battle over the Pentagon Papers*. New York: Dutton, 1972.

Urofsky, Melvin I. *Affirmative Action on Trial: Sex Discrimination in Johnson v. Santa Clara*. Lawrence: University Press of Kansas, 1997.

White, G. Edward. *Earl Warren: A Public Life*. New York: Oxford University Press, 1987.

Witt, Elder. *Guide to the U.S. Supreme Court*. Washington, D.C.: Congressional Quarterly, 1990.

———. *The Supreme Court at Work*. Washington, D.C.: Congressional Quarterly, 1997.

Woodward, Bob, and Scott Armstrong. *The Brethren: Inside the Supreme Court*. New York: Simon & Schuster, 1979.

Wunder, John R., ed. *Law and the Great Plains: Essays on the Legal History of the Heartland*. Westport, Conn.: Greenwood Press, 1996.

Yarbrough, Tinsley E. *The Burger Court: Justices, Rulings, and Legacy*. Santa Barbara, Calif.: ABC-CLIO, 2000.

———. *The Rehnquist Court and the Constitution*. New York: Oxford University Press, 2000.

Articles

Abbey, Thomas G. "Constitutional Law—Judicial Restraint of the Press—Nebraska Press Association v. Stuart." *Creighton Law Review* 9 (1976): 693–716.

Alberich, Glenn H. "*Nebraska Press Association v. Stuart:* Balancing Freedom of the Press against the Right to a Fair Trial." *New England Law Review* 12 (winter 1977): 763–788.

Berens, Charlyne. "Prior Restraint Threatens Free Speech." *NU College of Journalism & Mass Communication Alumni News* 11 (summer 2001): 1–2.

Bjork, Sheryl A. "Indirect Gag Orders and the Doctrine of Prior Restraint." *University of Miami Law Review* 44 (September 1989): 165–195.

Erickson, William H. "Fair Trial and Free Press: The Practical Dilemma." *Stanford Law Review* 29 (February 1977): 485–496.

Foote, Joseph. "Mr. Justice Blackmun." *Harvard Law School Bulletin* 21 (June 1970): 18–21.

Friendly, Fred W. "A Crime and Its Aftershock." *New York Times Magazine,* March 21, 1976, 16–18, 85–96.

Goodale, James C. "The Press Ungagged: The Practical Effect on Gag Order Litigation of Nebraska Press Association v. Stuart." *Stanford Law Review* 29 (February 1977): 497–514.

Howe, G. Woodson. "Fair Trial and Free Press: Who Won?" *Nebraska Newspaper* 28 (August 1976): 1–4.

Larson, Milton R. "Free Press v. Fair Trial in Nebraska: A Position Paper." *Nebraska Law Review* 55 (1976): 543–571.

Larson, Milton R., and John P. Murphy. "*Nebraska Press Association v. Stuart:* A Prosecutor's View of Pre-Trial Restraints on the Press." *DePaul Law Review* 26 (spring 1977): 417–446.

Marsell, R. S. "The Constitutional Jurisprudence of Justice Potter Stewart." *Tennessee Law Review* 55 (1987): 1–23.

Nakao, Cynthia M. "Constitutional Law: Gag Me with a Prior Restraint: A Chilling Effect That Sends Shivers down the Spines of Attorneys and the Media." *Loyola Entertainment Law Journal* 7 (1987): 353–369.

Norton, Will, Jr. "Nebraska Case Crucial to Freedom of Expression." *NU College of Journalism and Mass Communication Alumni News* 11 (summer 2001): 3–4.

Portman, Sheldon. "The Defense of Fair Trial from Sheppard to Nebraska Press Association: Benign Neglect to Affirmative Action and Beyond." *Stanford Law Review* 29 (February 1977): 393–410.

Seacrest, Joe R. "Gag! Nebraska Generates Most Important Freedom of Press Case since Pentagon Papers." *Nebraska Newspaper* 27 (December 1975): 1–8, 20.

Stephenson, D. Grier, Jr. "Fair Trial—Free Press: Rights in Continuing Conflict." *Brooklyn Law Review* 46 (fall 1979): 39–66.

Whitmore, Nancy J. "Nebraska Suppressed: How Gagging the News Media Intensified Pretrial Press Coverage of the Simants' Murder Case." *Journalism History* 29:3 (fall 2003): 107–122.

Dissertations/Theses

Whitmore, Nancy. "*Nebraska Press Association v. Stuart:* An Understanding of Prior Restraint." M.A. thesis, University of Nebraska at Omaha, 1995.

Zobin, Joseph. "Gag Orders and the First Amendment: The Legal Path to *Nebraska Press Association v. Stuart.*" Doctoral dissertation, University of Wisconsin—Madison, 1978.

Newspapers

Chicago Tribune (1975–2001).

Denver Post (1975–1979).

Kansas City Times (1975–1979).

Lincoln [NE] Journal (1975–2007).

Lincoln [NE] Star (1975–2003).

Los Angeles Times (1976).

New York Times (1975–2001).

North Platte [NE] Telegraph (1975–2007).

Omaha [NE] World-Herald (1975–2007).

Wall Street Journal (1976).

Washington Post (1975–1978).

index

Page numbers in *italics* refer to illustrations.

counsel, right to, 30
Cox Broadcasting Corp. v. Cohn, 105
Craig v. Harney, 105

Davis, Lila, 171
The Deadly Tower, 27, 131–132
death sentence, 111, 166, 171–174, 177,
    178, 217n24
Denver Post, 61, 168
dicta, defined, 204n88
Douglas, Paul, 76, 79
Douglas, William O., 145, 212–213n8
Dowd. See Irvin v. Dowd
due process, 174

Eddy, William (Bill), 44, 200n9
editorial cartoons, 68–69, *68, 69*
Eighth Amendment, 173
Eisenhower, Dwight, 117, 119
electric chair, 171, 173
English common law, 8–9, 11, 190n6
Estes v. Texas, 105
estoppel, 84, 203n72
evidence, 50, 137, 170
execution, stay of, 172, 173

Feldman, Don, 25–26, 178
fiber analysis, 137
fingerprint evidence, 137
First Amendment, xv. *See also* press,
    freedom of the
  absolutist view of, 110–111, 119
  Blackmun's decision on Stuart's gag
    order, 80
  Blackmun's record on, 75
  Burger on, 118
  conflict with Sixth Amendment, 17, 44,
    65, 80–81, 86–87, 100, 107, 109,
    111, 127, 135, 150–164, 187, 214n45
  interpretation and litigation, 7
  jurisprudence, xviii
  primacy of, 157–158
  provisions of, 11, 12, 72, 97, 105, 186
  Ruff's gag order and, 57

significance of *Nebraska Press Associa-
    tion v. Stuart*, 185
Fischer, George, *162*
Flood v. Kuhn, 75
Fogarty, Frank, 44
Ford, Gerald, 123
Foster, Miles, 50–51, 54, 64, 81
Fourteenth Amendment, 72, 173
Frankfurter, Felix, 15, 95, 212–213n8
Franks, Ronald, 180
Friendly, Fred, 55, 56, 187, 198n53

gag order. *See also* media coverage, gag
    order; *Nebraska Press Association
    v. Stuart*
  as amended by Nebraska Supreme
    Court, 82–89
  Blackmun's, xviii, 74–89, 151, 166,
    202n39
  constitutionality of, 65, 150–164, 185
  imposed by Ruff, 53–65, 71, 85–86,
    95, 102–103, 108, 137, 151, 196n9,
    199n84
  imposed by Stuart, 63–65, 67–89, 91,
    92, 96, 102–103, 108–109, 113, 122,
    124, 125, 137, 151, 166, 168, 199n84
  limited duration of, 140
  narrowness of, 132, 136, 199n84
  propriety of, 5
George III (king of England), 190n6
Georgetown University Law School, 38
Gibbons, Richard, 25
Gilster, Gordon (Hop)
  at arraignment, 30–31
  arrest of Simants, 29
  confession given to, 22–24, 51–53, 169
  information to media, 25–26, 39, 49
  media interviews of, 32, 54
  misconduct with jury, 174–177
  ordered to return Simants to Lincoln
    County, 182
  photographed in media, 33, *34*
  press conference, xvi
  testimony at preliminary hearing, 52,
    54
Globe Newspaper Company, 112